TRUEMAN BRADLEY

ASPIE DETECTIVE

Alexei Maxim Russell

D0310042

Jessica Kingsley *Publishers*
London and Philadelphia

First published in 2012
by Jessica Kingsley Publishers
116 Pentonville Road
London N1 9JB, UK
and
400 Market Street, Suite 400
Philadelphia, PA 19106, USA

www.jkp.com

Library of Congress Cataloging in Publication Data
Russell, Alexei Maxim.
 Trueman Bradley, aspie detective / Alexei Maxim Russell.
   p. cm.
 ISBN 978-1-84905-262-7 (alk. paper)
 1. Asperger's syndrome--Fiction. 2. Private investigators--New York
(State)--New York--Fiction. I. Title.
 PR9199.4.R857T78 2012
 813'.6--dc23

                                    2011025727

British Library Cataloguing in Publication Data
A CIP catalogue record for this book is available from the British Library

ISBN 978 1 84905 262 7
eISBN 978 0 85700 547 2

Printed and bound in Great Britain

CONTENTS

SLAM BRADLEY IS BACK IN NEW YORK CITY

I've always hated the sound of cars honking. In my new office on Reade Street, the traffic was loud and hurt my ears. I began to wonder if I had made a mistake by moving to New York City. It was much noisier here than I had expected.

Someone knocked at the door of my room and I opened it. A short, round man in a mover's uniform was standing there.

"You 201 Reade Street?" he asked.

"Am I what?" I asked. "No, I'm Trueman Bradley."

"Yeah, that's what I'm talking about, here," he said. "Mr. Trueman Bradley at 201 Reade Street, it says. I'm the guy what moved your furniture, right? I got the bill here. Now, we'll take off 10 percent if you pay cash, see? So, how about it?"

The mover was wearing a blue uniform with yellow stripes down the sides. He was unshaven. He had a lot of small burns on his trousers. I recognized the burns as the kind made by cigarette ashes. He smelled like smoke, and I could recognize the smell as being from Chesterfield brand cigarettes. The grease on the front of his shirt was recognizable as the kind of stains caused by French fries. I had read medical books and had learned to recognize the signs of many medical problems.

I could recognize all the symptoms that would indicate he suffered from the medical problem known as "high blood pressure."

I could see all these details about him, but I had no idea what he was saying to me. He spoke with a New York City accent. He was obviously speaking English, but his accent made it difficult to interpret. He wore a name tag that read "Ernie."

"Ernie?" I asked. "I don't understand your question."

"You serious?" asked Ernie. "It's pretty straightforward, pal. I just asked if you want to shell out now or do credit."

"Shell out?" I asked. "What do you mean?"

"I mean the green stuff!" said Ernie. "You got any?"

"I don't have any green shells," I said.

"Are you stupid?" asked Ernie. "I mean this stuff!"

Ernie pulled out a ten dollar bill and waved it in front of my face. He leaned closer and his strong smell of cigarettes made me dizzy. He had suddenly become aggressive and I didn't understand why. I started to feel tension in my stomach.

"I don't understand you!" I said. "I need to go!"

I closed the door to my room and locked it. Listening at the door, I could hear Ernie yelling. My heart beat fast as I listened to his aggressive words. They were incredibly ugly to me and made my head hurt. I fell down to the floor and covered my ears. I started doing math equations in my head.

"What on earth are you doing, Trueman?"

I was so affected by this confrontation with Ernie that I forgot that Mrs. Levi, my landlady, was visiting me. She was looking at me as if I was insane.

"I'm doing math," I said, getting up.

"Doing math, are you?" she said. "Well, of course you are. My question is, how come you're doing math on the floor?"

"I do math because it's comforting to me," I said.

"Oh?" she asked. "So you like math then? That's alright, dear. There's nothing in our lease about not doing math, but do you have to do it on the floor? You've got a perfectly good chair in here! Why use the floor?"

I patted the dust off my knees. I could feel my face burning with embarrassment. I remembered my childhood habit of falling to the floor when I got nervous or over-excited, but I hadn't done this for a long time. Usually, I could resist the urge to fall and would try my best to act as if nothing was wrong. Although my breath became rapid and I'd start to feel dizzy, I was always able to maintain my dignity. But this encounter with Ernie was so unexpected I had not been allowed any time to prepare myself for it. I was ashamed to think that Mrs. Levi had seen me falling down, like a frightened child.

"I don't usually fall to the floor like that…" I said, trying to hide my embarrassment. "It was just because, this time, I didn't have time to find a chair. I was surprised because a mover came to my door and yelled at me for no reason."

"Oh? You mean Ernie?" she asked.

"Yes, Ernie," I said.

"Well, I'm surprised at that!" she said. "Ernie's a nice guy! What did he say to you, dear? What was he yelling about?"

"I don't know," I said. "He wanted to know about green shells, and when I said I didn't have any, he became angry."

"Green shells?" she asked. "Strange thing for a guy like Ernie to be talking about. I didn't even know he liked shells! But never mind, dear, are you planning to tidy up a bit?"

"Yes. I'm going to unpack," I said.

"Okay, dear," she said. "Well, maybe I should get out of your hair, then. I really should be getting home for lunch."

I touched my hair.

"My hair?" I asked. "What are you going to do to my hair?"

"No, I didn't mean that, dear!" she said. "Bless you! It's just an expression! 'Out of your hair' means I'll go off and leave you alone. Don't tell me you never heard it before?"

"Oh, I see," I said. "Of course I heard of it before. I just didn't immediately realize you were using an expression. I don't understand why you need to talk about my hair if you are actually talking about leaving me alone. Next time, can you please just tell me that you are going to leave me alone? I prefer for you to speak with me using clear language, Mrs. Levi. Expressions and idiom are confusing to me sometimes."

"Oh, so this is some kind of symptom?" she asked. "Part of your condition, am I right? What's it called again, dear?"

"Asperger's Syndrome."

"Asperger's, right," she said. "So you're not joking, then, are you? I'm so sorry to hear you've got this condition, dear."

She looked at me with pity in her eyes, as if I was cursed. I felt as if she thought I was somehow abnormal, and I was embarrassed. She began speaking to me as if I was a child.

"Well, are you sure you can manage unpacking by yourself?" she asked. "I'll give you a hand. Oh, I'm sorry! I just used another expression, didn't I? I didn't mean I'd actually give you one of my hands, you understand? What I meant is, I'll help you unpack some of these things."

She opened a box and pulled out a book.

"Is this a 'Slam Bradley' comic book?" she asked. "Slam Bradley, the tough and cunning private detective! It's a classic. Why, I haven't seen one of these in years!"

I ran to grab the book from her hands.

"What's the matter with you?" she asked. "I was just helping you organize your stuff, dear! Why so grabby?"

I examined the comic, to be sure she hadn't damaged it.

"These are organized by issue number," I said. "You might disarrange them out of order. These are my most important possessions. I can't do my job without them."

I hugged the comic to my chest, lovingly, as if it were my child. For the second time, she looked at me like I was insane.

"Oh?" she asked. "What are you, a comic book dealer?"

"No, I'm a detective," I said. "Like Slam Bradley."

"You're joking!" she said. "You? You don't even know what 'out of your hair' means, and you're saying you solve crimes? You're pulling my leg! Criminals would eat you alive, dear!"

I couldn't understand her expressions, but I could recognize the ridicule in her voice. She was implying I couldn't succeed as a detective, just because I have Asperger's. Since I left home I'd had to deal with a lot of this kind of prejudice and it made me so angry, my cheeks would turn red.

"Who ever gave you the idea you could be a detective?" she asked. "Do you even know how much hard work that involves?"

"I'm not a child!" I said. "Please don't treat me like one. My granddad was a retired policeman and he taught me a lot about detective work. I have a very exceptional memory and I haven't forgotten anything he taught me. I'd like you to talk to me respectfully in the future, and don't yell at me."

She was quiet for a minute.

"Alright, dear," she said. "Whatever you say. It's not like I meant anything bad by it, you know! I was just concerned for you, that's all. I mean, you're not like the rest of us, are you? I don't want someone taking advantage of your... your condition."

"Taking what?" I asked.

"Oh, I used another one of those expressions!" she said. "I never even know when I'm using them, half the time. What I meant is, I don't want someone out there to victimize you, because they think you're weaker than them."

"Why would I be weaker?" I asked.

"Because of your problem!" she said. "Asperger's!"

"Asperger's is not a problem," I said. "It just means I think in a different way from you. It doesn't mean I can't be like Slam Bradley. I'll become a great detective and you'll see that it's not a problem. This has been my dream, since I was a child and first saw Granddad's comic book collection."

"Oh, is that where you got these from?" she asked. "I thought you were a little young to be a Slam Bradley fan. So, that's what this is all about? You're trying to be like that comic book detective, Slam Bradley?"

"Yes," I said. "After my granddad died, I got an inheritance of 5.2 million dollars."

"You've got 5.2 million bucks?" she asked.

"Yes," I said. "Before he died, my granddad told me to spend the 5.2 million dollars on whatever I've always dreamed of doing. So, I used some of it to move here to New York City to become a detective like Slam because that was my life-long dream. I'm sure you know, Slam Bradley was in New York City for most of his comic adventures. Although his adventures began in Cleveland. At first, I wasn't sure if I should go to Cleveland first and then come here. But then I decided to just come here immediately because my favorite comic books were the ones that happened in New York City. And my grandfather once told me that New York City is a lot more interesting than Cleveland."

"Well, he's got that right!" she said. "But you're not from here, then? Where are you from, dear? Originally, I mean."

"Heartville, Illinois," I said.

"Heartville?" she asked. "I never heard of it."

"It's just a small country town," I said.

"And you've never been to New York City before?" she asked.

"No," I said. "I've lived all my life in Heartville. In fact, I spent most of my life at my granddad's country house. He schooled me from home and I lived with him until his recent death. The only time I left home was to visit his workplace."

Mrs. Levi sighed.

"Look, I don't want to offend you," she said. "But really, I've just got to say something here. This isn't Heartville, dear! You understand? This is New York City and those are dangerous streets out there! There's more crime than even the professional detectives can deal with, so what chance have you got? If you'll take my advice, you'll pack up and go back home. Play your detective games in Heartville, where it's safer!"

"No, I can't," I said. "Slam didn't live in Heartville."

"Listen!" she said. "What's it matter where Slam lived? The point is not to get yourself clobbered! You say you've hardly left your granddad's side your whole life? Hardly left home or that dinky little town of yours? Why, you've been living a sheltered life out there! Too sheltered! You can't make it in the big city! You have no idea how different it is. And I can't just stand idly by and watch you put yourself in harm's way. You're a nice kid and I want to stop you before you get yourself hurt. Detectives have to be really tough! A country kid can't do it! Especially with your... condition."

She referred to my "condition" as if it were some horrible disease. I knew that she was referring to my Asperger's and, once again, her prejudice made my cheeks turn red from anger.

"I mean, what are you gonna do?" she continued. "Seriously, if you can't even understand expressions, how are you going to figure out mysteries and solve crimes? I mean, you just can't!"

"Yes, I can!" I said. "Just because I don't immediately understand some expressions doesn't mean I don't understand a lot of other things. I may be weak in a few areas like idioms but I'm strong in other subjects, like details, memory and seeing patterns. In fact, I'm better at these things than you or anyone else I know. I can notice details and memorize them better than you can!"

"Is that so?" she asked. "You don't know what 'out of your hair' means and yet you're telling me you're Sherlock Holmes?"

She shook her head. I could recognize what that meant. She was doubting me; she didn't believe me and didn't think I was telling the truth. It may have even meant that she thought I was stupid and incapable of being a detective. This thought made me angry. I was determined to prove my powers to her.

I examined her face and clothing and tried to memorize every detail. I was born with such a mind for detail that I can concentrate on something or somebody for a few seconds, and remember every little detail of it for months.

"I can see that you eat a lot of baloney," I said.

"What?" she asked.

"And you eat it while sitting in a chair," I said. "The stains on the lap of your dress are the kind made by greasy meats. You've dropped baloney in your lap many times. The dress was washed many times, but washing doesn't completely remove the oil stains. I've seen meat stains before and I remember how they look. I count twenty-one meat stains and your breath smells like baloney. Because all your stains are exactly the same diameter, they are probably all caused by the exact same kind of sliced meat. So, I can guess that you eat a lot of baloney, sitting in a chair, and drop it in your lap."

Her eyes opened wide and she silently stared at me.

"I can recognize the amazement on your face," I said. "Does that mean I'm right? Usually, if I'm wrong, people don't look amazed like that. I must be right. Now do you see what kind of skills of perception I have? I could be a great detective."

Mrs. Levi hid her face in her hands and moved quickly to the door. I was puzzled why she was leaving so suddenly. I had been speaking of baloney, so I thought perhaps my talk of greasy meats had made her hungry and she was going to eat.

"Enjoy your baloney!" I said.

Her eyes opened wider and her mouth opened. Tears formed in her eyes and she ran from my room.

"What's wrong?" I asked, but she was gone.

I stood there trying to understand what had happened. I can memorize details better than anyone else, but I sometimes have trouble interpreting the emotions of others.

"Was she surprised?" I asked myself. I walked into the hallway and looked at the door at the end of the hall. It had a red "24" written on it. This was where Mrs. Levi lived.

"Or was that embarrassment?" I asked.

I can only recognize emotions by experience. I learned what amazement and embarrassment look like, but they're similar.

"I always confuse those two emotions," I said.

Looking around, I felt a thrill to realize this was all mine. I had rented the whole floor of this building, except for Mrs. Levi's room at the end of the hall. This was where I would create my private detective business.

I looked fearfully at the door where Ernie had entered and exited from. I eyed it for a moment, apprehensively, hoping he was really gone. I ran into my room and locked myself inside.

"Why did he yell at me?" I asked myself. "Did I misinterpret his emotions, too? Or did I not understand an expression?"

I thought of Mrs. Levi, sitting in her room and crying from embarrassment, and it made me feel horrible. I felt guilty for embarrassing her and stupid for not knowing these social boundaries and these expressions that everyone else knew.

"God! I hate it!" I said, throwing my keys down on the floor, in frustration. "I don't even understand it! What's so embarrassing about eating baloney?"

I sighed and sat down on a box, to think of numbers and relax my mind. Number sequences are clear and predictable. They have patterns, and recognizing patterns is what my mind is best at. I can recognize patterns better than anyone I know.

That's why math relaxes me. It's a stable, comforting world where I can have confidence in myself.

A gust of wind blew through a nearby window and I heard a car horn. The sound of someone yelling in the street below gave me a headache. I shut the window and lowered the blinds to keep the noisy, confusing world away from me.

"Oh, I hate it!" I said, holding my head in my hands.

I felt overwhelmed. What if Mrs. Levi was right? Maybe this job is too difficult for someone like me? I sat on a box and thought about some of the things I have difficulties with.

"I sometimes have problems with idioms…" I said to myself. "I can't always interpret other people's emotions. But I have a great ability to see details. I have a powerful visual memory and I'm an expert at recognizing patterns. Those things will help me to be a great detective, won't they? Oh, I wish my granddad was still alive! He always supported me and gave me confidence when I doubted myself. He always reminded me to never give up and believe in myself. Granddad believed in me."

I looked at the window in fear, knowing how much noise was out there. In addition to my other difficulties, I am also sensitive to certain sounds, like traffic. They distract me and sometimes they're actually painful to my ears. I'm capable of great concentration, but I'm easily distracted by sudden noises or anything unexpected. Such things are very disturbing to me. I need everything to be neat, predictable and in perfect symmetrical order or I can become very tense.

"Maybe this messy room is making me feel bad," I said.

I looked at the disorganized mess of boxes around me and longed to organize my room in exactly the same way I had organized my room back home in Heartville. My room in Heartville had always been orderly and comforting; everything in its place, like a mathematical equation. I walked to a wall mirror I'd taken from home. I picked it up and moved to a nearby nail. I lifted up the mirror and hung it on the wall.

I could see myself in the yellow light of the ceiling lamp: my shaggy blond hair; my long face; my big cheek-bones; my big, blue eyes looking back at me from the mirror glass; my lanky arms and legs; my body—thin and frail, like a young tree. I didn't look like Slam Bradley. Slam was big and strong; I was thin and frail-looking. Also, Slam always had a look of confidence in his eyes. My eyes looked timid and uncertain.

"Can I really succeed as a detective?" I asked.

I looked at the comic book Mrs. Levi had removed.

"Number 4, 'The Hollywood Murders,'" I said. "This is in the wrong place. I knew Mrs. Levi would put them out of order."

I took them out, one by one, and propped them up on the shelving, displaying the cover of each one of them. I had every issue of the Slam Bradley series. Every comic was an original copy and in perfect condition. I stood and looked at them, proud of my collection and comforted to see them in order.

I stood, with my hands on my waist, savoring the familiar book covers. As I had always done, since childhood, I was so fascinated by the covers that, after a while, I'd imagine myself to be Slam Bradley. I felt confident and powerful, like Slam felt. Hung on a nearby coat rack was a trench coat and fedora, which I'd inherited from my granddad. He used to wear them when he did detective work. I took them and put them on.

"Now I look like Slam," I said.

Walking to the window, I lifted the blinds and opened the window wide. I stood with my hands on my hips, and looked down at the street, with cars honking and voices yelling.

"Slam Bradley is back in New York City," I said.

NEW YORK HOSPITALITY

I ran out of my office building and across the sidewalk. I stepped into a taxicab that was waiting for me on Reade Street. I slammed the door closed and breathed a sigh of relief.

"That wasn't so bad," I said.

I had been brave enough to run into the noisy, busy streets. The streets were unpredictable and disturbing, but I had just experienced the streets of New York City and I had survived. The cab I had called was parked exactly where I had asked it to park. Everything was going according to my plans.

"Maybe I can do this, after all," I said to myself.

"Maybe you can do what?" asked the cab driver. "You're the one who ordered a cab, yeah? Where you going to, mister?"

"Take me to the bank," I said.

"There's a lot of banks in this town, mister," he said.

"I meant the bank nearby," I said. "The bank on the corner of Broadway and Reade Street. I have a map I printed from the Internet, when I was still in Heartville. It's part of my plan to spend my first day banking and then to return home."

"You wanna go three blocks?" he asked. "You're three blocks from Broadway, pal! Why waste my time? Why don't you walk there?"

"But, that's not on my schedule," I said, "I haven't written any walking into my checklist of activities for today. See my checklist here? It says 'call a taxicab at 2:00 pm...'"

"Alright, alright!" he said.

He drove along Reade Street, cursing quietly to himself. I could see his face in the rearview mirror. I could recognize signs of annoyance on his face. His reaction confused me.

"What's wrong?" I asked.

"What's wrong?" he asked. "I'll tell you what's wrong, buddy! I drive for twenty minutes to pick you up here in Manhattan and what do I get? I get a two minute fare! It'll only take us a couple minutes. A couple bucks' pay for a half hour's work! That's what's wrong, pal."

"You don't like a couple bucks?" I asked.

"No, I don't like a couple bucks," he said. "I could've made fifty dollars in the time it takes to drive you around."

"Oh, I see," I said. "Well, if you want fifty dollars..."

I reached into my trench coat pocket and pulled out a roll of twenty dollar bills. I pulled sixty dollars from the roll.

"Here," I said, "Is sixty dollars okay? I know you want fifty, but I don't have any ten dollar bills. Are you happy now?"

He took the money and stared at me in silence.

"How much money you got in that roll?" he asked.

"2,940 dollars," I said. "In this one roll, I mean. I have another nine rolls in my trench coat pockets. Each roll has 3,000 dollars in it."

"You got 30,000 dollars in your pockets?" he asked.

"No," I said. "I have 29,940 dollars."

"And you wanna be let off on the street in the middle of Manhattan?" he asked. "You're gonna walk around with thirty grand?"

"Thirty what?" I asked.

"Grand!" he said. "You tellin' me you don't know what a grand is? It's a thousand bucks!"

"Oh, right," I said. "An expression. Yes, now I remember what that means. A thousand bucks. I prefer if you speak more clearly, please, mister taxi driver. I don't like expressions."

The cabbie looked at me as if I were from Mars.

"Are you foreign, or what?" he asked.

"No," I said. "I'm Trueman Bradley."

"Yeah, sure you are, buddy," he said. "This is your stop, here. But you're crazy if you're going out there with that kind of money. I suggest you go put that money in the bank!"

"That's what I'm going to do," I said.

We stopped on the corner of Broadway and Reade Street. I stepped out of the cab and onto the sidewalk. The street was full of people. I was intimidated by the crowds, but I thought about how brave Slam would be if he was in this situation. This thought made me feel courageous. I started walking across the sidewalk, towards the front door of the bank.

Before I took my first step, a bicyclist rode past me and startled me. I had expected to dodge people, not bicycles.

Unexpected events addle my mind so I panicked. I turned around to get back into the safety of the cab, but it had driven away. My confusion made me lose all my courage. I couldn't concentrate on being like Slam Bradley while there were so many unexpected distractions around me. I suddenly noticed all the noise around me and all the chaos of the busy sidewalk.

I sat on the side of the street and tried to calm my panicked nerves. I tried to focus on a triangular number sequence. Number sequences are mathematical number progressions that proceed in a logical pattern. Because of that logic, I find it comforting to recite these number sequences to myself and the triangular number sequence was my favorite.

"1, 3, 6, 10…" I said to myself.

A vision of the perfect triangles formed in my mind, and I felt comforted by their predictability. I could see the triangle, growing bigger and bigger, in my mind's eye. Each one of them was a flawless example of geometric symmetry. In a minute, the triangles had calmed me significantly and I opened my eyes. In front of me stood a man, dressed in a suede coat.

"36, 45, 55, 66…" I said.

"Say what?" the man asked. "You alright? You look kinda spooked. Are you sick? Here, I'll help you up."

He grabbed my arm and helped me get up.

"What're all those numbers you said?" he asked.

"A triangular number sequence," I said.

"Oh yeah?" he asked. "Say, I'll walk you over to where you need to be. Where you headed, buddy?"

"Why does everyone call me 'buddy' in this city?" I asked. "My name is Trueman Bradley."

"Trueman?" he asked. "I'm Seth. Where you going?"

"To the bank, across the street," I said.

"Here, I'll walk you there," he said. "These Broadway crowds can be a little tough to navigate for a newcomer, am I right? Don't I know it! I lived here all my life, so I know! You look like you're not from around here, am I right?"

"Right. I'm from Heartville, Illinois," I said.

"Yeah, I figured that," he said.

Seth grabbed my shoulder and led me across the street. He pushed his way through the crowds like an icebreaker through the ice-covered waters of the Arctic Sea. In ten seconds, we were walking through the doors of the bank. Seth led me to one of the teller's queues and shook my hand.

"Alright, Trueman," he said. "Here you are, now. How's that for New York hospitality? It's not true what they say, you know. We're not a bunch of cold, faceless robots in New York, not willing to give you the time of day unless it's to rob you."

"I'm glad for your help, Seth," I said.

"Forget about it," he said. "See you later, Trueman."

He walked out of the building and I wondered why he wanted me to forget about his help. I felt grateful to him, however, and so I obeyed his wishes. I forced myself to forget about Seth's existence and focused on my business at the bank.

I had to deposit 27,000 dollars of my money, and keep the roll of 2,940 dollars to use for my personal expenses. I had realized, before the cab driver had told me, that 30,000 dollars was too much money to carry around in New York City. Back home it was safe, because there wasn't much crime. But here, there were thieves on the streets. I took out my notebook and examined my checklist of today's activities. I checked off the item on the list that read "deposit 27,000 dollars."

A familiar smell distracted me from my thoughts. A mental image of the cab driver formed in my mind. I associated this aroma with the cab driver. I recognized the cab driver's cologne, which smelled like lavender, anise and vanilla.

Standing behind me was a man wearing a trench coat and a wide-brimmed hat. He had sunglasses on, but I could recognize him easily. He had ten small birthmarks on his right cheek, which formed a pattern similar to the constellation Orion. With my skill at patterns and my talent for memorizing details, I had been able to notice the pattern, and its similarity to the star system Orion, a few moments after having entered the taxicab.

The likelihood of someone else having the exact same configuration of small birthmarks on their cheek was close to zero. And the likelihood of anyone using the exact same cologne was also very low. I was convinced this man was the cab driver.

When he saw me looking at him, he walked away briskly. He picked up a nearby newspaper and seemed to be reading it. But every time I turned to look at him, I saw him staring at me.

"What does he want?" I asked myself.

He seemed to be trying to disguise his identity, and was following me. I hadn't expected someone to be following me.

It wasn't on my checklist, and I hadn't prepared for it. Because it was unexpected, it made me nervous. I took my notebook out of my pocket and added "be followed by a cab driver" to my list of today's activities. Adding it to my checklist helped, because now it was part of my scheduled activities; now it seemed less unexpected and troubling. But I still didn't know what to do about this situation. My confusion was making my stomach tense.

The queue moved forward and soon I was in front of the teller. The teller had a security guard standing behind her, and I thought of an idea. I added "report cab driver following me to the bank security guard" to my checklist.

"Can I help you, sir?" the teller asked.

"Yes," I said. "I have some items on my checklist that require your bank's services. First, I need to deposit money."

I started taking out my rolls of twenty dollar bills. I placed them in a neat line on top of the teller's desk.

"You're depositing all that money?" asked the teller.

"Yes," I said. "But wait... I'm missing 5,940 dollars."

"I think I might need my manager for this," she said. "Not many people come in with this much money. Just a moment, sir."

The teller walked away and I searched my pockets again. Two of my rolls were missing, totaling 5,940 dollars. They were the only two rolls that were in my side pockets. I had hidden the other rolls inside the lining of my coat.

"Thieves!" I said. "Someone stole them!"

I looked at the cab driver. He stood in the same place, peeking at me from behind his newspaper. He had been standing behind me; he was the only person who knew I had so much money in my pockets; he must have taken my money! I hastened to check off "report cab driver following me to the bank security guard" from my checklist and turned around to call for the security guard. But I was interrupted by the appearance of the teller.

"Sir," she said, "for a cash deposit this size, we need to call the local police station."

"What?" I asked, "Why?"

"Oh, it's just what we normally do," she said. "We have to check it out. Just a formality! You see, if someone deposits a lot of cash, the police think it's money from drug deals."

"They think my money's from drug deals?!" I asked.

The thought that local police thought I was a drug dealer terrified me. Being arrested definitely wasn't on the checklist of things to do today! I scratched out the items "deposit 27,000 dollars" and "report cab driver following me to the bank security guard" from my checklist and stuffed all my money into my coat.

I decided to cancel all my bank business and go home. I didn't understand how depositing this money made the police suspect me of drug dealing, but I was scared and ran out of the bank. I walked into the crowd and was hit by the elbows of pedestrians. The violent, unexpected bumps of the crowd made me panic and I ran along the street, turning into an alley. The alley was empty and gave me some comfort. I sat and leaned against a brick wall, where it smelled like trash and rotten eggs. I continued the triangle sequence from where I left off.

"78, 91, 105…" I said.

"Yo, Trueman!"

The voice caused a vision of Seth to form in my mind.

"You alright?" asked Seth. "I was walking by and saw you running from the bank. So, who you running from, buddy?"

"Buddy?" I asked.

"Trueman," he said. "I mean Trueman. What's happening?"

"The police think I'm a drug dealer," I said.

"Ha!" he said. "You've got to be kidding! A nice Heartville boy like you dealing drugs? Who told you that?"

"The bank," I said. "They said if someone deposits a lot of cash, the police think that person is a drug dealer."

"Oh…" he said. "You misunderstood, Trueman, my friend. All that means is the bank calls the police to check if you're a drug dealer. If you're not a drug dealer, the police will tell the bank you're not a drug dealer. Then they'll let you deposit the money, no problem! You see? It doesn't mean the police think you're a drug dealer. You misunderstood, my friend."

"Oh," I said. "Well, maybe I should go back to the bank, then. I didn't deposit my money. But there are big crowds on the street and they make me nervous. Can you take me there?"

"Sure thing, Trueman!" he said. "Just come with me."

Seth grabbed my arm and led me further along the alley, where it was shaded and dark. The stench of garbage was intense and unpleasant. It was so intense that I wondered if I'd vomit.

"But the bank is the other way!" I said.

"Hey, don't worry so much, buddy," he said. "This is a shortcut. If we go this way, there's less people. You don't like crowds, right? Come on then. It's just a little further."

We walked under a bridge. There was an oil drum here, full of burning trash. Burning smells always alarmed me, because I was once surprised by a fire that suddenly ignited when I was cooking bacon. Any burning smell causes me to panic and think something unexpected and terrifying will happen.

My anxiety was so powerful that I fell to the ground. I felt a need to escape from this disturbing reality. I leaned against the wall of the concrete bridge and continued reciting my number sequence.

To my surprise, Seth pulled me towards him and pushed my back against the wall. He breathed his sour-smelling breath into my face and held me tightly against the wall.

"Alright now, Trueman," he said. "Take off your coat."

I could recognize the anger in his face, but I didn't understand what he was angry about.

"What's wrong?" I asked. "I don't understand!"

"Don't bother trying to understand!" he said. "You're an idiot and I can't sit around all day waiting for you to understand. You're going to give me that coat, you moron!"

He spun me around and started to forcibly remove my trench coat. I tried to resist, but he was stronger than me.

"Freeze! Don't move!"

The voice caused me to see the cab driver in my mind's eye.

"Step away from him!" said the cab driver.

The cab driver was running towards us, holding a gun in his hand. Seth instantly started running, and he was gone before the cab driver got close. I wasn't sure if I should run too. Was the cab driver trying to rob me again? He was running at me with a gun and I was terrified. I fell to the ground and closed my eyes, trying to forget the disturbing situation I was in.

"120, 136, 153…" I said.

"Trueman!" said the cab driver.

I opened my eyes, and saw the cab driver, without his sunglasses, looking at me. I could recognize worry on his face. He had holstered his gun and was leaning over me.

"Trueman, are you okay?" he asked.

"No," I said. "I need to relax. I'm tense."

"No wonder!" he said. "You just got robbed!"

"I did?" I asked.

"Sure, you did!" said the cab driver. "That guy was trying to take all that cash in your coat. Lucky I was following you."

"Why were you following me?" I asked.

The cab driver pulled out a badge and showed it to me.

"Detective Sam Buckley, NYPD," he said.

"You mean New York Police Department?" I asked. "You're a police officer?"

"You could say that," he said. "I'm a detective. Chief of detectives, actually. I was in the middle of setting up an undercover operation when I picked you up. I followed you 'cause I figured someone would try to rob you, walking around with all that cash. And what do you know? I was right! But it looks like he didn't have the sense to take this with him."

He picked up the trench coat full of cash.

"I guess I spooked him, huh?" he asked.

He handed me the trench coat and helped me put it on.

"I'm still missing 5,940 dollars," I said. "Someone stole it from my pocket while I was in the teller's queue."

"Oh, yeah?" he asked. "Okay, well that must've been this same guy that just tried to rob you. I watched him walking with you into the bank. He must have picked your pocket while you were walking with him. Thieves like him are good at what they do. They can reach into your pocket and take your money so gently that you don't even notice."

"Seth stole my money?" I asked.

"So that's his name?" he asked. "Well, that helps. Listen, come with me. We'll write up a quick theft report and then I got to get back to the station. Come on, Trueman, let's go. This place stinks like hell and my cab's double-parked."

THE CRIME-FIGHTING EQUATION

Reade Street was busy. Pedestrians and disturbing sounds were everywhere. But we were safe inside a cab. Detective Sam Buckley and I were parked on the street, outside my office.

"So, you're not really a cab driver?" I asked.

"No," he said. "This is just part of an undercover job I was working on. I get to pretend to be a cabbie. Lucky me, huh? Now let's finish filling this report, alright?"

He was writing the details of the robbery in his notebook. I watched him as he wrote. His brow was furrowed from concentration and his jaw was clenched. He was handsome, with black hair. He had a powerful physique and a square jaw. He looked a lot like Superman, from the original comic book series.

"Did you know the Slam Bradley comic books were published before the first Superman comics?" I asked. "They say Slam was used as the model for Superman. That's why they look so similar. You look a lot like Slam."

"Slam?" he asked. "Is this about the robbery, here? No, I don't think so. I asked you about details. Let's stick to the subject, Trueman. I don't exactly have a lot of time on my hands, you know? Can you describe the guy that robbed you?"

"Yes," I said.

He had his pen positioned on the paper, ready to write.

"He was wearing a blue hat," I said.

"Good," he said.

"He was wearing navy blue jeans and a brown suede jacket," I said. "And his hair was brown. His eyes were gray."

"Okay, Trueman," he said, "I think that's all we need."

"He had six holes in his jeans," I said. "None of the holes were more than two inches in diameter. His shampoo smelled like coconuts. I recognized the smell of his wet hair. It smelled like someone who had just showered, maybe ten minutes earlier."

"Are you serious?" he asked.

"Yes," I said. "He had slight brown discoloration on the middle and index fingers of his left hand. From my experience, that means he smokes cigarettes with his left hand. I know it was cigarettes because I recognized the smell. It was the smell of a Marlborough Lite brand cigarette."

"Seth's a left-handed smoker?" he asked.

"Yes," I said. "I also noticed he had spray paint residue on his hands. I knew it was spray paint and not another kind of paint because it was a color called 'axe-handle' brown. That color is owned and copyrighted by the Hammer-Olgen spray paint company. I've seen their color sample books in the hardware store. He also had strange shoes with duct tape covering them. Maybe he repaired his shoes with duct tape because he can't afford new shoes."

"Well, he can afford a lot of new shoes now that he has your money," he said. "But listen, Trueman, are you seriously telling me the truth here? You really noticed all this?"

"Yes!" I said. "Of course! I'm not a liar."

"Well, I'll put it in the report," he said. "But I gotta tell you, Trueman, it's kind of hard to believe. I'm a trained detective and I have no idea how to tell when someone got out of the shower ten minutes ago. You're seriously on the level?"

"Am I on the level?" I asked. "On what level?"

"On the level!" he said. "You don't know what that means? If you're on the level, then it means you're telling the truth."

"Oh, it's an expression," I said. "I'd prefer if you speak to me in clear language. I sometimes have trouble with idioms."

He closed his notebook and put it in his pocket. I could recognize confusion on his face.

"Yeah," he said, "you also didn't know what 'a grand' was."

"I knew!" I said. "I just didn't immediately remember. Like I said, I sometimes have problems with expressions."

"Yeah?" he asked. "So how come?"

"I have Asperger's Syndrome," I said.

"So, you got Asperger's Syndrome," he said. "What's that?"

"It's a condition," I said. "It just means I might think a little differently from most people. Differently from you."

The detective stared at me and said nothing. It seemed to me I was confusing him even more. He opened his mouth to speak, but didn't say anything. Did he still not understand?

I couldn't think of a clearer way to explain it to him.

"Okay, Trueman," he said, "I don't understand that, but it's okay with me. Take it easy, and if you think of anything else about the robbery just call the number on my card, okay?"

He handed me a card and started the car. The card he gave me had the NYPD logo on it and Buckley's name and phone number.

"Wait!" I said. "Can you do me a favor?"

"What, Trueman?" he asked. "I'm already late here."

"Does the NYPD need any help?" I asked. "Because I'm a private detective and I still need to get my first case."

He turned off the car and stared at me again.

"You're joking," he said. "You? A private detective? Do you have any idea how much work that requires?"

"Yes!" I said. "I've studied detective work! I've studied the magazines too. The Slam Bradley magazines, I mean."

"Slam Bradley?" he asked. "That comic book detective from the forties?"

"Not just the forties," I said. "It began in March of 1937 and ended in October of 1949."

"It doesn't matter!" he said. "The point is, being a detective isn't like a comic book, kid! You're telling me you don't know what 'a grand' is, but you're gonna be a detective?"

"I'm not a kid!" I said. "And I know what 'a grand' is."

"Yeah, but I had to tell you!" he said.

He made a groaning noise.

"Look, Trueman," he said, "in order to succeed at being a detective, you need what is known as 'street smarts.' Now, if you don't know what that is, it means you already know what 'a grand' is and you can tell all about what someone's gonna do before they do it, just from reading their faces. You get me?"

"Get you?" I asked. "I don't understand, Mr. Buckley."

"Well, I'll spell it out for you," he said. "If this thing you've got, this syndrome, if it keeps you from being able to know what people are feeling and things like that, then you'll never make it as a detective. You need to be able to see that stuff! You're too naive, kid. New York will eat you alive!"

"Eat me?" I asked. "Are you saying there are cannibals in New York City? Cannibalism is illegal in the United States!"

"No, Trueman!" said Buckley. "I don't mean that literally. I mean you can't succeed as a detective! Not with your condition! You gotta be able to read between the lines and be cagey as a cat, and you can't if you take everyone literally."

I didn't understand what a cat or a cage had to do with any of this, but I could understand enough of what he was saying.

"You're wrong!" I said. "I noticed things you didn't notice about Seth. You saw him too, but you didn't notice all the details I noticed. I saw even more details than I told you about. Also, I knew it was you in the bank, because of the birthmarks on your right cheek that resemble the constellation of Orion and your lavender, anise and vanilla cologne!"

"So, you did know it was me," he said. "I kinda thought you did. You say I got the constellation of Orion on my cheek?"

"Yes," I said. "I wasn't fooled by the disguise of a professional detective. So, that means I'm a good detective, too. Correct? I recognize patterns and visual information better than anyone I know. I know I can use these skills to solve cases and detect criminals. Isn't it important for a detective to notice and analyze small details like I can?"

"Well, yeah," he said. "I admit I'm impressed by how well you can see and remember these things. And if there was an equation for finding criminals, you'd be the perfect man for the job, Trueman. Because it's clear you're a genius with math and logic and stuff. But the fact of the matter is, detective work is mostly running after people, not math or noticing patterns. Now, I ask you, if you're scared to even go in a crowd, then how you gonna chase a criminal down a busy Manhattan street, huh?

If you take my advice, you'll go straight back to where you came from and forget all about this, okay? Now, I gotta ask you to leave my cab, Trueman, 'cause they're expecting me back at the station. You take it easy, kid, and call me about those other details you talked about. I'm a busy guy, you know, but I'll get back to you some time."

I got out of the cab and stood there, unaware of my surroundings. I was concentrating on Buckley's cab, which drove slowly away from me and disappeared into the thick traffic.

Because Buckley looked a lot like Slam, I felt as if Slam Bradley himself had just told me I couldn't be a good detective. I was desperate to prove to him that I could be.

"An equation for finding criminals…" I said to myself.

I hadn't realized that no one had invented such an equation. I had assumed that some detective had invented it a long time ago. Everything in existence can be expressed by an equation. If there was such an equation, crime-fighting would be easy for me, because mathematical patterns are my greatest skill. I walked to my office door, oblivious to the crowds.

"An equation for finding criminals…" I repeated, as I walked into my building and climbed the stairs up to my room.

*

One single light bulb hung from the ceiling of my room and there was barely enough light to read what I was writing. I was using a piece of chalk to write numbers on a blackboard. I was playing music on my portable music player. I was listening to Symphony #41 in C major by Wolfgang Amadeus Mozart. Listening to this symphony always helped me to concentrate and so I played it repeatedly. The song's consistent pattern of musical notes inspired my mind to think logically and made me feel safe and secure.

The blackboard in my room was large. It was inherited from my granddad. They used it at the police station in Chicago, where he had worked. They used it to give lessons to new police officers. And now, I was using it to solve an important problem which could help to fight crime. I was inventing a mathematical equation that could find criminals and prevent their crimes.

In the dark, music-filled room, with the windows shut and the blinds lowered, I felt like I was in a different world; a comforting world of numbers and logical equations. It felt like I was in a bubble of safety, protected from the chaos of

New York City. Nothing unpredictable could happen in this bubble.

"Trueman!"

The voice was loud and made me drop my chalk. I saw an image of Mrs. Levi in my mind. She was calling through the door. There was a loud knock. I hadn't expected anything unpredictable to happen in my "bubble" and so I panicked. I hid behind my blackboard, hoping she'd go away.

Suddenly, I could smell raspberries. I closed my eyes and tried to remember the math I had been working on. I could smell raspberries and Earl Grey tea. I could also smell baloney.

"Mrs. Levi?" I asked, from behind the blackboard. "Could you come back another time, please?"

"What's that?" she asked. "I can't hear you, dear. Please open up. I've brought you some tea and cake."

It seemed Mrs. Levi wouldn't be going away, so I opened my eyes and came out from behind the blackboard. I liked Mrs. Levi and raspberries are one of my favorite foods. But I had planned to spend all evening inventing my crime-fighting equation and Mrs. Levi's interruption was upsetting and unwelcome.

I grabbed my notebook from a nearby table and added "have tea and cake with Mrs. Levi" onto my checklist of activities for today. Now that it was part of my plan, I felt better about the interruption. I opened the door and Mrs. Levi came into my room. She was carrying a tray, which held a blue and white striped teapot and a small, pink cake.

The raspberry scent of the cake made my mouth water.

"I just realized I haven't eaten since breakfast," I said.

"You haven't?" she asked. "My goodness, dear, it's nine at night! You have to eat! Here, take the whole cake. I shouldn't be eating it anyways. I'm trying to watch my figure."

"Watch what?" I asked.

"Oh, I'm sorry, Trueman," she said. "I'm trying to speak clearly to you, dear. What I meant is I'm trying to lose weight, so I shouldn't eat cake. It's fattening, you know."

"Yes," I said, "this looks like a raspberry lemon cake. It's small. I guess its weight at about 200 grams. So it would be about 600 calories. A pound of fat is 3,500 calories. So it is the equivalent of more than one seventh of a pound of fat."

"Really?" she asked. "How do you know all that?"

"I memorized nutritional information for over 200 different kinds of food," I said. "This cake has 168 calories per 50 grams."

"I've got to tell you," she said. "You've got a real talent for details, Trueman. I'm sorry I ever doubted that you're smart enough to be a detective."

"I forgive you," I said. "And I'm sorry I embarrassed you by mentioning the baloney. You were embarrassed, right?"

Mrs. Levi let out a deep sigh and said nothing. I assumed she had no answer and so I started eating the cake.

"I was just surprised, is all," she said. "We've all got our little private lives. You know, the things we do when we think no one's watching? It's one of my comforts to sit in front of the TV at night and eat baloney with mustard."

"Why is that embarrassing?" I asked.

"Well, it's not really embarrassing," she said. "Just surprising. If you know that, it's like you can see my private life. Who knows what else you might know about me? How you figured out about the baloney, I don't know! You were right, of course. I'm surprised you didn't know about the mustard."

"I did," I said. "I would have mentioned it if you didn't leave the room. I could recognize 121 small mustard stains."

Her face turned red and she averted her eyes from me.

"You're embarrassed again?" I asked.

"Well, maybe a little embarrassed," she said. "You must think I'm a slob, dropping food all over my dress. I assure you, I'm usually more lady-like."

"Aha. Good," I said.

I was not paying attention to her words. The cake was so delicious, I couldn't stop eating it. In a few minutes, there was only one small piece of cake left. I enjoyed the scent of raspberries so much, I didn't want to eat the last piece. I wanted to keep it, so I could smell it while I worked. My positive association with this smell would help inspire me.

"Thank you for the cake," I said.

"You're welcome!" she said. "I'm glad your Asperger's doesn't stop you from understanding good etiquette."

"My granddad taught me about it," I said. "I had some problems understanding the concept of etiquette, at first."

I sat up and checked off "have tea and cake with Mrs. Levi" from my checklist. I picked up my piece of chalk and continued inventing my crime-fighting equation.

"What are you doing there, dear?" she asked.

"I'm inventing a crime-fighting equation," I said.

"Pardon me?" she asked. "What sort of equation?"

"Well," I said. "It's an equation to determine when and where crime will take place in New York City."

I opened a box and pulled out some papers.

"I've ordered these statistics," I said. "They show when and where crime has occurred in New York City since 1951. If I can use this statistical data as variables, then I can make a mathematical equation that will determine where crime will happen next. I can't use a linear equation, because crime is very complicated and has many variables. But I think I might succeed if I use a path integral equation."

"Path integral?" she asked.

She looked completely confused.

"A path integral is an equation," I said. "It is usually used in physics to determine the probability of what a particle will do in a plane or medium, given an infinite variety of trajectories. First I need to define the medium. The medium, here, is New York City's criminal history. The trajectory can be any crime that has been committed or will be committed."

"My goodness!" she said. "You are clever, Trueman! I have no idea what you're talking about. You must be a mathematical genius! Can you really use equations to catch criminals?"

"Yes," I said. "You can use an equation for anything."

"Then, why hasn't it been invented before?" she asked.

"I don't know," I said. "Could you come back another time? I am scheduled to work on the crime-fighting equation right now and you are giving me a headache with all your questions."

"What?" she asked. "Well, so much for good etiquette!"

Mrs. Levi's voice had changed, but I couldn't interpret her emotions. My words seemed to have disturbed her somehow.

"What's wrong?" I asked. "Did I say something bad?"

"It's not good etiquette to tell a guest she's giving you a headache!" she said. "How do you think that makes me feel?"

"I don't know," I said. "You look disturbed."

"Well, yes I am," she said. "It's rude to say someone is 'giving you a headache.' I'll forgive you because of your Asperger's, but next time, remember it's a rude thing to say."

I felt guilty for offending her without meaning to. But I still couldn't see what I did wrong. How else will I be able to do my work, as scheduled, unless I tell her to leave? If her questions were giving me a headache, was I not supposed to mention it and pretend they didn't give me a headache?

"Am I supposed to lie?" I asked. "I was only telling the truth. How is that rude? I don't understand."

"Never mind, Trueman," she said. "I know that some things are hard for you to understand and I don't mind. But,

I guess, if I'm giving you such a headache, then I'll just be going."

She collected her cups and teapot and put them on the tray.

"I didn't say you give me a headache," I said. "I said your questions give me a headache. Because I am trying to work on my equation and listen to you at the same time."

"So?" she asked.

"I can't concentrate on more than one thing at once," I said. "It is very hard for me. It gives me a headache. That is why I make this checklist of my daily activities. See?"

I showed her my checklist and she became calmer.

"Oh, I see," she said. "You have trouble doing two things at once?"

"Yes," I said. "And so I schedule my activities in an orderly checklist. When I work on math, I listen to music and must be alone. I am glad you brought the cake, though, because the smell of raspberry will also help inspire my math."

"Oh, well," she said. "In that case I'll leave you alone."

She lifted her tray and walked towards the door. It seemed to me she understood my explanation, but she was silent and it was not normal for Mrs. Levi to be silent. I felt she might still be upset, so I made an effort to be friendly.

"You are welcome to come back later," I said. "I enjoy your company. I will schedule our next meeting in my checklist. Can you come at eight in the morning for breakfast?"

I was happy to recognize the pleasure on her face.

"Alright, dear," she said. "I'll make you a nice waffle. And if you like raspberries I'll go see my friend Mrs. Bernstein. She makes the most wonderful jam. You'll love it."

"Thank you," I said.

I started playing Mozart's Symphony #41 and placed the raspberry lemon cake nearby, so I could smell it. In one minute I was so concentrated on my equation that I had forgotten

Mrs. Levi. I had already entered a third of the variables for my crime-fighting equation and I was excited because my equation was beginning to form a mathematical shape in my mind.

"Trueman?" asked Mrs. Levi.

The interruption made me drop my chalk.

"You're still here?" I asked.

It was shocking for me to realize Mrs. Levi was here, when she was not supposed to be. This was the kind of unexpected occurrence that gave me stress. It made me feel slightly sick.

"Why are you still here?" I asked.

She was standing beside the open door, holding her tray.

"I just thought of something, dear," she said. "My daughter-in-law, Nora, would be very interested in your equation. She's a private detective too, you see. Why don't you talk to her? She could help you by teaching you a bit about how to be a detective. You might be of help to her, too, with your crime-fighting equation and how well you notice details."

"Okay," I said, trying to get rid of Mrs. Levi, so I could work. I was not interested in her talk, but I pretended I was interested so she would go away and let me work in solitude. "I will write her name in my notebook."

"Nora Lucca," she said. "Actually, it's Dr. Nora Lucca. She's a PhD in criminology. You two ought to get along really well. I hear she's good at math, so she'll be able to understand all your talk about equations and such."

I wrote Nora's name in my notebook, but then realized I didn't know how to contact her, so I couldn't put her on my checklist. I can't contact someone without an address.

"I can't contact her," I said. "I don't have her address."

"Oh, you don't need it," she said. "Nora will be at a convention for professional detectives, here in Manhattan, next week. Be at the Sentinel Hotel next Thursday, at noon. You can go to the convention and meet her there. I'll call her and tell her to meet you. Oh, I'm glad you're meeting Nora, dear. Now I don't have to worry about someone robbing you or taking advantage of you. Nora will take good care of you. She's a nice girl. And smart! Oh, she's smart as they come."

Mrs. Levi left the room and I wrote in my notebook.

"Thursday," I wrote. "At noon, at the Sentinel Hotel. Meet Dr. Nora Lucca at Professional Detective's Convention."

I looked at what I wrote. What was a Professional Detective's Convention? Is that where all the detectives meet? If that's so, then Sam Buckley might be there. Suddenly, I became excited and hopeful. If I could finish my equation and show it to Buckley, he would be impressed! He might change his mind and decide I'm a good detective. He might even let me solve a case with him!

I was inspired and lit a candle. Candlelight also helps me to concentrate. I needed all the concentration I could get. I had to finish my crime-fighting equation before the convention.

THE PROFESSIONAL DETECTIVE'S CONVENTION

"Three dogs, sixteen women and forty-nine men," I said.

"What?" asked Mr. Sal Valle, my driver.

Sal was driving me to the Professional Detective's Convention. We had started our drive in front of my office on Reade Street. We had turned left onto Greenwich Street and were now turning right onto Murray Street. Our destination, the Sentinel Hotel, was near the end of Murray Street.

"Three dogs, sixteen women and forty-nine men," I said.

"What are you talking about?" asked Sal.

"On Greenwich Street," I said. "On the area of Greenwich Street that is between Reade Street and Murray Street I counted three dogs, sixteen women and forty-nine men. I'm glad there were no bicycles on the sidewalk. They startle me. And it is illegal in New York City to ride a bicycle on the sidewalk."

"Why are you counting people on the street?" he asked.

"Because now I know how many people are on that area of Greenwich Street. Next time I come this way I'll know what to expect. I get nervous if I don't know what to expect."

"Well, there won't always be the same number of people on the street, you know," he said. "So why count them?"

"Because next time I can count again," I said. "And I can use an equation to estimate the number of people likely to be on the street. Every time I come this way and count the people, my estimation will improve, because I get more data for my equation. Do you now understand why I count the pedestrians?"

"Maybe my English is not perfect," he said. "But it seems to me you're not making any sense at all!"

Sal was a bald old man. He had a big white mustache with orange stains on it. I could recognize the stains were caused by tobacco. I knew from Sal's strong and aromatic scent that he sometimes smoked a pipe. He smoked his pipe in the car and it left a strong stink on his clothes. I was glad he wasn't smoking now, because smoke from a pipe makes me sneeze.

He spoke with an Italian accent. But because he was still learning to speak English, he used no expressions. I had no trouble communicating with him and so I enjoyed his company. It was also helpful to have someone to drive me to the hotel.

I had finished counting the pedestrians on Greenwich Street and I had written the data into my notebook. Now I was counting the people I saw on this area of Murray Street. Over the last week, I had written so many ideas into my notebook that I filled it up and I needed to get a new notebook. I had learned many things from the difficulties I had encountered on Broadway, that day Seth had robbed me. Since then, I had thought of a lot of solutions, so I wouldn't encounter any of these problems again. I had thought of dozens of great ideas.

One great idea was to wear special sunglasses whenever I needed to walk through a crowd. I painted over the sides of my sunglasses, so I could only see what is ahead of me. This way, when I'm in a crowd, I can look straight ahead without being distracted or startled by anything happening beside me. Another great idea I had was to carry my digital music player with me at all times. This way I could listen to music whenever I was in a crowd, and avoid being disturbed by sudden noises.

I checked off "get special sunglasses" and "get digital music player" from my checklist of today's activities. The next item on the checklist was "get chauffeur." I had the idea that if I had a chauffeur to drive me to my destinations, I could avoid walking on the busy streets as much as possible.

"Sal?" I asked. "Will you be my chauffeur?"

"Chauffeur?" he asked. "You mean to drive you around every place you want to go?"

"Yes," I said. "I need a chauffeur because walking on sidewalks and city streets is sometimes disturbing to me."

"No," he said, "I can't do that. I am only a poor old man. How can I pay to put gas in my car? I can't afford to drive you! I am driving you to the hotel only because Mrs. Levi asked me to do it. I owe her a lot of money for rent, so I do what she says. You understand? I can't be chauffeur for free."

I hadn't expected him to say no, so I felt sad and didn't ask him any more questions. I crossed "get chauffeur" off my checklist and continued to count the people on Murray Street.

"Forty-three men and thirty-nine women," I said.

"What?" he said. "Oh, you count again. Listen, even if you pay me, I can't do it. I have no good car."

"Oh, I'll pay you," I said. "And why do you say you have no good car? We can use this car. I don't mind the stink."

"No," he said, "I think you should call a professional chauffeur business. If you need a chauffeur, they can give you a good car. Maybe I would do it if I had a good car. But you see, this old car I've had for thirty years. It is old, like me. It will break down someday soon. It might break down while I'm driving you someplace important. You see? I have no good car, so I can't be reliable as a chauffeur."

The inside of the car was dirty, smelly and littered with old papers and food packages. Sal's clothing and old shoes were on the floor and the vinyl seats had holes in them, with seat-stuffing coming out of the holes. Sal was often blowing his nose as he drove, and many used tissue papers were on his lap. A photo of a car was on the dashboard.

"That photo," I said. "It's a photo of a 1942 Lincoln Continental Cabriolet."

"Yes, it is," he said. "How do you know?"

"I memorized the model car catalog I had when I was eleven years old," I said. "It had 215 types of cars in it. Is this a photo of your other car? This car looks good. Can you use this Lincoln car to be my chauffeur? Or is it also unreliable?"

"No, no. I don't own this Lincoln car," he said. "I wish I did! I keep this photo here because it is like the car my father had in Italy. A 1942 Cabriolet! That is what my father drove. I always loved that car. This car is for sale. I went to see it, but I didn't have enough money to buy it. I took a photo of the car and I keep it here with me. At least, I can look at it every day. It gives me good memories of my father."

"How much does the car cost?" I asked.

"This car?" he asked. "It's 60,000 dollars! Too much! I looked under the hood and noticed the engine has some problems. A car with engine problems should not cost so much! But, you see, my father was a car mechanic in Italy. I learned the trade from him. So, if I bought it, I could fix it. But, like I said, I am only a poor old man. I don't have 60,000 dollars."

I pulled the rolls of money from out of my pockets and threw them onto the front passenger seat, beside Sal.

"I don't have 60,000 dollars, either," I said. "I can only give you 21,000 dollars. I have 3,000 dollars more, but that is my personal expense money. I need it."

Our car turned violently to the left and then to the right.

"What's happening?" I shouted.

The car was swerving left and right in quick, jerky movements. These unexpected jolts made me panic. I covered my ears, closed my eyes and thought about path integrals.

"Sorry!" he said. "I lost control of the car, but I have control now. It's okay, now, Mr. Bradley! Are you okay?"

I opened my eyes and looked out the window. We were parked in front of a massive building. It had a neon sign that read "Sentinel Hotel" and, looking up, I counted forty floors. Sal was breathing heavily. He was holding one of my rolls of cash, staring at it. His eyes were wide open, like a fish.

"Don't throw a lot of money at me while I'm driving!" he said. "You almost made me crash, throwing this stuff around!"

"Why?" I asked. "You don't like money?"

"No!" he said. "I like the money! I like it a lot! But it surprised me, that's all! No one carries so much money around in cash. You're giving this to me, you said?"

"Yes," I said.

"But, why?" he asked. "Why are you so nice to me?"

"Because you said you can't be my chauffeur because your car will break down," I said. "If you buy this Lincoln car and fix it, then you can be my chauffeur. So I gave you money to buy the car. I only have 21,000 dollars with me in cash, but I can give you a personal check for the remaining 39,000 dollars."

"And I get paid a regular salary, too?" he asked.

"For being my chauffeur?" I said. "Yes."

Sal stared at the cash and smiled. I had never seen such a big smile. I assumed this meant he was even happier than a person with a normal smile. I imagined he was so happy because he could now be my chauffeur.

"I'm also glad you're my chauffeur," I said.

"Your chauffeur?" he asked. "Listen! If you give me this money and a salary too, then for sure I will be your chauffeur!

But, no need to give me the check right now. I will use this cash to make a down payment on the Lincoln car. I will go buy it while you are in the hotel. I'll be back with the car before you are done with your convention."

"Down payment?" I asked.

"Ah, never you mind, Mr. Bradley!" he said. "You just leave it to me. You go and enjoy your detective convention."

Sal opened his door and jumped out of the car. With great energy, he opened my door and bowed. I stepped out of the car and onto the sidewalk, in front of the hotel. I put on my special sunglasses and put my earphones into my ears. I played Mozart's Symphony #40 in G minor on my portable music player.

I felt like I was in a little "bubble," just like I did when I did math in my room at Reade Street. I felt safe and insulated from the world around me, as if I were wearing armor. I could see pedestrians walking in front of me, but I turned to avoid them and walked to the entrance of the Sentinel Hotel.

I was almost at the hotel entrance when I realized that Sal might smoke his pipe in the new Lincoln car. I didn't want my chauffeur car to smell like pipe-smoke. I turned around to go back and tell him not to smoke in it. I could see him in the driver's seat of his old car, throwing my rolls of cash into the air and laughing spasmodically. I was shocked to see him having so much fun with my money.

"He's very happy to be my chauffeur," I said to myself.

I suddenly remembered the 1942 Lincoln Continental Cabriolet was an open-topped car. So even if he smoked his pipe in the driver's seat, the open top would ventilate the car and prevent it from becoming too smelly. I was glad, because I thought it might be impolite to interrupt his money-throwing activities, which he was clearly enjoying so much.

I walked towards the hotel and entered the massive lobby. I could smell floor polish and could see moving water. There was a fountain in the lobby. The lobby's marble floor was shiny and polished; it was a huge and luxurious room. I saw a lot of people walking around, but my special sunglasses stopped me from being distracted. I found a sign that said "Professional Detective's Convention" and I followed the directional arrow beneath it, which pointed to the right.

I was proud of myself, knowing how thoroughly my various inventions were working. I was finding my way through the crowds with no problems whatsoever. I felt confident that I would go through this entire day without anything going wrong. I took out my notebook and checked off "enter Sentinel Hotel" and "find Professional Detective's Convention" from my checklist of today's activities. Next on my list was "meet Dr. Nora Lucca."

I walked to the right and soon was in a room that smelled like wine and cheese. The many different perfumes and colognes mingling in the air made me aware the room was full of hundreds of people, before I even entered the room. Looking around, I counted 221 people in the room. Some of them were standing in groups and talking and some were sitting in high-back chairs.

I didn't see anyone coming to meet me, so I sat in a nearby chair. Mrs. Levi had told me Nora Lucca would meet me here. I was alarmed that Nora hadn't met me immediately. Mrs. Levi hadn't informed me that I needed to wait for Nora. I began to get nervous that things weren't going according to my plan.

I was soon distracted from my worries by a very welcome sight. I took off my sunglasses to see better.

"Are you Slam and Shorty?" I asked.

A tall man with a square jaw sat in the seat next to me. Beside him sat a short, fat man with a big nose. They both turned to look at me, but said nothing.

"You look like Slam Bradley," I said to the tall man. "And you! You look like Slam's assistant, 'Shorty' Morgan! Shorty was short, fat and bald, with a big nose. Just like you!"

The two men looked at each other and then at me. I could recognize by the look on their faces that they were annoyed.

"Sorry," I said. "Did I annoy you?"

The short, bald man got up from his chair, put on a hat and walked away.

"Where is Shorty going?" I asked.

"Don't call him that!" said the tall man. "Don't you know who he is?"

"I thought he was Shorty," I said.

"He's the chief of the NYPD!" he said.

"Oh," I said. "Then he's not Shorty. Does that mean you aren't Slam Bradley?"

"I'm Malcolm Vrie," he said. "I'm a private investigator. I have no idea who Slam Bradley is. You've made a mistake."

He stared at me in a way that made me uncomfortable, but I could not interpret what it meant or what he was feeling.

"Slam Bradley," I said. "He was a comic book detective whose adventures were published by the 'Detective Comics' company. He was created by Jerry Siegel and Joe Shuster…"

"Yeah," he said. "I don't care, okay."

"You don't care?" I asked.

"No," he said. "Now, would you please go away? That seat you're sitting in belongs to someone else."

"Doesn't it belong to the hotel?" I asked.

Malcolm laughed loudly. "What are you, some kind of moron?" he asked.

I could now recognize the emotions on his face. His eyes expressed hatred and aggression. I tried to think of what I might have done to offend him, but I couldn't think of a reason.

"Didn't you hear me?" he asked. "I said get lost!"

His eyes expressed even greater hatred and they were starting to scare me. I thought about running from the hotel.

"Are you Trueman Bradley?" asked a female voice.

A tall, young woman with long black hair and wearing a violet suit had come towards us and extended her hand to me. My granddad taught me people do this when they want to shake my hand. I grabbed her hand and shook it.

"I'm Trueman Bradley," I said. "Who are you?"

"Dr. Nora Lucca," she said. "I'm sorry I didn't find you sooner. In a room full of detectives wearing trench coats and fedoras, finding you is like finding a needle in a haystack."

"How is it like finding a needle in a haystack?" I asked.

"Oh, sorry," she said. "That's an expression that means it's hard to find something. My mother-in-law, Mrs. Levi, told me you have Asperger's Syndrome. Don't worry about it. I had a cousin with Asperger's so I know a lot about it. I'll speak clearly and try not to use any more expressions."

"Thank you," I said.

"You know this clown?" asked Malcolm.

"I'm not a clown," I said. "I'm a detective."

Malcolm gave me another hate-filled look. His aggression was starting to make me nervous and upset. I couldn't understand why he had become suddenly aggressive.

"Why do you hate me?" I asked. "What did I do?"

"Hello, Malcolm," said Nora. "I haven't seen you for a while. Are you having some kind of problem with Trueman?"

"Yeah!" he said. "He just called the chief of police short, fat and bald. Then he was bugging me with questions."

Nora seemed to know Malcolm. But I could see from the look on her face that she didn't like him much. I interpreted that she was looking at him with eyes that expressed disgust.

"For one thing," she said, "did he lie? The chief of police is short, fat and bald. Are you denying that?"

"Well, no!" he said. "But you don't say stuff like that to people. It's rude! This guy has no manners. He's a jerk!"

"Malcolm," she said, "he has Asperger's Syndrome. He can't always tell what's rude and what's not. I'm sure you didn't know you were offending anybody, right Trueman?"

"Right," I said. "I didn't know I was being offensive!"

"There, you see?" asked Nora. "Now, Trueman, I think you and I should go somewhere else to talk."

"Why?" I asked.

Nora was quiet for a while and looked at Malcolm.

"Because I don't like Malcolm," she said. "He's a jerk. Let's leave him alone with his hate and go talk somewhere else."

Malcolm laughed. I could interpret from his face that he also hated Nora. She seemed like a kind, understanding woman and so I became even more emotional. This man seemed to hate innocent people for no reason, and it made me angry.

"You're just jealous, Nora," said Malcolm.

"Oh, am I?" she asked. "Why do you think that?"

"Because the Chief was talking to me," he said. "Do you know why he was talking to me? I think you do. He was talking to me because he was giving me a job. You've been trying to get a job from the Chief, but he didn't give it to you. Isn't that right? You're jealous, Nora, admit it! It's too obvious!"

I didn't entirely understand what Malcolm was talking about, but I could recognize the aggression in his voice. He was talking in a rude and threatening way to my new friend, Nora, and it enraged me. I jumped up from my chair.

"Shut up!" I said. "Just shut up, you bully! Stop threatening people! All you do is hate people for no reason! Don't threaten Nora! If you threaten us, I'll call the police!"

I had yelled so loudly that everyone in the room heard me. The room was silent and everyone was staring at us. Malcolm's face turned red and I recognized that he was embarrassed.

"Shut up!" he whispered. "Everyone's listening!"

"No, you shut up!" I said.

"Please, you two!" Nora said. "I mean, I think we should keep it quiet, okay Trueman? Could you sit down, please?"

She grabbed my shoulder and led me to my chair. Her voice was gentle and soothing and I started to feel calmer.

"Trueman," she said, "I know Malcolm aggravates you, but I'd like it if you could keep calm, okay?"

"Okay," I said.

"Malcolm," she said, "you have a lot to learn about good manners. I told you Trueman has Asperger's. You have to be careful what you say around him, because he doesn't always…"

"So, he's stupid," Malcolm said. "Who cares?"

"I'm not stupid!" I said.

"Malcolm," Nora said, "he's not stupid. He may not get all the subtleties of small talk or body language, but I'll tell you this: he's a lot more polite than you are. I don't imagine he'd intentionally insult anyone the way you just insulted him!"

"That's right!" I said. "And besides that, I'm not stupid! Maybe I'm smarter than you! Did you ever invent a crime-fighting equation?"

"I'm sorry?" he asked. "A crime-fighting equation?"

"Aha!" I said. "You don't even know what it means. Maybe you're the stupid one! I'm smarter than you! Buckley asked me to invent a mathematical equation to fight crime and I did."

"Sam Buckley?" he asked. "Yeah, right. I know him. I doubt Buckley would ask for help from someone like you."

"He did!" I said. "My equation can predict the cause and outcome of any crime. So, now you can see I'm not stupid."

Malcolm laughed and looked at me as if I was insane.

"You're seriously saying a mathematical equation can solve a crime?" he asked. "And just how does it manage to do that?"

"It's easy!" I said. "I just need the time and place of the crime, and what type of crime it was. Then I can use my equation to determine many things. Such as, where the criminal went, what neighborhood he lives in and many other things."

"There's no possible way a mathematical equation can do that," he said. "You really are stupid if you believe that."

"I'm not!" I said. "Maybe you're the stupid one!"

"If you're so smart, buddy…" he said.

"I'm Trueman Bradley!" I said.

"Fine…" he said. "If you're so smart, Mr. Trueman Bradley, then maybe you can use your miracle equation to solve the murder case that Chief Stokowski just gave me to solve."

"Sure I can!" I said.

"Okay," he said. "Now, we'll see if your equation really works! Here are the facts. A man named Eric Lendalainen was found dead outside 620 East 13th Street, last night. He was bludgeoned over the head. He had 50 bucks in his pocket, so it wasn't robbery. Is that all you need to know?"

"What time was it?" I asked.

"I told you it was last night," he said.

"I need the exact time!" I said. "Or the equation won't give an accurate result."

"We believe he was murdered at 11:15 pm," he said. "Go ahead, buddy. Use your magic equation and solve the crime!"

I was enraged by his taunting tone of voice. I was determined to show this aggressive bully that I was smarter than him. I had all the data I needed to use my crime-fighting equation and solve this crime. I put my earphones into my ears and closed my eyes, so I would not be distracted. I forgot about Malcolm and Nora and concentrated on my equation. I began to talk to myself.

"Man, murdered, 620 East 13th Street, 11:15 pm…"

I used the power of my mind to envision my crime-fighting equation, which had 357 variables. Although it was easy for me to do the math, it took me a few minutes to solve the equation, because there were so many variables and a lot of complex operations. Apart from the data he had given me, I had to determine the values of several hundred more variables, based on a variety of statistics I had memorized about New York City. The process was exceedingly complex and required all my formidable powers of concentration. After a few minutes of organizing the numbers in my head, I executed the equation and calculated an answer.

"I solved it!" I said. "The murderer is a man and lives near 545 East 13th Street and is currently at home. He is probably a plumber or a carpenter with a criminal history. He has a wife and family. He is an alcoholic who abuses his wife."

I opened my eyes, but Malcolm was gone. I had been savoring the thought of proving my intelligence to him. I was disappointed to realize he had not heard my successful solution. Nora was sitting in Malcolm's chair and staring at me.

"Where's Malcolm?" I asked.

"He left," she said.

"What happened?" I asked.

"Well, he gave you the details of the crime," she said. "Then he asked you to solve it with your equation."

"Yes, I remember that," I said.

"Then you closed your eyes," she said, "put in your earphones and started making a strange noise."

"What?" I asked.

"You made a noise like 'ung… ung,'" she said. "You went on making that sound for a few minutes. Malcolm started laughing, called you an idiot and then left."

"I make that noise sometimes when I'm concentrating very hard," I said. "I don't realize when I'm doing it. Why did he leave? I was using my equation to solve his murder case!"

Nora was quiet. I felt frustrated and looked around the room. I wanted to find Malcolm and tell him I solved his case.

"Did you really solve the case?" she asked.

"Yes," I said. "I told you that already. It was a man near 545 East 13th Street, like I said. I want to go there with Malcolm to prove to him that my crime-fighting equation works!"

"So, you really invented an equation that can solve crimes?" she asked. "That sounds too good to be true."

"What do you mean?" I asked. "Of course it's true! Do you think I'm a liar? I never lie!"

Nora stared at me silently. She looked calm and peaceful, but I thought I recognized confusion on her face. I guessed that she was not sure if she believed in my equation.

"I'm sure my equation works," I said.

"Really?" she asked. "Have you tested it yet?"

"No," I said. "But I tested it on old cases that are already solved. It was correct 98 percent of the time."

"Really?" she asked. "That equation of yours intrigues me. I'm still not sure I believe an equation can solve crime. But there's no harm in testing it. Would you mind coming with me to 545 East 13th Street to see if you're right?"

"But, I know I'm right!" I said. "I want to go with Malcolm. I want to make him realize he's wrong."

"Trueman," she said, "do you know what Malcolm meant when he said I was jealous of him?"

"No," I said. "But I knew he was being aggressive to you."

"Yes, he was," she said. "Thank you for trying to defend me, by the way. I appreciate your kindness, Trueman."

"You're welcome," I said. "I don't like cruel people."

"Me neither," she said. "Well, I'll explain to you what he meant when he said I was jealous. I'll tell you in clear language, since I know you like people to talk to you clearly. If the NYPD are too busy to solve a case, they sometimes give it to a private detective to solve. If you succeed in solving a case for them, the NYPD will be grateful to you. They will like you and give you more cases in the future. You understand?"

"Yes," I said.

"Well," she said, "I tried to convince the NYPD to let me solve this murder case of Eric Lendalainen. But instead they gave it to Malcolm. If Malcolm solves this case, the police will like him and give him more cases to solve. Now, maybe you guessed it, I don't like Malcolm. I hate him because he's aggressive and cruel. You don't like him either, do you?"

"No, I don't like aggressive, cruel people," I said.

"Then, if we can solve the case of Eric Lendalainen," she said, "we can make Malcolm look bad. The NYPD will be happy we solved their case and they'll like us and give us more cases. And they'll hate Malcolm for not solving the case. Understand?"

"Yes," I said. "If we go to 545 East 13th Street and find this murderer, then we'll cause that bully, Malcolm, to fail?"

"Yes, and the NYPD will be impressed with us," she said.

"And it will prove my equation works!" I said.

"Yes, and that detective you talked about..." she said. "Detective Sam Buckley?"

"Yes," I said. "That's his name."

"He'll be impressed too," she said. "We could get a lot of jobs from NYPD in the future if we succeed. That means a lot of money and a lot of cases to solve. If your equation is correct, then we could really make a name for ourselves in this city!"

"Make a name?" I said. "But I already have a name."

"No, Trueman," she said. "Sorry, I didn't mean to use an expression. I meant, if we solve this case we'll become famous and everyone will know we're great investigators. And if your equation really works, you'll be famous for inventing it!"

"Wow!" I said. "I didn't realize I'd be famous."

I felt a lot of pride imagining the NYPD publicly thanking me for inventing the crime-fighting equation.

"What should we do first, Nora?" I asked.

"Let's go to 545 East 13th Street!" she said.

5

MAGIC JERKS

We were driving our Lincoln car along East 13th Street. We passed by large buildings, with big windows. Every time we passed one of those big windows, I would look at our reflection in the glass. I loved the way we looked, driving in our car, towards 545 East 13th Street.

I looked like a detective, with my trench coat, fedora and big sunglasses. Nora was also dressed in a trench coat and sunglasses. She wore a gray hat with a wide brim. She had bright red lipstick and her black hair blew in the wind. Our driver, Sal, had used some of my money to buy a chauffeur's hat and uniform. Our 1942 Lincoln Cabriolet was the type of car I'd seen in Slam Bradley comics. I liked to look at our reflection in the windows, because we looked like an illustration from a Detective Comics book. I felt pride and pleasure to think my plans of becoming a detective in New York City were succeeding.

We had driven onto many streets to get to East 13th Street. As we went, I had counted the pedestrians on the sidewalks and wrote the totals into my notebook.

"If I add up all the pedestrians I've seen today," I said, "the sum is 612 men, 588 women, 52 people riding bicycles, 34 dogs, 20 cats and one alligator."

"An alligator?" asked Nora.

"Yes," I said. "When we drove past 14th Street Park, I saw a bald man who had an alligator on a leash. He looked weak and small. He was not very mature."

"Who wasn't mature?" she asked. "The bald man?"

"No!" I said. "The alligator! Its scientific species name is 'alligator mississipiensis.' It was not yet fully grown. A mature alligator of that species is about twelve feet long. This alligator was about four feet long. It is still maturing."

"How do you know so much about alligators?" she asked.

"Not only alligators," I said. "I read a book about zoology when I was fourteen years old. It contained details about 1001 different species of animals. I memorized it."

"Fourteen? And you still remember?" asked Nora.

"Of course," I said. "Why would I forget?"

"Most people would forget," said Nora.

"I know that alligator man!" said Sal. "He often walks on West 14th Street with his pet. They call him 'Stan the alligator man.'"

"Wow!" Nora said. "Only in New York City. Isn't it illegal, though, to have a pet alligator in the city?"

"No," I said. "There is no federal or New York state law prohibiting owning an alligator and housing it in a city."

"But what if it attacks someone?" she asked.

"Then it is illegal," I said. "It is against article 25-B of the 'Agriculture and Markets' law of the State of New York."

"Oh?" she asked.

"Yes," I said. "When I read the statute, I didn't understand it all. But it seemed to say that you will be charged with a misdemeanor if you have a dangerous animal and don't take precautions to protect other citizens from it. If the animal attacks somebody, then it will be a crime."

"You memorized New York state laws, too?" she asked.

"Yes," I said.

"Wow!" she said. "You have an amazing memory, Trueman! I wish I had your mind. You're like a real-life Sherlock Holmes. Having someone around who knows every state law is gonna be a big help to me. I'm glad I have you here with me."

"Good," I said. "But who is Sherlock Holmes?"

"You don't know?" she asked. "Well, I'll tell you later."

"Okay," I said. "You think it's important for a good detective to know these laws? And to have a good memory?"

"Yes," said Nora. "I think it's very important. Most of detective work is mental. You have a great mind, Trueman."

"I'm glad you think so," I said.

It was sunny and warm and I was feeling good. I was enjoying the feeling of the wind on my face. I was overjoyed to hear Nora tell me I could be a good detective. Detective Sam Buckley must have been wrong when he said I could never succeed as a detective.

I watched Nora's hair blowing in the wind and felt grateful for her understanding and her friendship. She admired my mind and I enjoyed her admiration. I wanted to use my mental powers to solve the case and impress her even more.

"Here we are, Mr. Bradley," said Sal. "That apartment building. It says '545 East 13th Street' on the front."

"Yes, it does," I said.

The apartment building was made of red bricks. I counted five stories. There was a fire escape on the front of the building and the four bottom windows had bars covering them. A small florist's shop was attached to the apartment building.

I could smell a cigarette, and soon noticed a man in a second floor window. He was leaning his arms on the window sill and blowing smoke out the window. He was wearing a white undershirt with many stains on it. He was bald and had tattoos on his forearms. I could recognize anger on his face.

"Stop whining at me, you shrew!" said the bald man.

He threw his cigarette onto the street.

"Was he talking to us?" I asked.

"No," said Nora. "I think he's talking to someone in the apartment. He's having an argument. Maybe with his wife."

"You keep your hands off me!"

The female voice had come from the bald man's apartment. Soon after, we heard the bald man shouting.

"Maybe he abuses his wife?" I asked.

"It sounds like it," said Nora. "I'd hate to be his wife, anyways. The way he's talking to her is just horrible!"

"And he's a carpenter!" I said.

"He is?" she asked. "How do you know?"

"Because he had a pencil behind his ear," I said. "That is a habit of carpenters. Of course, other people do it too. But there is another reason I know he is a carpenter."

"What reason?" she asked.

I pointed my finger at a nearby truck.

"That truck is full of carpenter's tools," I said.

"But, how do you know it's his truck?" she asked.

"Because there are Winston brand cigarettes littering the street beside that truck. I could recognize the smell of his cigarette. That bald man smokes Winston brand cigarettes."

"Wow! You're amazing, Trueman," she said.

"Yes," I said. "He must be the killer. Let's call the police! Let's call Malcolm and show him we solved the case!"

"But you don't have any proof!" she said. "We need to have some kind of evidence. We can't arrest somebody just because of our suspicions. How are you going to get evidence?"

I had never had a case to solve and I had never realized that my equation was not enough to send a criminal to jail. I was sure my equation was correct, but I still needed evidence. I had no idea how to get evidence. I had never even considered that question before. I felt embarrassed because I had no answer to Nora's question. She might not think I'm amazing anymore, if I had no idea what to do. My face turned red.

"You don't know what to do?" she asked. "Wow! Mrs. Levi told me you were new, but I didn't think you were quite so inexperienced as this. Have you even had one case yet?"

"No," I said. "This is my first case."

"Well, don't worry about it, Trueman," she said. "Leave this one to me. I'll show you how to get evidence! Just follow me and learn from what I do."

Nora stepped out of the car and I followed her.

"Sal," she said, "go park a block away and wait for us."

"Si, Signora Lucca," he said.

I expected Nora to walk into the apartment building. I was surprised when she walked into the florist's shop instead. Inside the shop, I could smell roses, magnolias, and nine other types of flowers. A young blonde woman in a blue dress sat behind the cashier's desk and smiled as we entered.

"Can I help you with something?" she asked.

"I think so," said Nora. "Can I get a half dozen red roses, please? And add a few lilies to the bouquet."

"They don't have lilies," I said.

"Yes, we do," said the cashier.

"No, you don't," I said. "I don't smell any."

"Well, what I meant is, we usually have them," said the cashier. "But we're sold out of them. We get more tomorrow."

"Aha," I said. "That's why I don't smell them."

"Well, then," said Nora, "in that case, just give me half a dozen roses, please."

Nora winked at me. My granddad told me that women winked at men when they are romantically attracted to them. I became shy and embarrassed. I hadn't realized Nora was romantically interested in me. I became confused and moved away from her.

"So…" said Nora, to the cashier, "this is a nice little shop. Do you get a lot of local people as customers?"

"Yeah," said the cashier. "They're all local."

"I just moved to this neighbourhood," said Nora. "I don't know anyone yet."

"Yeah," said the cashier. "I thought you were new. Like I said, we get all the locals. So, I know everyone around here."

"Oh, yeah?" asked Nora. "Say, do you know a carpenter in this neighborhood? I wanted to renovate my kitchen. But I can't find a carpenter. Are there any local carpenters?"

The cashier rubbed her chin and looked at the ceiling.

"Now that you mention it…" she said, "Eddie's a carpenter. He lives right next door in 545. But he's not too good, so I've heard. He's kind of lazy and I hear he's a drinker. So I wouldn't recommend him."

"A drinker?" asked Nora. "You mean he's an alcoholic?"

"Yeah, you could say that," said the cashier.

"Well, that's great!" I said.

"Pardon me?" asked the cashier. "You like alcoholics?"

"No," I said. "It means my equation was right! An alcoholic carpenter who abuses his wife, living at 545 East 13th Street! That is exactly what my equation predicted! This carpenter named Eddie must be the killer!"

"What?" asked the cashier. "Eddie killed somebody?"

"No, no!" said Nora. "Please don't listen to my friend here. He's joking. He's always telling jokes like that."

"I'm not joking!" I said. "Let's call the police!"

Nora stared at me and she seemed to be trying to communicate something to me. But I couldn't understand her facial expression. She put her finger in front of her mouth and I recognized what that meant.

"Why should I be quiet?" I asked.

"Give us our roses, please," said Nora, to the cashier. "Thanks. Can you give us the carpenter's apartment number?"

The cashier had become very quiet and seemed to no longer want to talk to us. I could recognize fear in her eyes.

"I'm sorry, lady," said the cashier. "I don't wanna get involved in whatever this is all about. Are you guys cops?"

"No, we're not," said Nora.

"And she's not a guy," I said. "She's a woman."

Nora sighed and paid for the roses.

We walked out of the shop and Nora whispered to me.

"Trueman!" she said. "You shouldn't have told her about our investigation! This is supposed to be a secret, right?"

"Oh," I said. "Well, why didn't you tell me that?"

"I'm sorry," she said. "You're right. I should've told you. I forgot this is your first investigation. If you tell people you're investigating a murder, they might get scared and not want to give you information. That's why she didn't want to give us Eddie's apartment number. She got scared when you mentioned a murder. Before that, she thought we were just normal customers, so she wasn't scared to give us information."

"I didn't know that," I said. "I'm sorry."

"It's my fault," she said. "I'm supposed to be teaching you detective work, so I'm responsible for your mistakes."

She grabbed my shoulders.

"But, Trueman," she said, "remember, from now on, our investigation is secret. That's your first detective lesson from me. Rule number one. Keep the investigation secret."

"Even from you?" I asked.

"Well, no," she said. "Not from other detectives."

"Should I tell Malcolm?" I asked. "He's a detective."

"We'll tell him after we solve the case," she said.

She winked at me. I was certain my granddad told me that women wink at men when they are romantically attracted. I was happy and excited to learn Nora was in love with me. I lifted my hand and touched her hair. It was thick and shiny and smelled like lilacs. I had always wanted to touch her hair.

"What are you doing?" she asked.

She pushed my hand away. She frowned and seemed to want to get away from me. I couldn't understand her reaction.

"Why did you do that?" she asked.

"I thought you wanted me to," I said.

I could recognize confusion on her face.

"I didn't ask you to touch my hair," she said.

We walked together, towards the apartment block. She had always walked close to me. But now she walked further from me. I realized she might be scared that I would touch her again.

She had winked at me, so she must have been in love with me. But now I had done something to make her afraid to be near me. I thought I must have done something wrong because of my difficulty understanding the subtleties of social rules. I felt frustrated and angry at myself for not understanding how to behave with other people and for losing the love of Nora.

"I hate this!" I said. "I can't do anything right!"

I sat on the sidewalk and hid my face behind my hands. Nora had walked to the front of the apartment and was looking at the intercom beside the door.

"What?" she asked. "What's wrong? Are you okay?"

"Nothing's wrong," I said.

That wasn't true, but I was so confused and frustrated that I didn't want to discuss the problem. I wanted to avoid her questions, fearing I might say something else to upset her.

"Well, in that case," said Nora, "come on and help me, Trueman. We have to find out where Eddie, the carpenter, lives. Now, we know he lives on the second floor because we saw him smoking out of a second floor window. So the apartment number probably starts with a two."

She waved her finger in front of the intercom buttons.

"Come on, Trueman," she said. "You're the smart one here. Can you help me and guess which apartment he lives in?"

I thought about it. I couldn't think of anything to help me determine which apartment the carpenter lived in. I hid my face behind my hands. She had already stopped loving me for some reason I didn't understand. If she knew I had no answer, she might start hating me. I didn't want to answer her.

"Ah, nuts!" she said.

"Nuts?" I asked. "Where?"

"No!" she said. "I don't mean real nuts. Sorry, that's an expression. 'Ah, nuts!' means I'm unhappy about something. I'm unhappy because this intercom doesn't even work. It's broken. How can we talk to Eddie if we can't call his apartment?"

"Can we go inside the apartment?" I asked. "We already know he lives in the front left apartment of the second floor."

"The front door of the building is locked," she said.

"Oh," I said.

I had given another wrong answer. I sighed.

"Trueman?" she asked. "I need your help. Do you have any ideas how to get into the building?"

"Can you climb that fire escape?" I asked.

The bottom ladder of the fire escape was on the second floor and she would need to jump very high to be able to grab it. Nora walked away from the building and looked up at the windows of the second floor.

"You're right!" she said. "One of those windows leads into the second floor hall! If I grab the fire escape ladder and climb on the fire escape, then I can get in the window. Then I can get into the building! I'll come down to the first floor and open the door for you. Then we'll knock on Eddie's door!"

Nora looked around. No one was on the sidewalks and no cars were passing. Nora ran towards the building. Just then a truck came round the corner. Nora stopped running and walked back towards me.

"Are you okay?" I asked.

"Yeah," she said, breathing heavily. "I'm okay, but that truck passed by and so I couldn't climb up to the fire escape."

"Why not?" I asked. "Why is the truck important?"

"Are you kidding?" she asked. "I thought you knew all the laws. It's illegal to trespass on a fire escape unless you live there. According to the law, this is an illegal entry."

"Really?" I asked. "You mean New York Penal Law, section 140.10?"

"Uh, yeah. I guess," she said.

"I don't think it would be 'criminal trespass in the second degree' because that only refers to trespassing in a 'dwelling.' The fire escape is not a private dwelling. And I don't think it is 'criminal trespass in the third degree' because the law says nothing about fire escapes. It says you should not cross property 'enclosed in a manner designed to exclude intruders.' I don't see how a fire escape is designed to exclude intruders. It's designed to help people escape fires."

"Maybe so," she said. "But, trust me, this is illegal."

"It is?" I asked. "But I don't want to commit a crime!"

"Look, Trueman," she said. "This is only a very little crime and all we're doing is getting into the hall because the intercom doesn't work. It's the apartment caretaker's fault for not fixing it! How are people supposed to talk to tenants?"

"Will the police arrest us if we trespass?" I asked.

"I doubt it," she said. "Besides, I'm the trespasser, not you. If they do discover us, I'll tell them you're innocent."

She winked at me. I was overjoyed. Her wink must have meant she was in love with me again. Even if I didn't understand why, I was happy to have her love. I forgot about my opposition to her trespassing. I decided to agree with everything she said, to ensure I wouldn't lose her love again.

"Okay, Nora," I said. "I don't mind if you trespass. Is that why you couldn't jump when the truck passed? Because you don't want anyone to witness your trespass?"

"Exactly," she said. "Now, watch for people, Trueman. I'll try to jump again. If you see someone coming, tell me."

Nora walked away from the building and prepared to jump up and grab the fire escape ladder. I saw no cars or pedestrians.

"There's no one around," I said.

"Good," she said.

She ran towards the building and jumped to catch the bottom of the ladder. She caught it and swung from it, like a monkey swinging from a tree branch. This thought amused me and I started laughing. A car sped very quickly down the street, its engine roaring. The shock of this unexpected noise made me fall down on the sidewalk and cover my ears with my hands. Nora dropped from the ladder and squatted beside me.

"Trueman!" said Nora. "Why didn't you warn me?"

"Sorry!" I said. "I was distracted by a funny thought and that noisy car came so fast! I had no time to warn you."

"Urg!" she said. "I hate people who speed down the street making a lot of noise. And he has to come just when it's most inconvenient too. It's like he does it on purpose, just because he's a jerk! That guy's got some serious jerk magic going!"

"What is jerk magic?" I asked.

"Oh, it's an expression I invented," she said. "Some people seem to know the worst, most inconvenient time to appear. It's as if they do that on purpose, because they're jerks. It's as if they can magically predict where to be at any given time of day, to ruin something for somebody. It's like they have magic powers. So I call it 'jerk magic.' That guy who sped past in the sports car, he's got a lot of that jerk magic!"

"That's not real magic, is it?" I asked.

"Of course not!" she said. "I just made it up."

"Oh, I see," I said. "Well, even if it was real, we could easily defeat the magic powers of these 'magic jerks.'"

Nora started laughing.

"Magic jerks," she said. "I like that. But what do you mean, defeat them? I'm trying to jump up to the fire escape without being seen, but these magic jerks keep coming. You're saying there's some way we can avoid them?"

"Sure," I said. "I do it all the time. It's a game I would play in my room at home, in Heartville. I sat at my window and watched the cars and pedestrians pass by. I counted the time it took for a pedestrian or a car to come and I made an algorithm to fit the data. This algorithm can predict when the next disturbance will come."

"What's an algorithm?" she asked.

"It's a kind of logical structure," I said. "A set of mental instructions. The steps in the algorithm are composed of Bernoulli probabilities and Bernoulli trials and…"

"Wait, Trueman," she said. "I don't understand any of this. Can you speak to me in clear, understandable English?"

"Oh," I said. "Usually I'm the one asking people to speak clearly. Okay, I'll explain it simply. I can use a calculation to determine if someone will arrive in the near future."

"Really?" she asked. "And it's always correct?"

"Well, about 75 percent of the time," I said.

"That's good enough for me," she said. "So I'll get ready to jump and you use that algorithm to tell me when no one will be coming for a while. Then I'll jump. Ready?"

"Yes," I said.

I closed my eyes and concentrated on the algorithm. I could see it in my mind, as if it was a physical thing in front of me. I remembered all the data I'd collected about the pedestrian traffic in this area of East 13th Street and calculated when the next person or car would arrive.

"After this old lady walks past us," I said, "then we will probably not be disturbed for four minutes and two seconds."

The old lady was walking past as I said this. I guessed she heard what I said because she stared at me. I turned my head so I couldn't see her. Suspicious stares always make me uncomfortable. I talked to Nora while I waited for the old lady to go away.

"I used to call this equation the 'disturbance detector' because I would use it to determine when loud sirens would pass our house. Loud sirens make me nervous if I don't expect them. But now that we're using it to defeat the magic of magic jerks, I think I'll call it the 'jerk magic detector.'"

Nora laughed. "I like that name," she said.

The old woman went into a neighboring apartment building.

"Okay, now it's safe!" I said.

Nora ran to the apartment building and jumped up to the fire escape. She grasped the bottom of the ladder with both hands and pulled herself up to the fire escape. She looked down at me and winked, then she walked into the second floor window.

I smelled smoke from a Winston brand cigarette. I could see Eddie leaning out of a window. I looked at my wristwatch.

"Oh, Eddie's here," I said, to myself. "That's a disturbance. He would have seen Nora if he came to the window a few seconds sooner. I was wrong. It was only thirty-two seconds before a disturbance came, not four minutes and two seconds. Well, my jerk magic detector is wrong 25 percent of the time."

I was at the front door of the apartment building and I could see Nora inside. She walked down the stairs and opened the door for me. As I entered the building, I could smell Eddie's cigarette smoke and I followed the scent. I followed it up the stairs to the second floor. We arrived at a brown wooden door with the number "20" written on it, with black paint.

"This is it," I said. "What do we do now?"

Nora stood there, biting her fingernails.

"Why are you biting your fingers?" I asked.

"Huh?" she asked. "I do it when I'm nervous."

"Why are you nervous?" I asked.

"Because I'm not sure what to do," she said. "We have to knock on his door. But I'm not sure what to say to them when they answer. We have to find out where Eddie was last night. We need to find out everything we can. We need some clue to let us know how to get evidence. But we can't let him know about our investigation. We need to pretend we're not detectives. Who can we pretend to be to ask him questions? Any ideas?"

The door to Eddie's apartment opened and a young boy with brown hair and a dirty shirt walked into the hall.

"Hi!" said Nora, to the kid. "Don't be scared, kid. We're friends. Are you Eddie's son?"

The kid nodded his head.

"You are?" she asked. "Okay, good. We're friends of your father. Can you answer a few questions for us?"

"Okay," said the kid.

Nora grabbed the kid's arm and gently shut the apartment door. Now we were alone in the dim light of the hallway.

"My name's Nora," she said. "What's your name?"

"Eddie," he said.

"Ah, Eddie Junior?" she asked. "Well, Eddie Junior. Do you know where your father was last night?"

"He was gone to his friend's apartment," he said.

"His friend's apartment?" she asked. "Where?"

"At 620. That big building," he said.

"You mean he was at 620 East 13th Street?" she asked.

"Yes," he said.

"When did he get home?" she asked.

"About 11:30, I think," he said.

"Aha!" I said. "The murder was at 11:15. So, Eddie must have come home immediately after he murdered Eric Lendalainen!"

"Trueman!" said Nora. "Remember rule one?"

"Yes, keep our investigation secret," I said.

"Don't say that out loud!" she said.

Eddie Junior ran back into his parents' apartment and slammed the door shut. I could hear him yelling and crying.

"Oh, great!" said Nora. "We have to get out of here, now!"

Nora grabbed my shoulder and led me down the stairs. We ran out of the apartment building. We ran so hard that I was breathing heavily. I could recognize panic on Nora's face.

"What's wrong?" I asked.

"That kid got scared!" she said. "Because you mentioned a murder! He ran to tell his parents that we were asking about the murder. If that Eddie guy is really the murderer, he'll get really angry. He looks like a violent guy! So, we have to get out of here, fast, before he finds us!"

We ran towards where Sal was waiting in the Lincoln car.

"Hey! What's the matter?" asked Sal.

"Nothing, Sal!" said Nora. "Just drive, okay?"

We got into the car and Sal drove onto East 13th Street, away from apartment building 545 and the violent carpenter.

"I'm sorry I ruined the investigation," I said.

"It's okay," said Nora.

"I just can't do anything right!" I said.

"That's not true!" she said. "It's true you mentioned our investigation twice and so we missed the chance to get some important information. But if it wasn't for your crime-fighting equation, we would not have even known the murderer lived at 545 East 13th Street. If it wasn't for your 'jerk magic detector' algorithm, I would never have gotten into the apartment. It's true, you're not perfect at everything. But you can understand things I couldn't possibly understand. Your different way of thinking does more help than it does harm. You understand?"

"I think so," I said.

I felt relieved that my mistake didn't make Nora stop loving me, this time. I was happy to feel my different way of thinking could be helpful to someone and not a hindrance. For all my life I'd felt like my different way of thinking was a problem, which others couldn't accept. But Nora not only accepted it, she saw good in it, and it made me feel confident and accepted.

Her acceptance meant a lot to me. Her gratitude for my help made me wish I could help her even more.

"Although, now I'm lost," she said. "We can't go back to Eddie's apartment. Because now he knows there's an investigator asking questions about him. If we get near, he'll probably chase us away. How are we going to ask questions and find evidence? I have no idea what to do about the case now."

"I wish I could help," I said.

"Well, did you get any clues?" she asked.

"What do you mean?" I asked.

"You know, clues," she said. "Did you see something suspicious, that might indicate a crime? Some hint that can lead us to evidence or something."

"I don't know," I said.

"Ah, nuts!" she said. "So, neither of us saw anything."

"I didn't say that," I said. "You asked me if I saw any clues. I don't know if what I saw was a clue. But I saw a lot of things. I saw Eddie Junior was wearing his father's baseball cap. I know that because it was too big for him and had glue on it. A lot of sawdust was stuck in the glue. So the cap must belong to his father, because his father's a carpenter and carpenters often get sawdust on their clothes."

"That's all you noticed?" she asked. "That doesn't help."

"There was also a lot of blood on the cap," I said.

"What?" she asked. "I didn't see blood!"

"You didn't?" I asked. "Well, the blood had been washed out of the hat. I noticed it because I've seen what blood stains look like after they're washed out, and I can remember how they look perfectly."

"How blood stains look when they're washed out?" she asked. "They're invisible if they're washed out, aren't they?"

"No," I said, "they're not. I see them. And they're easy to recognize. Only washed out blood stains look like that."

"Amazing," she said.

"Also, when the kid opened the door to apartment 20," I said, "I could see inside the apartment. I saw some rags on the closet floor. These rags also had blood stains on them. Also, there was a faint smell of blood and soap coming from inside the apartment. As if someone had recently cleaned away blood."

"You saw bloody rags?" she asked.

"Well, they were washed clean," I said. "But I saw the traces of blood that remained. Yes. And I smelled it, too."

Nora jumped up and down in her seat and her face had an expression I had only previously seen on children. Her sudden excitement alarmed me. She giggled so loudly that I had to cover my ears.

"What's wrong?" I asked.

"Nothing's wrong, Trueman!" she said. "This is great! If we can get back in there and take one of those rags, then we can send it to a laboratory to test if the blood belongs to the murder victim. Then we'll have the evidence to arrest!"

"Oh. You mean we can arrest Eddie the carpenter?" I asked.

"Yes!" she said. "But we have to think of a way to get back into the apartment. It might be dangerous. Are you willing to try this with me, Trueman?"

She grabbed my hand and looked into my eyes, smiling. I thought this must be another sign that she was in love with me. I didn't mind any danger. I wanted to keep Nora happy.

"I'm willing to face any danger with you," I said.

"Great!" she said. "Then we'll go back and try to out-smart the violent carpenter. And we'll try not to get killed in the process! Sal, can we go back to 545 East 13th Street?"

"Si, Signora Lucca!" he said. "We'll just turn right onto the East 14th Street loop and we'll be there in five minutes!"

OUT-SMARTING EDDIE

We were getting close to 545 East 13th Street.

"Stop the car!" shouted Nora.

The car stopped suddenly. This unexpected shout caused me to panic. I bent down and hid under my arms.

"What's happening?" I asked.

"Park here, Sal!" she said.

We parked on the side of the road.

"Raise the hood!" she said.

Sal pressed a button on the dashboard of the car. This type of Lincoln car has a leather hood. An electric button can raise the hood over the car. The leather hood began to unfold at the back of the car and covered the top of it.

Nora pushed me further down, against the seat.

"What are you doing?" I asked.

"Please stay down, Trueman!" she said. "It's Eddie!"

I stopped looking at the floor and noticed Nora and Sal were also bent down and hiding. Outside of the car, I could see Eddie, walking on the sidewalk.

I could not interpret the look on his face. But the way he was swinging his arms and spitting on the sidewalk told me that he was drunk and was acting aggressively. I became terrified.

"What is he doing?" I asked. "Looking for us?"

"Maybe," said Nora. "We need to be quiet. He might hear us. Here he comes! Stay down! Don't let him see you."

Eddie passed our car. I looked out the plastic window in the car hood and I could see his red, drunken eyes. They moved quickly, as if he was looking for someone. He passed by without seeing us and walked towards the café down the street.

"Why are we hiding from this man?" asked Sal.

"He's a murderer and he's looking for us," said Nora.

"He looks like he's ready to smash something!" he said.

"Well," she said, "I doubt he's looking for us because he wants to make friends. He's probably thinking of smashing us."

"I know you detectives make enemies sometimes," said Sal, "but do you have to make such big enemies? He's a giant!"

"What do we do?" I asked.

"Well, I don't know," she said. "I hoped we'd have more time to think about it. Stay down! He might come back!"

I hid my head under my arms. I could hear the familiar sound of Nora biting her fingernails. That meant she was nervous. I was scared of Eddie, but I wanted to make Nora happy. I decided to try to get the rag myself, without anyone's help. If I did that, I could impress Nora and she would be sure to remain in love with me. Also, if I got the evidence, without any help, I could make amends for exposing our investigation twice. I could also prove to myself that I could be a great detective. Detective Sam Buckley and Malcolm Vrie would be forced to agree that I'm a great detective if I succeeded at this mission. I opened the car door and stepped outside.

"What are you doing?" asked Nora. "Get back in!"

"No," I said. "I'll get the rag myself."

"You can't!" she said. "You'll get killed! That Eddie guy might be coming back, any time! If he sees you, you're dead!"

"Don't worry," I said. "I used my jerk magic detector. No one will be on the street for the next three and a half minutes! That gives me time to get into the apartment."

I closed the car door. Nora rolled down the car window and stuck her head out. I recognized fear and concern on her face.

"Trueman!" she said. "You can't do this by yourself!"

"Yes, I can," I said. "You said I have a great mind, so I can think of a way to get the rag. Please, Nora, if you have confidence in me then let me accomplish this myself. I want to make amends for ruining our investigation. Let me do this myself, without help. I will think of a way to get the rag."

I could not recognize the emotions on Nora's face, but she touched my hand and squeezed it. I guessed this was another sign of love and it made my face turn red from pleasure.

"I have confidence in you, Trueman," she said. "I'll let you do it alone if it will prove my confidence in you. But remember we'll be watching you. If you get into any serious trouble, just shout my name. I'll come and help you."

Nora rolled up the car window and looked at me. I recognized the affection on her face and it made me smile. I looked fearfully at where Eddie had gone. I couldn't see him. I hoped my jerk magic equation was correct and I really had about two minutes of privacy. It was wrong 25 percent of the time.

I walked as fast as I could towards 545 East 13th Street. I hoped Eddie had left the front door of the apartment building unlocked, but it was locked. I looked up at the second floor of the building. The window of Eddie's apartment was open and I heard a woman crying inside. I thought of jumping to catch the fire escape, like Nora did. But I soon realized Nora was more athletic than me. I have always been clumsy and not very good at sports. It was not possible for me to jump as high as Nora.

"What will I do?" I asked myself.

I looked at my wristwatch.

"I only have one minute and ten seconds!" I said.

I looked to where our Lincoln car was parked and saw Nora in the window. She waved her hand at me. After a few seconds, she opened the door and looked like she was coming to help me.

"No!" I shouted. "Don't help me! I can do this!"

Nora must have heard me, because she stayed in the car and closed the door. I tried to think of a solution to this problem, but I couldn't think of anything. I kicked at the sidewalk, from frustration. If I can't think of anything, Nora will be disappointed. I'll never prove I'm a good detective and I might even be killed by Eddie. I felt like crying.

"Trueman!" shouted Nora.

I saw Nora waving at me and pointing her finger towards the end of the street. Far away, I could see Eddie approaching. I backed against the front wall of the apartment building and looked at my wristwatch.

"Ah! My equation was right!" I said to myself. "A disturbance came, exactly when I predicted."

I saw that Eddie was getting closer. He was moving towards me very quickly, as if he had seen me and was chasing me.

"I didn't know the disturbance would be Eddie!" I said.

I stood with my back against the wall and felt a strong desire to think of my triangular number sequence and forget all about this dangerous job of being a detective.

"Oh, I wish I didn't try to do this without help!" I said to myself. "Nora! Help me!"

The front door of the apartment building opened and Eddie Junior walked out onto the sidewalk. He saw me immediately and ran back into the apartment. I grabbed the door before it could close and followed him into the apartment building.

I closed the door and made sure it was locked.

"Oh, he probably has the key!" I said, to myself.

Eddie would be here any second, so I knew I had to hide myself from him. There was no place to hide in the first floor hall of this building. I saw nothing but a stairwell to the second floor and two doors that were locked. I thought of disguising myself, but I hadn't brought any disguises with me.

There was a baseball cap on the floor. I took off my fedora and trench coat and sunglasses and hid them under some old newspapers. I put on the baseball cap and hid my face under the cap's visor. I leaned against the wall and tried to look like an innocent bystander. Maybe he wouldn't recognize me?

I saw the horrible face of Eddie through the glass of the front door. My heart started beating fast and sweat dripped down my face. I could recognize the anger on his face and I was terrified. I closed my eyes and hoped he wouldn't notice me.

I heard Eddie unlocking the door and felt the draft caused by the door opening. Soon I felt breath on my face. It stank horribly like alcohol and Winston brand cigarettes. I was too afraid to open my eyes, even when he started talking to me.

"Who are you?" he asked.

His words sounded harsh and aggressive and the stink of his breath was making me dizzy.

"Leave me alone!" I said.

I tried to run past him, but my dizziness caused me to trip over my own feet. I stumbled across the hall and when I turned around, I saw Eddie running towards me and trying to send his fist into my face. His punch missed, because I tripped again.

I fell down on the floor, near the front door, and protected my head with my arms. I expected Eddie to start hitting me soon and I was too scared to even think of numbers.

"Stop right there!" shouted Nora. "Don't move, Eddie! You're under arrest for assault and battery!"

I looked up and saw Nora through the glass of the front door. She held a gun in her two hands and was pointing it at Eddie. Eddie had a look on his face that I couldn't interpret. He stood still and slowly raised his hands over his head.

"Trueman!" said Nora. "Open the door for me, will you?"

I got up and unlocked the front door. Nora opened it and stepped inside. She pointed her gun at Eddie's face.

"Stay perfectly still, Eddie," she said.

Eddie's facial expression hadn't altered.

"What do you want?" he asked. "I didn't do nothing."

"You didn't do nothing?" I asked. "So, you mean you did do something?"

"He means he did nothing," said Nora.

"But he said he didn't do nothing!" I said.

"Yeah, I know," she said. "That's just how he talks."

"Oh," I said. "I thought he was confessing his crime."

"What do you mean?" he asked. "I did nothing wrong."

"Yes, you did!" I said. "You killed Eric Lendalainen last night at 11:15 pm outside the apartment building at 620 East 13th Street."

"Who says I did?" he asked. "Where's the evidence?"

I looked at Nora. I had failed to get the rag, so we had no evidence. I expected to recognize disappointment on her face. But she was looking at my head and smiling wide.

"Trueman has the evidence," she said.

"What?" I asked. "But I wasn't able to get the rag."

"Look at that hat on your head," she said.

I took off my cap and looked at it. It was the cap Eddie Junior had been wearing. Eddie Junior's cap must have fallen off his head when he ran away from me. I was so panicked, when I was trying to hide from Eddie, that I didn't notice whose hat this was. I recognized the faint blood stains on the hat.

"Of course!" I said. "This is evidence! There is blood on this hat. Were you wearing this hat last night?"

"Yeah, so?" he asked. "There's no blood on that hat."

"Yes, there is," I said. "You tried to wash it, but there are still faint blood stains on it. Someone like me who can see minute details can see the faint blood stains, even after you wash it. I can smell the blood too."

"Good job, Trueman," said Nora. "I had confidence that you could get the evidence."

She smiled at me and I smiled back. I had only gotten the evidence because of good luck, not because of my intelligent planning, but I didn't mention this to Nora. I was happy to be a success, and to have succeeded at impressing her. I didn't want to ruin it by admitting I succeeded only because of luck.

Eddie's facial expression changed and I recognized that he was feeling hatred for us. Nora's face became more serious and she seemed ready to shoot him if he did anything threatening.

"Even if there was blood on that hat," he said, "so what? Maybe it's my blood. I cut myself sometimes when I'm working. You've got no proof it's the blood of a murder victim."

"We'll send it to the crime lab," said Nora. "They'll discover whose blood it is. We know it's the victim's blood."

"Oh, you know it, huh?" he asked. "Well, that doesn't mean anything. You can't arrest me just because you suspect it's the victim's blood. I know the law! Until you know for sure whose blood it is, I'm free to go. You've got no right to point a gun in my face! You're the one that's in trouble, lady. Not me! You'll get in a lot of trouble for making this illegal arrest!"

"I don't think so," she said. "I witnessed you assaulting Trueman and I have a perfect right to arrest you for it. I'm a private detective and so is Trueman."

"So, you're not cops," he said. "In that case, you got no right to arrest me. Only real cops have that right!"

"Wrong," she said. "You said you know the law? If you knew the law, you'd know any citizen can make an arrest. We don't have to be cops. But if you want cops so bad, we'll get you some. Will that make you happy, Eddie? I'm sure they'll be happy to know we found the murderer of Eric Lendalainen."

She took a mobile phone from her pocket and gave it to me.

"Trueman," she said, "would you please call the police and tell them how we solved the case that Malcolm Vrie could not solve? I'll let you call them, since I know how much you're going to enjoy making Malcolm look stupid."

I was overjoyed at the thought of calling Detective Sam Buckley and telling him about my success. He would probably admit that I'm a great detective and maybe he'd let me help with some of his cases. I also loved the thought of proving to Malcolm Vrie that I wasn't stupid. I had not only proven that my crime-fighting equation works, I had also proven that I was a better detective than Malcolm Vrie. I felt intensely happy.

I collected my trench coat, hat and sunglasses from under the newspapers and found the business card that Buckley had given me. I dialed his phone number and it rang three times.

"Hello," said the voice on the phone. "This is Detective Buckley. Who's this?"

"Detective!" I said. "This is Trueman Bradley!"

"Oh, Trueman," he said. "Yeah, I remember you. Look, if you're calling to talk about the details of that robbery, then please call me in about an hour, okay? I'm kinda busy now."

"No, Detective!" I said. "I solved a murder! I found the man who murdered Eric Lendalainen! We are keeping the criminal here for you and we have some evidence. We're at the apartment building at 545 East 13th Street. Can you come arrest him?"

"What?" he said. "You've got the murderer of Eric Lendalainen? But Malcolm Vrie is working on that case!"

"I know," I said. "And we're better detectives, because we solved the case, and he didn't! I've proven my crime-fighting equation works. Do you think I'm a good detective now?"

"You say you have the murderer there with you?" he asked.

"Yes," I said. "My friend Nora is pointing a gun at him."

"What?" he said. "A gun? Look, Trueman. Just don't move. We're in Central Park. We're not too far away from you. Just stay there. We'll be there in ten minutes, okay?"

"Okay," I said.

I hung up the phone and smiled. I couldn't recognize the emotion in Buckley's voice, but I was sure he was impressed that we solved the case of Eric Lendalainen.

"So, what's happening?" asked Nora.

"He's coming," I said. "They'll be here in ten minutes."

*

Fifteen minutes had passed, and we were sitting in the first floor hall of 545 East 13th Street. Nora was sitting with her back to the wall. She laid her gun on her thigh, but every time Eddie moved, she lifted her gun and pointed it at him.

"Why is the detective late?" I asked. "He said he'd be here in ten minutes!"

"Maybe there's a lot of traffic," said Nora.

"But he said ten minutes!" I said. "How am I supposed to know when he'll come if he doesn't tell me the correct time?"

"People can't always predict when they'll come," she said.

It makes me nervous when people are late, because I am comforted by predictable routines. I like to make plans and know exactly what will happen. I need to know who I will meet and exactly when they will come. If they don't come on time, my day is no longer predictable, and I don't like to alter my plans.

I took out my notebook and looked at my list of today's activities. After I had talked with Buckley on the mobile phone, I had written "wait for ten minutes for Detective Sam Buckley to come." I crossed it off my list and wrote "wait for fifteen minutes for Detective Sam Buckley to come." I felt a bit better, now that it was part of the plan. But I feared I'd need to change it again if he didn't come soon.

I had spent the fifteen minutes watching Eddie. He sat on the bottom stair and I had been able to recognize a lot of emotions on his face: fear, hatred, anger and worry. He was still drunk and was breathing heavily. The smell of alcohol on his breath caused the entire first floor hallway to stink. The hallway smelled like alcohol, cigarettes and Eddie's strong body odor. The smell was making my stomach sick.

But what interested me most were the stains on Eddie's trousers. He wore torn blue jeans, covered in paint, glue and urine stains. But the most interesting stains were on his knees. He had ink stains on his knees, as if he had kneeled down in a puddle of ink. I knew from experience that only ink made that type of stain. But I wasn't sure what kind of ink it was. It didn't appear to be India ink. For fifteen minutes, I had been trying to imagine the explanation for these stains.

"Why do you have ink stains on your knees?" I asked.

"What?" he asked. "That's not ink. It's oil from my car. I was fixing my truck. It was leaking oil and I kneeled in it."

"Why are you lying?" I asked. "That's not an oil stain."

"Like hell it isn't!" he said.

He stood up and started moving around the room. I couldn't interpret his emotion, but his movements were frightening. My question about the ink seemed to make him aggressive.

"Sit back down, Eddie," said Nora.

She had stood up and pointed her gun at his face.

"And what if I don't?" he asked. "I'm not gonna sit here all day answering stupid questions about ink stains! What would you do if I left? Would you really shoot me? Huh?"

Eddie started yelling and Nora's arm stiffened. She closed one eye and aimed the gun. It seemed she was ready to shoot.

"Oh, you're going to shoot, are you?" he asked. "I could knock that gun out of your hand before you could even get a chance to shoot! Then I could beat both of you into putty! A little girl playing with a gun! You don't scare me, lady!"

"Oh yeah?" she asked. "Well, if you could take the gun from me so easily, then let's see you try it."

I could now recognize the emotion on Eddie's face. He was trying to threaten Nora. He wanted to dominate her and take the gun. He moved closer to her and her body became very stiff.

"Watch out, Nora!" I shouted.

Eddie threw one of his fists into Nora's hand, knocking the gun from her hand. He sent his other fist towards Nora's face, but she moved to the side and grabbed his hand. She pulled him and he tripped over her foot. Nora pulled the massive man over her back and he fell down on his stomach.

"Trueman!" she said. "Get my gun, please."

The stress of the situation had caused me to drop down to the floor and cover my face with my hands. Eddie's attack had been so sudden and his fall so violent that it made me shake with tension. I had never experienced such violence before.

"Trueman," she said, "are you okay?"

"I think so," I said. "But I can't stop shaking."

Nora pointed her finger towards the corner of the hall where the gun had slid after being knocked from her hand. I grabbed it and handed it to her.

"How did you knock him to the floor like that?" I asked.

"I know judo," she said. "It's a fighting skill designed to defend yourself against people bigger than you. I don't like to use it, because you can really hurt someone with it. But he gave me no choice. He would've killed me if I hadn't used it."

Eddie was making sounds that indicated he had been hurt. I noticed his arm had hit the glass panel of the front door and caused it to crack. The cracks formed a pattern that looked like a spider's web. I saw that two men were watching us through the glass. It was Detective Buckley and Malcolm Vrie.

"Detective!" I said. "Here's the murderer!"

I opened the door and they stepped inside.

"What the hell's going on in here?" asked Buckley. "Why's this guy groaning on the floor?"

"He just attacked me," said Nora. "I had to defend myself. I used a judo flip on him. I had no choice, Detective Buckley."

"I know you," said Buckley. "You're that detective, Nora Lucca. What's the deal with this broken glass? You did that?"

"He must have done it when he fell," said Nora.

"Oh, for the love of…" said Buckley. "Okay, now please tell me what's going on here. I'm confused as hell. Trueman said this guy murdered Eric Lendalainen. You got evidence?"

"This hat!" I said.

I handed him the baseball cap with the blood on it.

"So what?" he asked. "It's a hat. What about it?"

"It has blood on it!" I said.

Detective Buckley took off his sunglasses and examined the baseball cap very carefully.

"There's no blood on this thing!" he said.

He gave me the cap and turned away from me. I wasn't sure if I interpreted his emotions correctly, but it seemed to me he had a look of annoyance on his face. I had expected him to be overjoyed that we solved the case; I had expected him to congratulate me for my success and give me more cases to solve.

"There is blood on it!" I said.

Buckley turned his back to me and spoke to Nora.

"Look, Miss Lucca," said Buckley.

"Mrs. Lucca," she said.

"Okay, Mrs. Lucca," said Buckley. "You've got no right to be investigating this case. My boss, Chief Stokowski, gave this case to Mr. Vrie over here to solve. And I don't like it when people do things to put my boss in a bad mood. Because if he's in a bad mood, I'm the one that's gotta listen to him gripe. You understand? This case doesn't belong to you or Trueman!"

"Listen to the detective, Nora," said Malcolm.

"I understand that, Detective Buckley," said Nora. "But we got a hot lead on this case, which Malcolm over here was not following up. We felt it was our duty to solve the case, because Malcolm didn't seem capable of it."

"Well, that's between you and Mr. Vrie!" said Buckley. "If you've got a problem with one another, you solve it between yourselves. Don't interfere in criminal cases that aren't yours to solve. Understand?"

"Yes, Detective," said Nora.

Nora looked at me and frowned. I could recognize the sorrow and disappointment on her face. It made me miserable to imagine Nora was unhappy. I didn't understand why Detective Buckley was annoyed with us or why he didn't believe the cap had blood on it. I could see the blood stains clearly.

"Look, Detective!" I said. "Look right here! Can't you see the blood stains? There are three blood droplets!"

"I already looked. I don't see any blood," said Buckley.

"Well, you have to look closely!" I said. "The blood has been washed out. But if you look closely, you can still see the faint traces of blood."

"That's impossible, Trueman!" said Buckley. "No one can see blood stains if they've been washed out!"

"Trueman can," said Nora. "If you take this hat to the crime lab and test it, I think you'll find traces of blood."

"I'm not gonna be doing that!" said Buckley. "Listen close, Mrs. Lucca. Don't encourage this guy. Trueman's a good guy and I like him a lot. But he's got no right calling himself a detective. He's just an inexperienced kid from Heartville and he doesn't understand how dangerous New York City is. If you're really his friend, you'll tell him to stop trying to pretend he's a detective and tell him to head back home to Heartville."

"But, Detective..." I said.

"You heard me, Trueman!" said Buckley. "You could've gotten killed here and next time I might not be around to save you. You're not a detective, okay? I don't want to ever hear of you interfering with police investigations again. Now, you made a big mess here. You pointed a gun at this guy without evidence. You assaulted him. You broke the glass in the window. This is all illegal. But I'm gonna ignore all this."

"Thank you, Detective Buckley," said Nora.

"Yeah," said Buckley. "But in return, you've got to promise me something. Promise me you don't ever interfere with another police investigation. Now, can I get a promise?"

"I promise," said Nora.

Detective Buckley looked at me. I couldn't read the expression on his face. I still didn't understand why he wasn't thanking Nora and me for solving the case. Instead, he was lecturing us, as if we were a couple of naughty children.

"Why aren't you happy we solved the case?" I asked.

Buckley sighed and put his face in his hands.

"Trueman," he said, "first, you didn't have permission to solve this case. Second, you aren't an experienced detective, so you shouldn't be trying to solve anything! And third, you didn't solve the case. There's no blood on this cap. So you got no evidence. You can't arrest someone without evidence. You arrested this guy with no evidence and that's very illegal."

"Oh," I said.

"Now, I like you Trueman," said Buckley, "so, I'm gonna forget this happened. I'm gonna let you walk away. I'm not gonna arrest you. But you have to promise me not to interfere with police cases. If you wanna play detective… well, fine. Go find your own cases, okay? But if you're smart, you'll take my advice and forget all about trying to be a detective. Now, promise you won't try to solve any more police cases and I won't arrest you. I'll let you go home, understand? You promise?"

"Okay. I promise," I said.

"Good," said Buckley. "Malcolm. Take over."

Buckley handed the baseball cap to Malcolm. Malcolm put the baseball cap into his coat pocket and smiled at us.

"I think you two should leave now," said Malcolm.

Nora walked out of the building and I followed her. We walked to our Lincoln car and climbed inside.

"What happened?" asked Sal. "I saw you pull your gun. Then the police arrived. I was expecting to hear gunfire! Quite an exciting show to watch. Better than television!"

"We caught him," said Nora. "But then Malcolm came and took all the credit. I could tell by the look on his face. That jerk's going to take all the credit for this!"

"What do you mean 'take credit'?" I asked.

"He took the baseball cap!" she said. "He's going to take it to the lab and discover it has Eric Lendalainen's blood on it! Then he'll tell the NYPD that he solved the case, although it was actually us who solved it!"

"How do you know he'll do that?" I asked.

"I don't know," she said. "Just a hunch. I could tell by the look on his face. I can't explain it, exactly. Something about his smile told me clearly that he'll take credit for it."

"What's a hunch?" I asked.

"Oh," she said. "It's kind of like a suspicion. If a detective suspects something, but doesn't have evidence yet, then it's called a hunch."

"A hunch…" I said.

I also had an interesting hunch. Before Malcolm had suggested we leave the apartment building, I had seen ink stains on his coat sleeves. He had fifty-one small ink stains, and they were made from the same kind of ink that had stained Eddie's knees.

Normally, I would not think that is very interesting. But I had just thought of another thing that connected Eddie and Malcolm. Both of them had small cuts beside their left eye. Both cuts looked like they had been made by exactly the same material and were exactly the same shape. What is the likelihood that two people would have the same kind of cut on the same part of their face? What is the likelihood they would both have stains from the same mysterious type of ink—an ink that I had never seen before.

"That is not very likely," I said to myself.

"What?" asked Nora. "You mean that he'll take credit?"

"Oh, no," I said. "Sorry, I was talking to myself."

I put on my sunglasses and put my earphones in my ears. I closed my eyes and tried to think of more similarities between Eddie and Malcolm. I had a hunch that all these similarities meant something important and I wanted to solve the puzzle.

"There's some connection between them," I said.

THE TRUEMAN BRADLEY
DETECTIVE AGENCY

My room at 201 Reade Street was a mess, but I didn't mind. I had been trying to discover the connection between Eddie, the carpenter, and Malcolm Vrie for the last eight hours.

I had written all my thoughts about the case on small pieces of paper and organized them into piles, which were placed all over the room. If someone else looked at the paper-strewn room, they might've thought it was a mess. But to me, who understood the pattern of their placement, it was perfectly organized. The one dim light bulb that hung from the ceiling was not bright enough for me to work. So I had lit six candles and put them all over the room. I had closed the window and lowered the blinds, so I would not be disturbed.

I played Mozart's Symphony #41 in C major on my music player. The music filled the room and echoed off the walls. I felt as if the perfectly arranged notes of the music were filling the room with logic and order. I felt as if it helped me to organize my piles of papers and helped me solve this case.

The door opened quickly and caused a draft to enter my room. All my papers flew around the room and four of my candle flames were extinguished. It felt like a tornado had suddenly appeared in my room and blown away all the order and calmness that had surrounded me. Everything was chaos and it caused me to panic. I grabbed my head and fell to the floor.

"What's happening?" I shouted.

"Trueman!" said Nora. "I'm sorry!"

I lay on the floor, protecting my head with my arms and shaking with fear. I thought something horrible had happened. Did a tornado hit? Or did a plane crash into my office?

"No!" I said. "There have only been sixty-five plane crashes in New York City since August 11th, 1920! The odds are too low!"

I felt someone touch my shoulder and I moved my hands from my face. There was no tornado or burning wreckage from a plane crash. Nora was standing above me, looking down at me.

"I'm sorry, Trueman," she said. "I didn't know my opening the door would make so much wind. Did I mess up your papers?"

Nora helped me to get up and sit in my chair. I looked at the mess of papers that surrounded me. The draft had blown the papers everywhere, and now it was truly a mess. All my organized thoughts had become chaos. I was horrified to think all my hours of organizing were wasted. I was even more alarmed because I could smell something burning.

"Oh!" said Nora. "It's on fire!"

Nora ran to the corner of the room, where one of my candles was still burning. One of the papers had been blown onto the candle flame and was now on fire. Nora stomped her foot down on the paper and extinguished the fire. She kept stomping on the candle until it was broken into tiny pieces of wax.

I couldn't endure it anymore. All this unexpected chaos, interrupting my calm organizing, was too much for me to handle.

"But it was all organized!" I shouted. "What happened?"

This confusing and horribly unexpected event was too horrifying for me to accept. I needed to escape reality. I closed my eyes and began thinking of prime numbers. Prime numbers are numbers that are not divisible by anything other than themselves to yield an integer. The mathematical solidity of these numbers comforts me, somehow. They always relax me when I'm confused. I pictured each of them in my head, and could see them as clearly as if I was looking at them.

"2, 3, 5, 7, 11, 13…" I said.

I felt hands on my shoulders, but I didn't stop counting.

"17, 19, 23…" I said.

"Trueman?" asked Nora. "I'm sorry I surprised you."

I felt her arms embracing me and I could smell her lilac shampoo. I could smell a slight dampness in her hair, so I knew she had showered about twenty minutes earlier. I could feel a wool sweater, covering her arms, and it felt very comforting.

I was drawn from out of my imagining of prime numbers by the attractive sensations of Nora's embrace. I looked up at her. She smiled and put her hand on my head. I imagined her embrace meant she was in love with me again. I felt comforted knowing this and stopped shaking. I touched her hair.

"I forgive you, Nora," I said. "I'm glad you're in love with me again. Maybe we can get married soon."

"Married?" asked Nora.

She moved away from me quickly.

"What's wrong?" I asked. "Aren't you in love with me?"

"What?" she asked. "No! Why did you think I was?"

"Because you winked at me," I said. "My granddad told me that women wink at men when they're in love with them."

"Well, sometimes!" she said. "But a wink can mean a lot of things. It doesn't always mean love. Sometimes I wink at people if I'm doing something slightly naughty, or I'll wink because we have a secret between us… there's lots of reasons!"

"So, you aren't in love with me?" I asked.

"No, I never said I was!" she said.

"You never were in love with me?" I asked.

I was confused why my granddad told me a wink meant a girl was in love. I was now entirely confused about what a wink meant. I started to feel a horribly unpleasant emotion. Nora wasn't in love with me and I had also embarrassed her with my silly idea that she was in love. I didn't want to acknowledge this reality or deal with these horrible emotions. I hid my face behind my hands and continued imagining prime numbers.

"29, 31, 37…" I said.

"Trueman?" she asked.

"41, 43, 47…" I said.

"Are you okay?" she asked. "You're counting prime numbers, right? Why are you doing that?"

"They relax me," I said. "53, 59…"

"Did I stress you out because I entered the room so fast and blew away all your notes?" she asked.

"Yes," I said. "61, 67…"

"I'm sorry I did that," she said. "I know sudden, unexpected things are hard for you. I feel bad for disturbing you, Trueman. I'll make you a sign to put on your door that says 'Do not disturb.' So nobody will surprise you again."

"Thanks," I said. "71, 73…"

"Then I made your stress worse by telling you I'm not in love with you?" she asked. "Because you thought I was? Trueman, just because my wink didn't mean I was in love with you doesn't mean I don't like you. I like you very much."

"But you're not in love with me?" I asked. "You don't want to marry me?"

"Well, no," she said. "But I like you a lot."

I sighed. I was happy she liked me, but I had already thought we would get married and now I was disappointed. I had even written an item on my checklist of things to do in my day, "propose marriage to Nora." Now I would need to cross it off the checklist and change my plans. I looked at the mess of papers on the floor and I felt like my life, also, was a mess.

"Trueman…" said Nora.

She walked to me and put a hand on my shoulder. She looked at me with an emotion I recognized as affection. She was very gentle and to feel her soft touch made me feel better.

"I see you're still upset," she said. "I know you can't always interpret people's emotions and you got the wrong idea about my winks. But I understand and so you don't need to feel embarrassed. I'm flattered by your love for me, Trueman, but I'd be lying if I didn't say that we could never be a couple."

"Why not?" I asked. "Is it because you are Mrs. Nora Lucca? Because you already have a husband and are monogamous?"

"Well, no," she said. "I used to be married to Mrs. Levi's son, Julius. But we've been divorced for three years now. I changed back to my unmarried name but kept the title 'Mrs' because it's often easier to talk to people if they think I'm married."

"Three years?" I asked. "And you didn't marry again?"

"No," she said.

"Why not?" I asked.

"I don't know," she said. "I haven't found the right man."

"Can I be the right man?" I asked.

Nora stood very still and stared at me. I couldn't interpret her emotions. I was camping with my granddad once, and accidently surprised a raccoon in the forest. The raccoon had a similar look on its face as Nora now had on her face.

Nora started laughing.

"Trueman," she said, "you're not like anyone I met before. You're honest and sincere. Most people I know say nice things, but are hiding a lot of cruelty or hatred. You can't trust them. It's like they talk in riddles and you're never sure exactly what they mean. You talk clearly and truthfully. It's refreshing talking to you. That's probably why I came tonight."

"Why did you come here tonight?" I asked.

"I wanted to talk to you," she said.

"You missed me?" I asked.

"I guess so, yeah," she said.

I felt better knowing Nora had missed me, but I was still sad and disappointed. I wanted her to be my wife, because then she would not leave me. Unexpected surprises make me nervous, so I like my life to be predictable. And ever since I began believing Nora was in love with me, I was thinking how nice it would be to have a wife. Someone who will always be there for me; someone reliable who is always predictably present and willing to help me. I had become very attracted to the idea of being married. I was also attracted to Nora's beauty. If she were my wife, I could touch her hair as often as I wished.

I sighed.

"What's wrong?" she asked. "You're still upset?"

"A little bit," I said. "I thought we'd be married."

She looked at me, but didn't say anything to comfort me. I couldn't interpret her emotions and wondered if she didn't care about my upset or if she wasn't sure how to help me feel better.

"We'll talk about this more, okay?" she asked. "But for now, can you come with me? Mrs. Levi, Sal and I are playing cards. I came into your office to ask you if you want to join us in our card game. So, how about it, Trueman?"

"I can't come," I said. "I have to organize my papers."

Nora looked at the mess of papers and her shoulders dropped. I recognized the frown on her face—it meant she felt guilty and ashamed.

"I'm sorry I messed up your papers," she said. "I promise I'll help you organize them, after the card game."

"You will?" I asked. "It might take five hours."

Nora smiled at me.

"I don't mind," she said. "That gives us lots of time to talk. I said we'll talk about your feelings more, right?"

"Yes," I said.

"Then, we'll organize and talk," she said.

"For five hours?" I asked.

"Sure," she said.

I couldn't stop smiling. I was always happy and comforted in Nora's presence and the thought of spending five hours with her, involved in the peaceful task of organizing, seemed as blissful as heaven. Maybe she liked being with me so much that we could have a reliable, trustworthy friendship, without needing to be married.

"So, ready to play cards?" she asked.

"Yes," I said. "I'll do what makes you happy."

"Well, then," she said, "let's go!"

I followed her out of my room and into the hall. The hall was dark and smelled like the streets of New York City. A draft was blowing through the hall and so I knew many windows were open. She opened the double doors that led into a very big office, which I had rented but not yet used.

Inside, there was very little furniture. There were no coverings on the windows. The flashing lights of Reade Street were visible and the full moon could be seen in the sky. Pale blue moonlight lit everything. All of the thirteen windows were open and there was a cool breeze blowing through the room.

There was only one table, with four chairs. Sal and Mrs. Levi sat at the table, playing cards. Nora and I walked to the table and sat down. On the table was a pot of tea and a cake.

"Trueman, dear!" said Mrs. Levi. "I'm so glad you could join us! I baked you another raspberry lemon cake. I know you must like it, since you ate the other one so quickly!"

"Thank you," I said. "You're playing poker?"

"We sure are!" said Sal.

"I know this game," I said. "I watched my granddad playing it with his police officer friends. I was six years old."

"Six?" asked Sal. "Well then, I guess you're out of practice. Maybe you will play for a while? I'll teach you."

Sal gave each of us five cards and we started playing.

"Sal was just telling me about your adventures on East 13th Street," said Mrs. Levi. "So, did you really catch a murderer?"

"We sure did!" said Nora, "but I have a feeling Detective Malcolm Vrie is going to try and make everyone believe he's the one who caught him."

"Malcolm Vrie?" asked Mrs. Levi. "Now, why does that name sound so familiar to me, dear?"

"Ah yes, it was a spine-chilling adventure!" said Sal. "Just like out of a Dick Tracy comic book! It does my old heart good to watch these two young detectives chase criminals!"

"Who is Dick Tracy?" I asked.

"You never heard of him?" asked Mrs. Levi. "Oh, you've got to be joking! He's a famous comic book detective. A lot like that detective you always talk about. What's his name? Bam?"

"Slam," I said. "Dick Tracy is like Slam?"

"Well, sort of," said Nora, "but Dick Tracy uses a lot more research and intelligent investigation to catch criminals."

"Yes," said Sal. "Slam Bradley uses his fists instead!"

I had never heard of Dick Tracy. But I had been so focused on Slam Bradley that I hadn't even thought of the possibility of there being other comic book detectives who I might like better.

Ever since my meeting with Eddie, the violent carpenter, I had doubted my ability to be like Slam. In the comic books, Slam always punched people and used his fists to defeat criminals and solve crimes. I was too clumsy and easily frightened to punch people. When Eddie attacked me, I was helpless. Even if I had wanted to punch him, I didn't know how. I wanted to be like Slam, but I had to admit that I was nothing like him. But if there were other comic book detectives that used intelligence, not punches, to solve crimes, then maybe I could try to be like those detectives instead.

"What?" exclaimed Sal. "A royal flush!"

We had been playing poker while I was thinking.

"Yes. It is a royal flush," I said.

"But that's the best hand in the game!" said Sal.

"When we're talking about poker..." I said, "and you say I have a good 'hand.' That means I have a strategically beneficial configuration of cards, right?"

"What?" asked Sal. "I don't understand that."

"Yes, dear," said Mrs. Levi. "That's what it means."

"Aha. I thought so," I said. "I learned that from my granddad. Yes... an ace, a king, a queen, a jack and a ten. All of them of the hearts suit. It is a royal flush. The best hand in poker. Better than your hands. I win, correct?"

"I thought you said you haven't seen this game played since you were five years old?" asked Sal.

"Six," I said.

"And you get a royal flush?" he asked.

"Sure," I said. "Why not?"

"Trueman has an exceptional memory," said Nora.

"Mio dio!" said Sal. "You should go to Monte Carlo and gamble at the casinos! With your powerful brain, you could make millions of dollars!"

"I don't need it," I said. "I have enough money."

"Well," said Sal, "then make millions and give it to me!"

Nora and Mrs. Levi laughed and we started playing again.

"You know, I love to hear about your adventures, Trueman," said Mrs. Levi. "Back when I was a girl living in Brooklyn, my father had a friend named Mordy. He was a private detective and worked for a detective agency. He looked just like Dick Tracy! He'd always have a smile for me or a piece of candy. I just loved Mordy! I'd read my old Dick Tracy comics and imagine Mordy was Dick. Oh, how I'd be happy at the end when he solved the case! I always wanted to work in a detective agency and be like Mordy. I regret that I never did. I married young and never really had a career besides being a landlady."

Mrs. Levi looked down at her lap. For a moment I thought she had found more baloney stains on her dress. But soon I recognized the look in her eyes. Her memories had made her sad.

"Why are you sad?" I asked.

"Oh nothing, dear," she said. "I just sometimes wonder how life could have been different if I had followed my dreams in life."

"Oh," I said. "You wish you worked in a detective agency?"

Mrs. Levi didn't answer, but continued staring at her lap.

"I know what you mean, Mrs. Levi," said Sal. "I had wanted to join the police when I was a young man in Palermo, Italy. I also had the dream to become a detective. But what did I do instead? I became a taxi driver! There's no excitement in driving people to airports and sitting on my rump all day. Why did I start to drive a taxi? Why did I not become a detective? Every day, I ask myself this. I regret my choices in life."

"A straight flush?" asked Sal. "How do you do this?"

I put my cards on the table and showed them to everyone.

"Yes," I said. "The second best hand in poker. My straight flush beats all your hands. I win again."

"You're quite the card shark, Trueman," said Nora. "Remind me to take you Vegas with me one of these days."

"Vegas?" I said. "You mean the city of Las Vegas?"

"Yeah," said Nora. "Vegas is full of card sharks."

"I don't understand," I said. "How can there be sharks in Las Vegas? That city is in the state of Nevada. Isn't Nevada a big desert? Sharks need water to live and deserts are dry."

"No, Trueman," said Nora. "Sorry, that's an expression. 'Card shark' means someone who's good at playing card games."

"Oh," I said. "Now I understand."

Nora collected the cards and we started playing again.

"I always wanted to be a detective too," said Nora.

"What do you mean?" I asked. "You are a detective!"

"Well, yeah," said Nora. "I am now. But for a long time, I worked as a waitress in Brooklyn. During my whole marriage."

"But you're divorced now?" I asked.

"Yeah," said Nora. "It wasn't until after my divorce that I followed my dream to become a detective. I got my doctorate in criminology before my marriage, but I never actually did anything practical with my education. I thought of becoming a detective. But I never had the courage to do it until after my divorce. I only started trying to become a detective about a year ago. And, I gotta tell you, so far, I've hardly been able to make any money from detective work. So, you're right, I am a detective. But I'm still not a successful detective."

"A successful detective?" I asked. "What does that mean, exactly? You are saying that you're an unsuccessful detective?"

"Well, yes," said Nora. "So far, I have been unsuccessful. And if I don't become successful soon, I'll run out of money. No cases equals no money. See? If I'm not successful, I'll need to give up detective work and go back to being a waitress."

Everyone frowned. I could interpret they were sad because Nora might have to stop being a detective. I was sad too. If she stopped being a detective, she would never work on another case with me. Maybe I would never see her again. I felt a strong desire to make it so that would never happen.

"Then we will help you to become a successful detective!" I said. "What, exactly, do you need to become successful?"

"I need cases to solve!" she said. "And I need to solve them successfully. If people read about me in the newspaper, successfully solving cases, then they'll call me and hire me."

"But we did solve a case," I said.

"You mean the Eric Lendalainen case?" asked Nora. "Sure, but we didn't get credit for it. Malcolm will take the credit. So, no one knows we solved it. So that doesn't help."

"Well, maybe we can solve a new case," I said. "This time, we'll get the credit. How can we get new cases to solve?"

"I can go to the NYPD and ask if they'll give me a case to solve," said Nora. "But I already tried that and they gave it to Malcolm instead. And now we promised not to interfere in police cases, right? So I can't hope for NYPD cases anymore."

"Is there another way to get new cases?" I asked.

"Well…" said Nora, "if I could join a detective agency, they would give me cases to solve. If I was part of an agency I could always have cases to solve and I could quickly become a successful detective. But I've tried applying for jobs with detective agencies. They've never replied to my applications. I guess the agencies don't want to hire me."

Nora frowned and looked at her lap. I could interpret sorrow and pain on her face. It looked like she was trying not to cry. Mrs. Levi also looked like she would start to cry.

"Maybe Julius was right," said Nora, "when he said my dream to become a detective was silly. He said I'm not strong enough to do that kind of work, and maybe he was right. I'll never succeed. I'm destined to be a waitress all my life."

"I'll never forgive my son for how he treated you," said Mrs. Levi. She reached across the table and held Nora's hand.

Everyone at the table was frowning, and I could recognize misery on their faces. I felt miserable too, knowing everyone was unhappy. I couldn't understand exactly what had caused their upset, but I knew that it could be solved if Nora could become a successful detective. I also felt horrible to think she'd leave me and go to work somewhere as a waitress, instead.

"What if we create a detective agency?" I asked.

"We can't do that," said Nora. "That takes lots of cash!"

"Really?" I asked. "How much?"

"A million bucks!" said Nora. "At the very least!"

"Oh, good," I said. "That leaves me 4.2 million."

"What?" asked Nora.

"Didn't you know, dear?" asked Mrs. Levi.

"Trueman's got millions!" said Sal. "Where do you think we got that beautiful old Lincoln Cabriolet? Trueman bought it!"

"Is that true?" asked Nora.

"Yes," I said. "My granddad left me 5.2 million dollars as an inheritance. But I've spent some of it."

"How much?" asked Nora.

"Hm… about 66,461 dollars," I said.

"That's all?" asked Nora.

"Yes," I said.

Nora looked down at her lap again, and I couldn't interpret her emotions. Everyone had stopped playing, put down their cards and were silent. Sometimes they looked at each other, and it seemed to me they were communicating to each other in some non-verbal way I couldn't understand. It made me uncomfortable, as if they were speaking in a foreign language in my presence.

"What are you talking about?" I asked.

"What?" asked Nora. "We didn't say anything."

"No," I said, "but you're communicating non-verbally. I can recognize what you're doing. Please remember that I can't understand that kind of communication. I don't like being excluded from the conversation. Can you speak aloud, please?"

They all looked at each other.

"Trueman?" asked Nora.

"Yes?" I asked.

She leaned towards me and grabbed my hand.

"If we make an agency, it'll solve everything!" she said.

"It will?" I asked. "How?"

"Because," said Nora, "I could get cases and become a successful detective. Then I don't have to go back to waitressing and could prove my ex-husband wrong! That would solve all my problems. You understand?"

"Yes," I said.

"Also," said Nora, "Mrs. Levi could work for us and so she could fulfill her life-long dream of working in a detective agency! That solves the problems of two people, right?"

"Oh, but dear," said Mrs. Levi, "I'm too old to be a detective. No, you should find a younger woman to hire."

"You don't have to be a detective," said Nora. "You can work in the office. We need someone to organize this place!"

"Well, in that case," said Mrs. Levi, "I'd love to!"

"And I could fulfill my dream to be a detective too!" said Sal. "Of course, I'd drive you around, Mr. Trueman, but now and then I could do a little detective work too. You think so?"

"Sure," I said. "I would appreciate your help."

"Then that solves three people's problems!" said Nora.

"Four people," I said.

"Huh?" asked Nora.

"You won't need to leave me," I said. "You won't leave me to become a waitress. I want to keep you in my life, so that solves my problem. Now we've solved four people's problems."

Nora's face turned red and I guessed this meant she was embarrassed. But she was smiling, so I knew her embarrassment was not a bad thing. Mrs. Levi smiled at me and held my hand.

"Not only that, dear," said Mrs. Levi. "You can also become a successful detective yourself! You can solve a few cases and you'll be famous in no time! With that mind of yours—why, you'll be the talk of the town! How about that, dear?"

"Yes!" said Sal. "You could be another Dick Tracy!"

"And you can name it after yourself," said Nora.

"Name what after myself?" I asked.

"The agency!" said Nora. "How about it? We could call it 'The Bradley Detective Agency.'"

"Hey! I like the sound of that!" said Sal.

"I like it, too," said Mrs. Levi. "But are you sure it's not already taken? I mean, maybe there's already an agency called 'The Bradley Detective Agency.' You think of that?"

"There can't be two of them?" I asked.

"No," said Mrs. Levi. "It's against the law."

"Well, then I think I will call it 'The Trueman Bradley Detective Agency,'" I said. "I doubt that name is in use already. But how do I make sure the name hasn't been used?"

"Well, you see," said Mrs. Levi, "you can't just call yourself something and start a business, you know? You've got to register with the state of New York. You've got to go to the county clerk's office. That's located on Centre Street…"

"Okay, okay," said Nora. "It sounds like you know a lot about how to start a business. Maybe that can be your job, Mrs. Levi? You can get all the permits and stuff that our agency needs. Any kind of paperwork or permit can be your job, okay?"

"Of course!" said Mrs. Levi. "From owning property in New York City for over thirty years, I know all about that kind of thing. I can take care of everybody! You know, keep it legal. Like you, Sal, need to get an investigator's license if you wanna do any detective work. Wouldn't hurt to get a chauffeur's license too, dear. Just to make sure it's all legal, you know."

"Great!" said Nora. "So Mrs. Levi can be our office manager, taking care of all the paperwork and what-not."

"And I…" said Sal, "I can be chauffeur. But also, I know a lot about how to run a business. I operated my taxi business for twenty years. I know how to do maintenance, how to manage employees, how to order supplies. Over the years, I learned everything needed to run a business. I can run the whole show! That is, if you say so. You're the boss, Mr. Bradley. But, if you will trust me for the job, I'll be 'general manager.' I'll operate the whole business, top to bottom! What do you say?"

"Of course I trust you, Sal," I said. "You're hired."

Sal smiled and leaned his chair back. I could recognize the happiness on everyone's face. I was also very pleased with the idea of creating a detective agency. It solved everyone's problems, and it was even more than I had been dreaming of.

"This is a dream come true," I said. "I'm not only a detective, I'm also the owner of a detective agency!"

"This is so exciting!" said Nora.

"Yes," I said. "So, Mrs. Levi will be office manager, doing paperwork and answering calls. Sal will be the general manager, doing everything that isn't paperwork. I'm a detective and owner of the agency. What will be your job, Nora?"

"I'm a detective, of course!" said Nora. "You can't do the investigations all by yourself, can you?"

Nora grabbed my hand and squeezed it. She had told me her winks weren't romantic, so I assumed she also didn't mean anything romantic by squeezing my hand. But I still smiled and felt my face get warm with the pleasure of her touch.

"Then all our problems are solved," I said.

For a few moments everyone was quiet and didn't move. I couldn't interpret the look in their eyes, but I imagined they felt similar to me. I was incredibly excited at the thought of beginning work on our detective agency. I was so excited that I wanted to start immediately, although it was already evening.

"I don't want to play cards anymore," I said. "Now, I'm so excited about our detective agency, I want to work on it now!"

"Me too!" said Nora.

"Yes!" said Sal. "First thing I am going to do is order a large neon sign with the name 'The Trueman Bradley Detective Agency' written on it! We will hang it over the front door!"

"I can't wait either!" said Mrs. Levi. She got up from her chair and put all the dishes on her tea tray. "I'm going to print the registration forms!" she continued. "First thing in the morning I'll have all the forms into the county office and we can open for business right away."

Mrs. Levi walked away with her tea tray. She had a big smile on her face and was shaking with excitement. Sal had turned on the lights to the big office and was busy designing a neon sign on a piece of paper. His joy was also easy to interpret. I could feel the excitement in the room and it was infecting me.

"What do we do first, boss?" asked Nora.

She was looking at me and smiling. I looked around the big, empty office. I closed my eyes for a second and I imagined what it would look like cleaned up, with furniture, in the morning. No longer would it be an empty, abandoned office. It would soon be an organized, busy detective agency office. Emerging from my imaginings, I wanted to make it a reality.

"We'll start by cleaning this office!" I said.

I grabbed a nearby broom and began sweeping the dusty floor. Nora found a garbage can and began collecting trash.

"Sal, can you go and buy some cleaning supplies in the morning? We'll make this place look like a real detective agency," I said.

"Yes, boss!" said Sal. "Just give me the cash."

I took out a roll of 3,000 dollars and gave it to Sal.

"Mio dio! This buys a lot of cleaning supplies!" said Sal.

"It's not all for cleaning supplies," I said. "I am giving you some extra money to buy some furniture for this office. We need desks and chairs. Oh, and some computers."

"Some computers?" asked Sal. "They cost more than this! Besides that, it is already evening. No furniture store will deliver. Well, they might deliver if we give them a tip."

"A tip?" I asked.

"Yes," said Sal. "If we give them some extra cash. You can buy anything in this city if you have enough cash. If we give them a nice big tip, they might deliver our furniture."

I took out my credit cards and gave them to him.

"Here," I said. "You can use these. When I had no money I couldn't get a credit card. Then when I became rich, they gave me credit cards with a lot of money on them. I can spend up to 250,000 dollars with these cards. Is that enough?"

"A quarter million!" said Sal. "Mio dio! Yes, boss!"

"Okay," I said. "Then buy whatever kind of furniture suits a detective agency. Oh, and if you find any Dick Tracy comic books, buy them. I need to read them before we can begin."

"Sure thing, boss!" said Sal.

Sal left the building and I continued cleaning. I was almost finished cleaning all the dust and spider webs, when I remembered my daily checklist. My plans had changed, very drastically. I needed to alter my checklist.

I took out my notebook from my pocket and looked at my checklist of activities for today. I crossed off "discover connection between Malcolm Vrie and Eddie." I looked at Nora cleaning the windows, with a smile on her face. I was happy that now she would be my employee and would never leave me.

I wrote on my checklist, "make agency and so ensure Nora will never leave me." I looked at it, then crossed it out. I wrote, "make agency and so ensure Nora, Mrs. Levi and Sal will never leave me." I looked at it, but it still looked wrong.

I crossed it off my checklist and wrote "make agency and so ensure my friends and I will make our dreams come true." I looked at this and it made me smile. I checked it off. I then wrote, "spend night cleaning and organizing detective agency."

I checked it off and continued sweeping. I felt happy with my future and secure with my present. For the first time in my life, I felt accepted and content. I felt I had real friends and I was confident that I could be a great detective and make my dreams come true. I was so happy, I couldn't concentrate.

I looked out the window at the full moon. It was pale and shiny and seemed to be smiling at me. It seemed to be telling me that my lonely days were over. It seemed to tell me that the days when I felt like an outcast, unaccepted and misunderstood, were over. I knew the moon was telling me nothing, and it was only my imagination. But I enjoyed my imaginings, and so I continued to listen to the moon. I closed my eyes and sighed. The moon told me this was the first night of a new and better future.

8

THERE ARE SEVENTY-ONE PUBLIC TELEPHONES IN MANHATTAN

Sunlight was shining on the table and illuminating a chart I was making. This chart showed the location of every public pay telephone in Manhattan. This was an important chart for solving the case of the connection between Eddie and Malcolm, the first case of our new Trueman Bradley Detective Agency.

"We're open for business!" shouted Sal.

Sal walked towards me, across the sunlit office. Our office was entirely different from how it had been last week. Now it was decorated with artworks, fine furniture and elegant window curtains. There was a large clock on the wall, filing cabinets for our paperwork and cork bulletin boards for pinning case details to the wall. Sal had ordered placards with our names on them. The placard on my desk said "Detective Trueman Bradley." Piles of paper were on my desk. This was all my research and notes about the case of Eddie and Malcolm.

Nora and I had been awake until late, reorganizing my notes, and now they were neatly arranged on my desk.

"Did you hear me?" asked Sal. "We're open for business! The sign is installed! You want to come out and see it?"

I couldn't understand his words, because I was focusing on my chart and the solution of the Eddie and Malcolm case.

"I can't concentrate on two things at once!" I shouted.

I covered my ears with my hands and closed my eyes, trying to block out the sounds and movements of the busy office. I tried to sit in my chair, but I have always been clumsy. When I'm dizzy from loud distractions, I am even clumsier. I tripped over my chair's legs and fell down on the floor.

"Trueman!" shouted Nora.

She ran to me and helped me to get up. She led me to my chair and I sat, breathing heavily.

"What happened?" asked Nora.

"I was confused," I said, "because Sal came and said something loud while I was busy concentrating on my chart."

"Sal!" shouted Nora.

"What?" he asked. "I was only telling him about the sign! How could I guess that would make him fall down?"

"Well, now you know!" she said. "Trueman sometimes finds it hard to concentrate on more than one thing at a time! Especially if he's focusing on something, don't interrupt him."

"That's very odd!" he said.

"I'm not odd!" I said.

"Okay, I'm sorry," he said. "I don't mean you're odd, Mr. Bradley. But how can I guess that shouting disturbs you so much, unless you tell me? I didn't know this! You treat me like I punched his face, Mrs. Lucca. I meant no harm!"

"Okay," she said. "Relax, Sal. No one's blaming you. Now you know not to interrupt Trueman if he's concentrating, okay?"

"Okay. I'm sorry," said Sal. "I will remember that."

Sal walked away and Nora knelt beside my chair. She stroked my face and talked to me gently. She took a comic book from my desk and opened it to a page we had bookmarked.

"Remember our talk last night?" she asked.

"Yes," I said.

"After we organized your papers," she said, "we read these comic books together. I asked you why you told Sal to buy you Dick Tracy comic books. You said it helps you concentrate on being a detective if you can imitate a detective hero, right?"

"Yes," I said. "That's true."

"So, if you're feeling confused right now," she said, "we'll read this part of the comic you said you liked most. That'll restore your concentration, right?"

"Probably," I said.

She held the comic book in front of me and I recognized it. Sal had found five Dick Tracy comic books and I had already read them all, fifteen times. I had learned there were 140 more Dick Tracy comic books, and a lot of movies and radio plays. But these five comic books were good enough for me to get an idea of Dick Tracy's methods and his detective skills.

"That is issue number 25," I said, "from March 1950."

"Yes," she said, "this is page 25 of issue number 25. I remember you really liked this part when we read it last night. You said it helped give you confidence as a detective. Here, Dick Tracy asks the reader 'can you solve the murder mystery?'"

"Yes," I said. "I remember. A man named Mr. Playhard was found dead. The police thought it was a suicide. But Dick Tracy was suspicious because Playhard was found wearing a green tie. Witnesses who had met Playhard that day said he had been wearing a red tie earlier in the day. Dick didn't think he'd change his tie before committing suicide. So, someone must have murdered Playhard, and replaced his tie for some reason."

"And you solved the case easily," she said.

"Yes," I said. "It was easy. There were three suspects. The suspect named Wilbur Smoothtalk killed him. I knew it was him, because he was color blind. He was the only one of the suspected murderers who would not notice the difference between a red tie and a green tie. Smoothtalk had murdered Playhard by strangling him with his own tie. To hide his crime, Smoothtalk replaced the tie around Playhard's neck. But because he was color blind, Smoothtalk put the wrong colored tie on Playhard."

"Yeah," she said. "That's the right answer. You solved it. And reading this helps you feel confident. Why's that?"

"Because of what it says at the beginning," I said. "It says 'we challenge you to see how good a detective you are! Can you solve the case as Dick Tracy did?' I solved the case easily, so it means I'm a good detective, like Dick Tracy."

"I see," said Nora. "So you feel less confused now?"

"Yes," I said.

I got up and leaned against my desk.

"I think I can continue working now," I said.

Sal had returned and was staring at us.

"I don't understand you, Mr. Bradley!" he said. "Why you get scared so easily? How will you fight the bad guys if you are so easy to scare? I'm sorry, I don't mean to insult you, but why you need to read these comic books? How is it helping you? I don't understand. These comics are for little kids!"

Sal picked up a comic book from my desk and threw it back down. I could recognize irritation on his face.

"I wasn't scared," I said.

"But when I came to talk to you, you panicked and fell down!" he said. "I'm sorry to say it, but that is strange!"

"Sal!" said Nora. "Trueman has Asperger's Syndrome."

"He has what?" he asked. "I never heard of that."

"His mind operates a little bit differently," she said. "For one thing, he can easily get alarmed by unexpected or sudden interruptions. Crowds or loud noises are hard for him."

"Oh…" he said, "so that is why you can't walk on the busy street? That's why you need a chauffeur to drive you?"

"Yes," I said.

"Okay, okay." he said. "I am sorry, Mr. Bradley. I didn't know you have this condition. How can I know if no one tells me, huh? But I still don't see why you need these comic books."

"I need them," I said, "so I can imitate the details in the books and become like Dick Tracy. I do sometimes have some problems because I can't do some things other people can do, but I also have some mental powers other people don't have. I am better at remembering small details and patterns than anyone else I know. So, I can memorize every detail of Dick Tracy perfectly, until I can learn to imitate him exactly. I can even see patterns in his behavior that others don't see. It helps me to become like him. I used to try to imitate Slam Bradley this way, but I prefer Dick Tracy now, because he is more intelligent. Do you see why I need the comic books now?"

"Not really," he said. "Why don't you join the police and become a normal detective? After all, Dick Tracy isn't real, you know! He is a fictional character. Some man invented him to entertain kids. There are not really any men like him!"

"Why not?" I asked.

"Well, I don't know," he said. "There just aren't."

"I don't understand your answer." I said. "Why aren't there? Is it illegal or harmful to be like Dick Tracy?"

"Well, no," he said. "But no one tries to be like him!"

"Okay," I said. "Then I'll be the first to be like him."

Sal sighed and shrugged his shoulders.

"Well, do what you like, boss," he said. "I just don't understand why you want to know everything about this comic book. Why Dick Tracy? Why choose him for your obsession?"

"Why?" I asked. "Because I like him."

Nora put her hand on Sal's shoulder.

"Don't call it an 'obsession,' Sal," Nora said. "It's true, people with Asperger's will sometimes develop a very strong interest in a certain subject. More of a concentrated interest than you or I might have, but there's no reason to make it sound like it's 'strange' or an 'obsession.' He likes comic book detectives because he enjoys memorizing every tiny detail of them. He likes looking for the patterns in the detective's behavior and in criminal behavior. Most people aren't as interested because all these details and patterns are invisible to them. Maybe most people don't try to act like Dick Tracy because they're not good enough at observing details, so they can't possibly mimic Dick Tracy as well as Trueman could."

"But how can he?" he asked. "Dick Tracy was a very smart man. If, as you say, Mr. Bradley has some kind of mental problem, how can he be smart like this?"

"I don't have a mental problem!" I said.

Nora grabbed Sal's shoulders and spoke firmly.

"Sal," she said, "what Trueman lacks in social skills and the ability to concentrate on many things at once, he makes up for in an incredibly strong intelligence in other areas. He just kicked your butt at cards! So don't think he's stupid!"

"Okay! I'm sorry!" he said.

Nora was grasping Sal very hard and I recognized anger in her eyes. She looked ferocious, like an angry cat. I imagined what she'd look like if she were a cat, spitting on Sal's face. I realized she was defending me from Sal and I was grateful to her. She was a loyal friend, willing to protect me from anyone who insulted me or tried to hurt me.

"You're like Tess Trueheart," I said.

Nora was concentrating on Sal so hard that she didn't immediately notice what I said. I couldn't interpret Sal's emotions, but he was trying to free himself from Nora's grasp.

"I didn't mean to insult Mr. Bradley!" he said. "I would not do that. I like Mr. Bradley very much. I didn't know he was so smart! I'm sorry! Yes, of course he must be a genius, right? After all, he is the best poker player I ever saw!"

Nora released Sal and leaned against the table. She was recovering from her strong emotions and was breathing heavily.

"Did you say something, Trueman?" asked Nora.

"You're like Tess Trueheart," I said. "The loyal friend of Dick Tracy. You look like her. Maybe when I imagine myself to be Dick Tracy, you can pretend to be Tess Trueheart."

Nora's face turned red.

"Isn't Tess his girlfriend?" she asked.

"Yes," I said.

"Why do you want me to be Tess?" she asked.

"Because you accurately explained to Sal how I think," I said. "You know me better than anyone else. Tess Trueheart also knows Dick Tracy better than anyone else. Also, you defended me when you felt I was being attacked or insulted. It means you are a loyal friend. Tess Trueheart is also a loyal friend to Dick Tracy. Of course, she is his girlfriend too. But you don't need to be my girlfriend, unless you want to."

Nora's face became redder. I thought this might mean she was embarrassed by what I said. But then I thought it might be caused by her anger and her heavy breathing. Sal was looking down at the floor and I could recognize sorrow on his face.

"Mr. Bradley…" he said, "I am sorry I misunderstood. I wasn't intending to attack or insult you. I did not know about your different way of thinking. But now I understand you better. I hope that both of you will forgive my mistake."

Nora put her hand on Sal's shoulder and embraced him. I thought this was a non-verbal method of saying she forgave him. I felt I should use the same method, so I embraced them both.

"I forgive you, Sal," I said.

Wind came through a window and blew papers off my desk.

"Catch them!" I shouted.

Nora, Sal and I grabbed the papers as they flew through the air. After we caught them all, I walked to my desk and tried to remember where these papers were meant to be. My desk had been perfectly organized. Nora went to close the window.

"I hope that didn't disturb you," she said. "We should get a carpenter to come in here and build walls around your desk. Having your desk in the middle of this big office isn't good. We should build some walls to make you a private office. Then people, sounds and drafts can't disturb you like this!"

"Sure," I said. "But don't hire Eddie the carpenter."

"No, of course not him!" she said.

"Say, what is this map you are working on?" asked Sal.

Sal pointed at the chart I was making. It was marked by little papers, with numbers on them.

"This chart is important for our first case," I said. "The first case of our agency is to discover the connection between Eddie the carpenter and Malcolm Vrie."

"Why is that so important to discover?" he asked.

"Because," said Nora, "Eddie is a murderer. If they have a connection, maybe they were both involved in the murder."

"No," I said. "They were probably both involved in another crime. It is a big coincidence that Malcolm Vrie was given a case to solve, and the murderer in that case is someone who has a connection to him. I have learned that big coincidences, in criminal cases, usually means there is a second, hidden, crime."

"Interesting," she said. "How did you learn that?"

"I studied and memorized all the criminal cases in New York City since 1951," I said. "I memorized all the details. It is easy to notice that pattern. In 95 percent of cases where there were coincidences, there was a second, hidden crime."

"I wish I had your brains!" said Sal. "You memorized cases since 1951? I'm sorry I doubted you, boss. You're a genius!"

"You think I'm a genius?" I asked. "Well, maybe other people can't recognize the patterns so easily. But I'd like to continue explaining the case. I don't like interruptions."

"Sorry, boss," he said.

"When we were at 545 East 13th Street," I said, "I had noticed two similarities between Eddie and Malcolm. They both had stains on their clothes, made by the same ink, and they both had little cuts in exactly the same place on their faces. The likelihood of two people having these similarities is very low. After I came home and spent five hours thinking about it, I remembered more details. I recalled twenty-five more similarities between Eddie and Malcolm. The likelihood of two people having twenty-seven similarities is so low, it is impossible for these two men to not be very much involved in each other's lives."

"I agree," said Nora.

"Yeah, sure," said Sal. "But what does it mean?"

"When you consider that their lives are very closely connected," I said, "and also consider the statistic that 95 percent of big coincidences mean there is a hidden crime, then you can be at least 99.9 percent certain Eddie and Malcolm are criminal partners."

"You don't say!" said Sal.

"Yes, I did," I said. "I just said it now."

"No, Trueman," said Nora. "That's just an expression. It means 'that's amazing.'"

"Oh," I said. "Your expressions make no sense. You are saying the opposite of what is true and its meaning is unrelated to what you're saying. Expressions are illogical."

"Yeah, they are," said Nora. "Please continue explaining."

"Yes, Mr. Bradley," said Sal. "Please continue. I am very impressed by how you can logically solve these problems! You said something earlier about a crime-fighting equation? Is that how you will discover what crimes Eddie and Malcolm have done?"

"No," I said. "I have no equation to determine what crime someone might have committed. My equation only works on crimes that I already know about. I don't know the location and date of their crimes or what kind of crimes they were. Without a date and time, it is hard to use the equation to solve the crime. At least, I need to know what kind of crime it is. I need that information for my equation to execute properly."

"Okay," said Nora. "Can we guess what the crime was?"

"Guess?" I said. "You mean to randomly select a possibility?"

"Yeah, I guess so," she said.

"But why?" I asked. "In that case, the likelihood of being correct is very low. I don't like guessing. It's not logical."

"Okay, never mind," she said. "How do we solve it then?"

"Solve it?" I asked. "I already solved it."

"Oh," she said. "Well, what crime did they do then?"

"The statistics," I said, "of crimes in New York City since 1951 helped me. The twenty-seven clues I observed on Eddie and Malcolm were also observed in fifteen old police cases. Of those fifteen cases, seven of them were cases of counterfeiting money and eight of them were cases of illegally cutting stolen diamonds. So there is a 47 percent chance they are counterfeiting money and a 53 percent chance they are illegally cutting stolen diamonds."

"Wow!" she said. "Then what should we do about it?"

"Well, now that I know what kind of crime it is," I said, "I can use my crime-fighting equation. But I don't know if their crime was counterfeiting or cutting diamonds. So I used the equation for both possible crimes. If they counterfeited, their crime happened eight days ago in a warehouse beside the Hudson River. If they are diamond-cutters, their crime happened on the fifth floor of an apartment building in the area of New York City that is called 'Queens.'"

"So, tomorrow we'll check these places for evidence of their crimes?" she asked.

"Correct," I said. "Except it's not correct that we will do it tomorrow. Mrs. Levi has gone to get our agency permits. We won't be allowed to investigate our first case until we get the permits. Mrs. Levi said we'll get them later this month."

Sal picked up a geometric compass I had been using to create my telephone booth chart.

"You are ingenious, Mr. Bradley," he said. "But I still don't understand what is the purpose of this chart?"

"It is my chart of all the public pay telephones in Manhattan," I said. "I learned yesterday that Manhattan has seventy-one public pay telephones."

"So?" he asked. "Most of them are too dirty to use!"

"Please don't interrupt," I said. "Seventy-one is a prime number. I realized that I could indicate on a chart where all the seventy-one public telephones are. Because it is a prime number, I can make the location of the telephones into an Ulam spiral."

Sal and Nora were silent. I'd expected them to understand immediately, but I could recognize confusion on their faces.

"You don't understand?" I asked.

"No," said Nora. "What's an Ulam spiral?"

"You don't know?" I asked. "An Ulam spiral is composed of a natural progression of numbers, arranged into a spiral. In the spiral, the positions of the prime numbers form diagonal lines. Nobody knows why the prime numbers form diagonals. It is a mysterious law of nature. But because it forms diagonals, it makes a non-random geometric pattern. Sometimes, maybe because of my Asperger's, my sense of direction isn't good. I often get lost trying to walk through the city. But I am good at recognizing numbers and patterns. I am also good at visualizing geometric shapes. So if I imagine the locations of the public telephones are prime numbers and envision Manhattan as an Ulam spiral, the configuration of Manhattan is now logical to me. I will never get lost in Manhattan again. Do you understand now?"

"Ah, this is too much math for me!" said Sal. "Can we change the subject, please? This is hard for me to understand."

"Yeah, me too," said Nora. "But I think I get some of your meaning. You see numbers and patterns better than real objects, so you made a mathematical pattern out of locations of the public telephones. So, now, you can use this prime number pattern to better remember where everything is in Manhattan. Is that what you're saying?"

"Yes, Tess," I said. "You know me better than anyone!"

Nora's face turned red again.

"Well, that's great, Trueman," she said. "I'm glad you won't get lost in Manhattan. But why is that so important for solving the case of Eddie and Malcolm?"

"It's very important!" I said. "Because this Ulam spiral can be used for more than one purpose. Discovery of this Ulam spiral pattern in Manhattan has allowed me to invent a new equation. This equation can locate criminal evidence."

"You made a new equation?" she asked.

"Yes," I said. "This equation finds evidence. How it works is… I can add the prime number aggregate onto my crime-fighting equation, and it adds a location variable…"

"No, please!" said Sal. "No more math! My brain is hurting from all this! Let's take a break from math!"

"Okay," I said. "I'll explain it later. I'll test my new 'Ulam spiral evidence-finding equation' later this month when we look for evidence of Eddie's and Malcolm's crimes."

Nora picked up a comic book and looked at it. She started pacing around the floor. She walked so briskly, she bounced. I could recognize she was excited about our investigation.

"I can't wait!" she said. "We'll get that jerk, Malcolm! We'll get him thrown in jail! I always knew he was bad news!"

"I am still amazed at you, Mr. Bradley," said Sal. "You are a modern Sherlock Holmes!"

"Who is he?" I asked.

"I'll tell you later," said Nora.

"You are a master crime-solver!" said Sal. "It is amazing! How do you do it? Is it just because you are good at math?"

"No," I said. "As I said, I concentrate on Dick Tracy and memorize it all and recognize the patterns. That helps me concentrate so much on detective work that I think of very helpful and ingenious solutions to our cases. I don't know the exact cause. It results from my intense concentration."

"I start to see how Dick Tracy helps you," he said. "The more you know of Dick Tracy, the better your detective skills?"

"Yes," I said. "I will become better if I can get the other 140 comic books and learn everything I can about him."

"Well, in that case, I will do everything I can to help fill your mind with Dick Tracy!" he said. "I would even pretend to be Dick Tracy's partner, if you wished it! What was the name of Dick's partner? Was it Sam Catchem?"

"Yes," I said. "But I'd prefer if you'd pretend to be Bob Oscar 'B.O.' Plenty. He was a good friend of Dick Tracy."

"Okay," he said. "But why you want me to be this man?"

"Because," I said, "you're a good friend."

"A good friend, am I?" he asked. "That is flattering."

"Also," I said, "Oscar Plenty's house was messy, just like your old car was. And sometimes Oscar smelled bad, just like you sometimes smell bad because you smoke a pipe."

Sal's face turned red and I could recognize that he was embarrassed. He put his hands in his pockets and coughed.

"Well…" he said, "maybe I won't pretend to be him yet. At least, not until we go on our investigation later this month and I know, for sure, that all your equations really work."

"But you'll find more Dick Tracy comic books?" I asked.

"Of course!" he said. "I was not able to find any more comic books last time I searched. But I know I will find some next time! Last time, I only found someone who was selling a cheap two-way wrist TV. The kind Dick used in the comic books."

I became excited at the thought of owning a two-way wrist TV, like Dick Tracy used in his comic books. He wore it on his wrist and used it to communicate with his friends during a case. It would be useful for me to have a two-way wrist TV and be able to communicate with Nora, Sal and Mrs. Levi during our investigations. Also, it would help me to feel like Dick Tracy.

"I'd be a lot more confident as a detective if I had a wrist TV!" I said. "Go buy it, Sal! I'll give you the money."

"No, no, Mr. Bradley!" he said. "It is just a toy! It doesn't really work. In the 1960s they made fake two-way TVs for children to play with. They aren't real. You understand?"

I understood, and I was disappointed. I had gotten so excited, imagining the two-way wrist TV on my wrist, that it felt like the case would be much more difficult without it. I must have looked very upset, because Nora comforted me with a hug.

"Ah, Trueman," she said. "You forget, you've got a lot of cash! We can probably buy some real two-way wrist TVs somewhere. Back in the 1960s they couldn't make real wrist TVs like that. But nowadays, I'm sure someone's invented them."

"Really?" I asked. "Someone's invented them?"

"Well, I'm not sure if someone did," she said. "But if they've not been invented, we can pay someone to invent them for us!"

"That's right," I said. "We have a lot of money."

"Hey!" said Sal. "If you are looking for an inventor, I know a good one! She is an old Italian lady. She's an old friend of mine. Her name is Dr. Lucretia Rozzozzo. From an old, rich family. She is eccentric. Very strange lady. I think all people from old, rich families are strange like that. They can afford to be! She would help us. A two-way wrist TV is exactly the unusual kind of invention she likes to create."

"Really?" I asked. "Can we talk to her now? I would love to have the two-way wrist TVs before we go on our investigation!"

"Sure!" he said. "I have the Lincoln car ready to go! Just put on your coats and we'll go see my strange, old friend. On the way, I can show you our new neon sign! It is a beauty!"

The sky had become cloudy and rain was falling. I could smell the humidity coming in, through an open window. Rain on the streets of New York City smelled like wet dust. We walked to the front hallway and put on our coats.

"We should bring our umbrellas," I said. "I think the volume of rain will increase as time progresses."

Sal laughed.

"Let me guess…" he said. "You know this because you have invented an ingenious equation for predicting the weather?"

"No," I said. "I know this because I can hear the sound of the rain getting louder as time passes. Can you hear it?"

"Oh," he said. "I guess so. My hearing's not so good."

"But a weather-predicting equation is a good idea," I said. "Maybe I'll work on that later. I'll need weather statistics."

We walked out the front door and onto the sidewalks of Reade Street. Everything was gray, because the sun was hidden behind thick rainclouds. Water covered everything. The sound of cars driving through puddles made noises like waves on the shore of an ocean. The whole city smelled like wet dust.

The three of us stood under our umbrellas. We were lit from above, by a yellow light. A big square sign hung above the front door of 201 Reade Street. It said "The Trueman Bradley Detective Agency." The words were made of glass pipes filled with neon gas. The words glowed yellow and could be seen from far away. The bright yellow words glowed on the gray, rainy street like the light of a lighthouse, shining through fog. Pedestrians and people in cars stared at our sign as they passed by it.

"How do you like it, boss?" asked Sal.

I was very pleased with our new sign, but I was too concentrated on my thoughts to answer Sal. I was inspired by how much this gray, rainy street looked like an illustration from a Dick Tracy comic book. I was allowing myself to experience the similarity between my life and the fictional world of the comic books. The more my world resembled Dick Tracy, the more I could concentrate on solving cases and the more confident I became in my ability. I had learned from my granddad that success would come if I had confidence in myself. The neon sign made me feel I was now a real detective, with my own recognizable and deserved place in New York City. But more than that, it made me feel confident. Because the sign reminded me of something from a comic book illustration, it made me confident that I was like Dick Tracy.

"I need a yellow outfit..." I said.

"What's that, Trueman?" asked Nora.

Nora touched my arm and I emerged from my daydreaming.

"Oh," I said. "The yellow light of our neon sign reminded me that Dick Tracy wears a yellow hat and trench coat. I shouldn't be wearing gray. Also, am I in the right city? Did Dick Tracy live in New York City?"

"I don't know where he lived," she said. "The comic books we have don't mention anything about where he lived."

"I think Dick Tracy was living in Chicago," said Sal.

"Well," I said. "Maybe. But that doesn't matter to me. It is too late to change. And I like New York City better."

"Why?" asked Nora.

"Because," I said, "you and Sal and Mrs. Levi are here. I would not have met you in Chicago, and I'm glad I met you."

Nora squeezed my arm. I didn't understand the meaning of the squeeze, but it made me smile.

"Maybe I can pretend this is Chicago," I said. "Then I can feel like the real Dick Tracy without moving there."

I looked at the street, trying to imagine it was Chicago. I was beginning to convince myself, when I was distracted by an unexpected sight.

A man was crossing Reade Street, walking towards me. His stride was aggressive and I could recognize anger on his face.

"Detective Buckley?" I asked.

The man approached us and I could recognize Detective Sam Buckley. He was wearing a soaking wet fedora and trench coat.

"Yeah, I'm Buckley!" he said. "Who do you think I am?"

He removed the fedora from his head and shook the water from it. He looked at our sign and pointed his finger at it.

"What's that?" he asked.

"That's the sign of our new detective agency," I said.

"Yeah, I can see that!" he said. "What do you know about opening a detective agency? Didn't I tell you to go back to Heartville, or wherever it is you're from? You're setting yourself up for a fall, kid! Get rid of that sign and forget all about this detective agency business, you understand?"

"No," I said. "Why are you ordering me to leave?"

"Because you're gonna get yourself hurt!" he said. "You're a nice kid and I like you a lot. But you have no idea how dangerous this kind of work is! That's why I'm telling you to go home and stop trying to be a detective, you understand?"

"You're worried I'll get hurt?" I asked.

"Yeah!" he said. "Because you're in way over your head! What do you know about running a detective agency?"

"I know what I've read in Dick Tracy comic books," I said.

"Comics?" he asked. "Are you still talking about your comic books? Listen kid, this is no comic book! This is real-life criminals and real guns and a good chance of getting yourself killed! You can't run an agency! I mean, what do you even know about managing a business, huh? You're just a kid!"

"I'm not a kid!" I said.

"And he does not need to know everything about managing a business," said Sal. "Because I already know everything about it. I ran and operated my own business for many decades."

Buckley became silent. He stared at Nora and Sal as if he hadn't noticed them until now.

"Who are these guys?" he asked.

"I'm not a guy," said Nora. "I'm a woman."

"Fine!" said Buckley. "Trueman, who are these people?"

"I am the man who manages his agency!" said Sal. "Like I said, I know all about running a business. So, Trueman doesn't need to know anything about it. You asked Trueman how he can manage and operate a business? Well, I'm telling you how!"

"Yes," I said. "Sal operates the agency for me."

Buckley shook his head and sighed. He put his wet hat on his head. He walked closer to me and grabbed my shoulder.

"Listen, Trueman," he said. "Okay. So, maybe you can get someone to manage your agency for you. But what are you gonna do when you have to chase down criminals, huh? You couldn't even cross Broadway! Remember? That criminal had to help you cross the sidewalk! Now, I ask you, buddy, how you gonna do detective work? You can't even cross a street alone!"

"He's got me to help him!" said Nora.

Nora moved to stand between Buckley and me. I interpreted the anger on her face and I realized she was defending me again.

"Trueman has some difficulties doing things that are easy for you and me," she said, "but he's a genius in other ways, which you don't understand. You're trying to say he couldn't possibly be successful as a detective, but he's thought of ways to solve crimes that you're not smart enough to think of."

Buckley stared at Nora. It seemed to me he was not certain how to respond to Nora's opposition.

"Who is this lady?" he asked.

"She's my friend," I said.

Nora removed her sunglasses and wide-brimmed hat.

"We've met before, Detective," she said.

"Oh yeah," he said. "Now I recognize you, Detective Lucca. Don't tell me you're in on this too? What are you doing here?"

"I'm one of the detectives in his agency now," she said.

"Are you kidding?" he asked. "Didn't I tell you, Ms. Lucca, not to encourage this guy? I mean, I know he really wants to be a detective. But, I mean, come on, the guy's got some kind of mental disorder, right? You're just gonna get him killed or something by encouraging him and making him believe he can be a detective! This guy's not right in the head!"

Sal started making noises that reminded me of a growling dog. He moved and stood between Buckley and me. I could recognize the anger on his face. I realized that both Nora and Sal were defending me now. They stared angrily at Buckley.

"You listen to me, Detective!" said Sal. "Mr. Bradley's Asperger's Syndrome doesn't mean he's a stupid guy! You understand? It does not mean he is 'not right in the head'! It does not mean he has a mental disorder! He can think of brilliant ideas and equations, better than you could ever think of! So, I tell you, when compared to Mr. Bradley, you are stupid! So, maybe you are the one with a mental disorder!"

Buckley stepped backwards, away from the two angry faces. He was silent for a while and seemed like he would walk away, without a word. But, instead, he put one of his arms around my shoulders and whispered to me in a kindly way.

"Okay, Trueman," he said. "Sorry, maybe I don't understand enough about this Asperger's thing. Maybe I should read a book about it or something. If I said something offensive, well I'm sorry, alright? But I'm saying this for your own good. There's a real good chance you'll get hurt or something. You understand? Like I said, I like you, and I don't want you getting hurt, understand? That's why I'm telling you to forget about this detective work. I'll tell you one more time, alright? Just go back home. Forget about all this. You're gonna get yourself hurt. Okay, maybe I made a mistake, kid. Maybe you're smarter than I gave you credit for. But you can't deal with a big city like this, right? What are you gonna do next time you get nervous on a busy city street? Is another criminal gonna victimize you like last time? Next time, I might not be around to rescue you. You just can't succeed as a detective."

Buckley's words made me feel terrible, because I still was not entirely sure if I could succeed. His discouraging words caused my doubts to intensify and I felt my confidence lowering. But I remembered Nora's willingness to help me, by reading me Dick Tracy; I remembered how impressed Sal was, when he heard about my equations and my solutions; I remembered the times when I felt like I was really Dick Tracy. I looked up at the yellow neon sign, which looked so much like a sign from a comic book.

"That was a long time ago," I said.

"What?" asked Buckley.

"When we first met," I said. "That day when Seth tried to rob me. That was a long time ago, Detective."

"It wasn't!" he said. "It was nine days ago, Trueman!"

"Yes, I know," I said. "It was 216 hours ago. I meant, it was a long time ago because many things have happened since then. Maybe it only feels like a very long time ago, to me, because my life is much different now. Everything is different now. Now, I am stronger and more confident in myself."

"Now he has friends to help him," said Nora.

Nora and Sal stood in front of Buckley, staring at him. Buckley didn't say anything. I couldn't interpret his emotions, but I imagined he was too confused to say anything. He grabbed the sides of his coat and pulled it tightly against his body.

Mrs. Levi's antique car, a 1966 Volvo Saloon, arrived on Reade Street and parked beside us. Mrs. Levi, dressed in a blue dress and a flowery hat, waved at us. Buckley looked at the Volvo and frowned. Then, without saying a word, he walked away.

"Trueman!" said Mrs. Levi.

"Hello, Mrs. Levi!" I said. "Did you get the permits?"

Mrs. Levi moved quickly, and it seemed to me she was excited about something. She had a newspaper in her hands.

"Yes, dear," she said. "We get our permits later this month. But when I was waiting in the office, I happened to pick up this newspaper. And look what I found! There's a story here about that detective, Malcolm Vrie!"

Nora grabbed the newspaper from Mrs. Levi's hands.

"Listen to this…" said Nora. "Murder in East Village solved by private detective!" she read aloud. "A case of murder was solved by a Manhattan private detective named Malcolm Vrie. Mr. Eddie Sipple, a forty-six-year-old carpenter, was arrested for the murder of Eric Lendalainen, in front of an East 13th Street apartment building, a week ago. Vrie was able to identify Sipple as the murderer when he discovered traces of the victim's blood on a baseball cap belonging to Sipple."

"That scumbag!" said Nora. "I knew he'd steal our evidence and take the credit! Now everyone thinks he solved it!"

Sal, Nora and Mrs. Levi stood close to each other, under one umbrella, reading the story. But I was too focused on my thoughts to give any more attention to the newspaper. I was thinking why Malcolm would arrest Eddie, the carpenter, if they were both involved in criminal acts together. This seemed to indicate they were not actually involved in crime together.

"That's not possible…" I said. "There are too many clues to connect them as criminal partners. Why would Malcolm arrest Eddie if they're partners in crime?"

"What did you say, Trueman?" asked Nora.

I had been talking to myself, not Nora. And I was too concentrated on my own thoughts to answer her question. I began to think of my crime-fighting equation. I had some new information now. Malcolm had arrested his criminal partner, Eddie. I wanted to insert this new information into my crime-fighting equation and see what the results would be. I closed my eyes and tried to concentrate on the equation.

"Well, let's get to the car, friends!" said Sal.

Nora pulled my arm and we walked along the sidewalk, towards the Lincoln car. The rain started coming down heavily and we rushed to get into the car. Sal opened the driver's side door and sat in the driver's seat. He operated the controls and the leather hood of the car began to lower. Nora, Mrs. Levi and I stood outside the car, watching the rain fall into the car, soaking the luxurious leather seats.

"Mannaggia!" said Sal. "I pressed the wrong button! Now I lowered the hood and it won't come back up!"

Sal jumped out of the car and tried to raise the hood with his hands. Mrs. Levi and Nora helped him. After a minute or so, their efforts were successful and the hood came up.

"I told you!" said Sal. "This old car has some problems. Sometimes it does not function correctly. Now, let's get in!"

We opened the car doors and sat in the wet seats. I could feel the water soaking into my clothes and every time I moved, the wet leather made a squeaking sound, rubbing against my trench coat. After a few minutes, we were driving away.

"Are you okay, Trueman?" asked Nora.

Nora and I sat on the back seat together.

"Yes. Why?" I asked.

"Well, ever since Mrs. Levi showed us that newspaper," she said, "you haven't responded to anything I said to you. You just stared at nothing and made a sound like 'ung, ung…'"

"Oh," I said. "I didn't notice you were talking to me, because I was concentrating on my crime-fighting equation.

Malcolm arrested his own criminal partner and I was trying to equate what it means. I was trying to determine the result."

"So, what was the result?" she asked. "What does it mean?"

I was not sure of the result. In my equation, Malcolm and Eddie were represented by algebraic variables. For some reason, when I executed the equation including this new information, Malcolm and Eddie both equaled zero. Any time I had used this equation, no variable had ever equaled zero. I didn't know what that meant. I had not designed the equation in a way that allowed for answers to equal zero. This was an anomaly and I started to wonder if my crime-fighting equation was imperfect.

"Is something wrong?" asked Nora.

Nora must have been capable of reading my emotions, because she was looking at me and I could recognize worry on her face. She knew that I was doubtful of myself. I didn't want her to know about my doubts. Sal and Nora were so impressed by my equations and I didn't want to lose their good opinion of me by admitting that my equations might be flawed.

"Nothing's wrong," I said. "Don't worry. I was just thinking about it. We can still go searching for evidence later this month. Like you said, we'll expose Malcolm's crimes."

"It's so exciting!" she said. "Our agency's first case!"

Nora put her arm around me and hugged me. She had said she wasn't in love with me, but the warmth of her arms still made me smile and my face turn red from pleasure. I didn't want to risk changing Nora's loving attitude towards me. Although I was full of doubt, I tried not to let it show.

"I'm excited too," I said.

I smiled and tried to act confident, like Dick Tracy would. But my mind was distracted by the strange result of my equation.

"What does zero mean?" I asked.

"What?" asked Nora.

"Oh, nothing," I said. "I was just talking to myself."

HICKSON WAREHOUSE

The Hudson River is close to my office on Reade Street. At night, the city lights reflect off the river and these reflections look like a sea of shining stars. These imaginary stars fascinated me. But I resisted the desire to stop and memorize them. I forced myself to continue walking along the boardwalk. I couldn't be late, because I was on a mission. I was working on my agency's first case. I was on my first mission alone, without help. I was alone on the boardwalk, hunting for evidence to expose the crimes of Malcolm Vrie.

I had been walking along the boardwalk for thirty minutes, but I hadn't met anyone. This is because I had improved my jerk magic detector equation, and I had successfully predicted when pedestrians would be coming. This way, I had been able to avoid meeting anyone. I was glad, because I had made a detailed checklist of how I would complete this mission. The first item on the list read "go to Hickson warehouse without meeting anyone." So far, everything was going according to my plan.

Sometimes I would pass a window or a mirror and I would look at myself. I was wearing a long, yellow trench coat and a yellow hat—just like Dick Tracy. My special sunglasses made me look mysterious, as a detective should look. I liked to look at myself, because I looked exactly how I had planned to look. I was comforted to know my plan was going as I had expected.

The river, at night, was the perfect setting for detective work. It looked like a scene from a comic book. I was excited to be able to prove to everyone that I could solve a case and go on a mission without anyone's help. I'd prove to them my Asperger's doesn't stop me from becoming a great detective.

"Trueman!" said Nora.

The sudden, unexpected voice made me jump and trip over my feet. I fell to the ground and hid my face behind my hands.

"Trueman!" said Nora. "Are you there?"

I had left my wrist TV on. One month had passed since we'd visited Sal's friend, the inventor, and she had made four two-way wrist TVs for us. I had forgotten I was wearing it.

"Yes, Nora?" I asked. "Is that you, Nora?"

I looked at my wrist TV and saw Nora's face on the small screen. She looked like she was walking down a busy street.

"Yes, it's me," said Nora. "What's wrong? You look scared. Are you lying on the ground?"

"Um, yes," I said. "You scared me with your voice."

"Oh," she said. "Did you forget you were wearing the wrist TV? Maybe we should have designed them to beep or something, before we can talk to each other. That way you won't get surprised or scared by the unexpected voice."

"But then the beep would surprise me," I said.

"Okay," she said. "Never mind. I'm just calling to tell you that Sal and I have arrived at the apartment block in the neighborhood of Queens. We're going to search for evidence."

"Good," I said. "Malcolm and Eddie are either counterfeiting money or illegally cutting diamonds. If they counterfeited, their crime happened in Hickson warehouse, beside the Hudson River. If they are diamond-cutters, their crime happened on the fifth floor of an apartment building in

Queens. The plan is for you to search the apartment building and I will search the warehouse. One of us will find evidence and then we will know if Malcolm and Eddie are counterfeiters or diamond-cutters. The first step of my plan is to go to…"

"Trueman," said Nora, "you're repeating yourself. You already told me about your plan many times in the last month."

"Oh, okay…" I said.

Sometimes I repeat myself, and don't realize I am boring other people. My plan interested me so much that I couldn't imagine why someone else wouldn't want to hear about the details of it. I am not bored by repetition if the topic being repeated is interesting to me. I had repeated my plan in my mind hundreds of times. The neat, logical perfection of my plan's details fascinated me and I never became bored of it.

"What do you want to talk to me about?" I asked.

"I want to ask if we can change the plan," she said.

"No!" I said. "We can't! I finalized this plan a week ago and it is very specially designed! It is perfect and we must do it exactly as planned. No changes or surprises are allowed!"

"I know you don't like surprises, Trueman," she said. "I have the plan you printed out and gave me. Me and Sal have done it all, just like you said. But the only thing…"

"But you didn't!" I said. "There was no item on your checklist saying 'call Trueman.' That is why your voice surprised me. Now you forced me to change the plan. Please write 'call Trueman at 9:38 pm' into your plan. I'll write 'receive call from Nora at 9:38 pm' into my plan. Please don't force me to change the plan again, or I'll get very nervous!"

"Why should I write it into the plan if I already did it?" she asked.

"Because," I said, "it will make me less nervous if our conversation is part of the plan."

"But we already…" she said. "Okay, never mind. We'll write it into our checklist if it's important to you. But the reason I called you, Trueman, is because I'm worried about you."

"Worried?" I asked. "Why?"

"Why?" she asked. "Because you're all alone, at night, on the boardwalk. The boardwalk has a lot of crime at night. Muggers and robbers and crazy people! If you were a kickboxing champion, carrying a machine gun in your back pocket, I would still be worried about you. It's just not safe! I'm worried you'll get killed or something! Why did you insist on searching the warehouse alone? Sal could've gone with you."

"I wanted to do it alone because…" I said.

I saw a shadow moving along the sidewalk. I was horrified to realize someone was walking towards me. I was still lying on the ground. I crawled into a nearby bush, hiding from the unexpected pedestrian. I remained still, hoping he wouldn't see me. I was relieved when he walked past without noticing me.

"Nora!" I said. "You made me forget to use my jerk magic equation. Someone approached me and almost saw me!"

"Oh, I'm sorry!" she said. "I didn't know you were using that equation. So, you haven't met anyone on the boardwalk?"

"No," I said. "The inventor put my equation into my two-way wrist TV. So now I can enter the data into the watch and it does the jerk magic equation for me. So, I've been able to improve the equation. I met no one, until you distracted me!"

"I said I'm sorry!" she said. "Wait… you said you put the jerk magic equation into the computer of our wrist TVs?"

"Yes," I said. "And the crime-fighting equation too. The inventor helped me to put the equations into the wrist TVs."

"Does that mean we can use your equations?" asked Nora.

"Well, yes, I guess you can use them…" I said.

I stopped myself from saying any more. I hadn't meant to tell Nora that. Ever since I had been confused by Malcolm and

Eddie equaling zero, I had begun to doubt that my equations worked. If my equations were flawed, I didn't want my friends to know about it. I didn't want them to use my equations on their wrist TVs or they might discover my equations are imperfect. I needed to end this conversation.

"I need to go now," I said. "I will write on my schedule, 'receive call from Nora at 10:05 pm.' Write 'call Trueman at 10:05 pm' on your checklist. Please don't call before then. We need to execute the plan very precisely or it won't succeed."

Nora sighed.

"Okay, Trueman," she said. "I guess I'm not as worried if you are using your jerk magic equation to avoid people. But I would like it if…"

"Okay, bye!" I said.

I interrupted her because I was scared she might say something about my equations again. I cut off my connection to Nora's wrist TV and began inputting the data of my jerk magic equation to predict when it was safe to emerge from hiding and continue walking to Hickson warehouse.

But inputting data made me impatient.

"Maybe putting the equations into the wrist TV wasn't a good idea," I said. "I can execute it faster in my head."

I closed my eyes and concentrated on the jerk magic equation. Within a few seconds, I calculated the answer.

"Great," I said. "Ten minutes and three seconds with no people. I'll get to Hickson warehouse with no interruptions."

I emerged from my hiding place and started walking along the boardwalk. I thought about my equations.

"Maybe putting the equations into the wrist TV's computer was a bad idea," I said to myself.

Because of my thoughts, I hadn't been concentrating on where I was going. I suddenly felt very confused about my surroundings. I have a poor sense of direction. I often get lost and confused, even in places I've visited before. I had been sure of my location only a few seconds earlier, but from a moment of not paying attention, I had completely forgotten where I was. I panicked, and wasn't sure if I should continue walking or hide somewhere until my panic stopped.

"I need the telephones!" I said.

I pressed a button on my wrist TV and saw the Ulam spiral I had invented. The location of all the public pay telephones in Manhattan were entered into my wrist TV's computer and arranged into a mathematical Ulam spiral. I was comforted by the logic and order of prime numbers in the spiral. Their diagonal symmetry calmed me and I was able to remember where I was. I was walking along the fifth diagonal on the Ulam spiral. Because of my skill at math and visualizing numbers, having a mathematical map of Manhattan helped me to visualize my location. I continued walking confidently along the boardwalk.

"Only eight minutes until someone comes!" I said.

I could see a large, square silhouette beside the river. It was at exactly the location where Hickson warehouse should be. There was a short distance of forested parkland between the boardwalk and the warehouse. I needed to climb over a fence, walk across the parkland and enter Hickson warehouse through the back door. My equations indicated that no one would disturb me.

I looked at the metal fence and tried to think of how to climb it. I had expected to simply jump over it, like I had seen Dick Tracy do in comic books. But now that I was in front of the fence, I could see it was too high for me to jump over and I didn't know how to climb it. I put my hands on the bars of the fence, but I was not strong enough to climb over it. In the comic books, Dick Tracy simply flew over fences. There was no explanation about his method of jumping a fence.

I looked at the item on my checklist that read, "jump fence and walk across parkland." It seemed to me I would fail at this task and never be able to cross that item off my list. I noticed an open gate nearby, leading into the parkland. I hated to change anything in my plan, but when I made the plan I didn't realize there was a gate. So, maybe it was not so bad to change this one detail. I would have planned to use the gate, if I knew it existed. I crossed "jump fence" off my checklist and replaced it with "use gate."

A wind came in from over the Hudson River and my yellow trench coat flapped. The cold wind caused me to shiver. I pulled my coat tightly around my body and hurried through the wind, past the gate and into the dark shadows of the parkland. The darkness was disturbing to me, and because I was wearing my special sunglasses it was difficult for me to see where I was going. Although everything was going according to plan, and the changes I'd made had been minor, I could not stop feeling tense. The darkness made me nervous. Even the cold breeze scared me. It all made me feel a paralyzing anxiety.

The trees looked sinister in the shadows and sometimes looked like people. But I knew my jerk detector equation was improved. It was now correct 92 percent of the time. So, every time I thought I saw a person, I reminded myself that nobody was around. There was only an 8 percent chance of anyone being around.

"That's a very low percentage," I said, comforting myself.

As I said this, I saw the silhouette of a man, leaning against a fence. I tried to deny that it was a man; I tried to remind myself the likelihood of seeing someone was only 8 percent, but I couldn't. The silhouette was too clear and too obviously human. I ran towards the nearest tree and hid behind it.

I was breathing heavily and it was hard to keep quiet. All my anxiety and fear had now been justified. I covered my mouth with my yellow scarf, trying to keep my breathing silent. I peeked around the tree to see if the man had heard me. He was standing in exactly the same position, leaning on the fence.

I was horrified to realize this 8 percent chance possibility had come true. I was either having incredibly bad luck or my equation was somehow flawed. Either way, I was unhappy and terrified. My plan was ruined. Now, too much had gone wrong. I had the strong desire to cancel the mission and run away.

I looked at my wrist TV and was tempted to call Nora, even though calling her now wasn't on the checklist. My checklist plan was ruined now, so it didn't matter anymore. Besides that, I was scared of what this man might do to me and wanted the comfort of feeling I wasn't alone. Because of the wrist TVs, I was never really alone. I switched on the wrist TV.

"Nora?" I asked, trying to speak quietly.

There was no answer. I peeked behind me, to see if the mysterious stranger had heard me, but he stood in the same position. He was so perfectly still, it was frightening.

"Nora!" I said, slightly louder.

Nora's face appeared on the wrist TV.

"Trueman?" she asked.

Her voice was loud and it made me jump from fear that the man would hear us. I lowered the volume. I could see from the TV screen that Nora was high above the street. I could see the lights of New York City below her.

"Please speak quietly," I said. "I know it is not on the checklist for me to call you right now, but I have a problem."

"What is it, Trueman?" asked Nora.

"Trueman?" asked Mrs. Levi.

Shocked, I looked around the dark forest for Mrs. Levi, but all I saw was the mysterious man, still leaning on the fence.

"Trueman?" asked Mrs. Levi. "Is that you, dear? My goodness, this wrist TV really works! I can see your face!"

I realized Mrs. Levi was using her wrist TV to talk to me. I could now see two faces on my wrist TV: Nora and Mrs. Levi. Mrs. Levi appeared to be sitting in our office, drinking tea.

"Mrs. Levi," I said, "this is not a good time for talking."

"Oh, are you busy, dear?" she asked.

"Yes," I said. "I have a problem."

"Oh, you don't say?" she asked. "Well, I won't take too much of your time. You know, I was just wondering, Trueman... me and Nora were talking a little while ago..."

"Mrs. Levi," I said, "I really need to talk to Nora."

Mrs. Levi continued talking.

"...and Nora told me all about how you put that equation of yours on these wrist TVs... so, I was just wondering. Does it mean any one of us could solve crimes like you now? We can all use your equations and solve crimes now?"

"Yes," I said.

"Well, then, dear," she said, "in that case, there's all kinds of crimes in New York City. There's murders and robberies that could be solved by any one of us, right? I think we should be using this thing to saved kidnapped children, recover the purses of poor old ladies... you know, that kind of thing. Isn't it kind of... immoral, if we have the secret to solve these crimes and make people happy, and we don't use it?"

"Immoral?" I asked. "What do you mean?"

"Well," she said, "we're really no better than the criminals if we have the key to rescuing kids or to finding some poor old lady's stolen money and we decide not to use it."

"Key?" I asked. "What key? I only have the key to the office and the key to my granddad's house in Heartville."

"No, Trueman," said Nora. "That's just an expression. What Mrs. Levi means is... if we have the power to help save kidnapped children, for instance, and we decide not to help them, that's kind of immoral. Because we're not helping the children when we are able to. That's bad, right?"

"Yes," I said.

"Well, we have the power to help them with your equations!" said Nora. "So I think we have an obligation to do things like save kidnapped kids. If we don't, we're just deciding to let them suffer! Then, we're really just as bad as the criminals, right? Mrs. Levi and I decided we'd use our wrist TVs to rescue all the kidnapped children in New York City. I think we could do it. I've seen how well your equation works. Mrs. Levi and I just need you to show us how to enter data into our wrist TVs and use your equation. So, what do you think? Will you help?"

I had never really thought of this before. My equations had always been a fascinating hobby for me and a means of succeeding as a detective. I hadn't realized they could also do a lot of good. Just by inputting data into the computer of my wrist TV, I could end the miseries of a kidnapped child. The innocent victim's horrible ordeal could be stopped by me, in just a few minutes. I suddenly felt as if I were responsible for all the unsolved crimes in the world, because I had a tool on my wrist that could solve every one of them. All the criminals were free because I was so selfish that I didn't choose to spend a few minutes to solve their crimes.

"You're right, Nora," I said. "I didn't realize that."

"Great!" said Nora. "Then when we're done this mission, you can show me and Mrs. Levi how to use your equation."

"Wait!" I said. "No! I can't help you!"

"What?" asked Nora. "Why not?"

I had remembered that my equations seemed to be flawed. I didn't want Nora or Mrs. Levi or anyone to use my equations until I was sure they were working perfectly. I couldn't endure the embarrassment if they discovered my equations didn't work.

"I can't show you how to use them," I said. "Sorry."

"But what about saving kids?" asked Nora. "Trueman, you can't be saying you refuse to help us. Don't you know there are innocent victims of crime out there suffering all kind of awful things? And you don't want to help them! Why not?"

"I don't want to talk about this!" I said. "I have some trouble here. A man is leaning on the fence and he doesn't move. I think I might need to cancel the mission."

"What?" asked Nora. "Why? Trueman, is something wrong? You're acting very strange. If there's something you're not telling us or if something's bothering you, please tell me."

"There's nothing I'm not telling you," I said. "I don't want to talk about it! Items on my checklist plan are going wrong. Maybe I'll go back to the office and make a new plan."

"We can't start over, Trueman!" said Nora. "I'm already on the roof of the apartment block. What exactly is going wrong?"

"There's a man here in the park," I said.

"Well, just hide!" said Nora. "Wait for him to go away."

"But he doesn't move!" I said. "He hasn't moved at all for the last five minutes. He's scaring me. I need to cancel."

"I don't understand!" said Nora. "You said you're using your jerk magic equation to avoid people. So, how come you couldn't avoid this guy? Just use your equation!"

I didn't answer. I had accidently let her know my jerk magic equation seemed not to be working. I felt a terrible fear that all my equations had stopped working. I would fail at this mission; fail at being a detective and Nora, Sal and Mrs. Levi would no longer admire my mind. I felt paralyzed by anxiety.

"Wait a minute, Mr. Bradley!" said Sal.

"Sal?" I asked. "You're using the wrist TV too?"

Three faces now appeared on the screen of my wrist TV. Sal was inside the driver's seat of the Lincoln car.

"Yes, Mr. Bradley," he said. "I was listening to your conversation. You said there is a man leaning on a fence? And he is standing very still? Is that correct, Mr. Bradley?"

I looked around the tree and saw the mysterious man leaning on the fence. He hadn't moved from his original position.

"That's correct, Sal," I said.

"Okay, I thought so," he said. "Tell me, is there a bear standing nearby?"

"A bear?" I asked.

"Yes," said Sal. "Have a look around. See a bear?"

I looked around the grassy lawn where the man was leaning on the fence and I saw the outline of a bear, in the distance.

"A bear!" I said. "Now I know I need to cancel the mission. Sal! Please drive here and get me. Fast!"

"No, no, Mr. Bradley!" he said. "I do not need to get you, although I know exactly where you are! You are close to the street called River Terrace. That is correct?"

"Yes," I said. "But how do you know that?"

Sal laughed.

"Because, Mr. Bradley," he said, "there are many statues in the parkland beside River Terrace. That man is a cast-iron statue! The bear is also a statue. If you walk further, you will see a statue of a giant fist. That man is not a real man!"

I looked at the mysterious man, but couldn't determine if he was real or a statue. I removed my sunglasses and could instantly see that he was, indeed, a statue. I could see the moonlight reflecting on his metal body. I felt incredibly relieved and sighed deeply.

"Oh," I said. "Then the cancellation is cancelled."

"Okay," said Nora. "But we still have to talk about why you won't help me and Mrs. Levi to help rescue kidnapped kids!"

I felt suddenly embarrassed that I had mistaken a statue for a man and defensive about my equations, which I still suspected were not working. I didn't want to have this conversation right now. It caused me stress and I didn't want any more stress. All these mistakes already stressed me so much, I was shaking.

"I can't talk now," I said. "Please write 'receive call from Trueman at 9:52 pm' on your checklist. Thanks. Bye."

I switched off my wrist TV to avoid hearing her reaction.

"Only three minutes until someone comes!" I said.

I ran across the grassy lawn, towards the warehouse.

"Oh, I wasted so much time because of that statue!" I said.

As I ran past the statue of the man leaning on the fence, I hit him on the head, as his punishment for making me late. I ran past the statue of the bear and was soon at the back door of Hickson warehouse. The moon was beautiful, reflected on the waves of the Hudson River, but I had no time to admire it. I had only a few minutes to execute the next item on my plan.

I crossed off "go to Hickson warehouse without meeting anyone" from my checklist. The next item read "pick lock of the back door of Hickson warehouse." I had only a few minutes to open the lock of the warehouse's back door before someone came to disturb me. But it shouldn't be a problem for me, because I have been picking locks since I was a small child.

"Picking locks" is an expression used to describe a method of opening locks without using a key. Instead of using a key, I use long metal rods called "picks." When I was seven years old, I had an obsession with keys and locks. One day, I had found an old dead-bolt lock in my granddad's garage and, after examining it, I became fascinated with locks and keys. I didn't play with toy cars or teddy bears; I played with locks and keys. I would study lock and key catalogs and memorize every detail. I could recognize the brand, model number and style of any lock. When I was nine, I found a book about picking locks, which my granddad had hidden between the "S" and

"T" encyclopedias in his library. In a few days, I was able to pick locks and had practiced on every lock in the house.

My granddad became suspicious of my activities after finding all of his doors, filing cabinets and briefcases unlocked. But instead of getting angry when he learned about my lock-picking, he was proud of me for becoming such a good lock-picker at such a young age. He explained to me that picking locks was a useful skill for a police detective, but it should never be used to break into private property illegally.

Over the years, my granddad had trained me to be an expert at lock-picking. I was proficient at opening all types of locks and could usually open them within two minutes. I knelt before the back door of Hickson warehouse. The door was solid and made of blue metal. I recognized its lock as an Iver brand lock, model number 1A-114. I knew from my memories of the lock and key catalogs that Iver locks were simple "pin and tumbler" locks. These were the easiest types of locks to pick, so I felt optimistic that I could open the door before I was disturbed.

I took a leather case out of my trench coat pocket. This case contained my granddad's collection of lock-picking tools, which I'd inherited from him. I unrolled the leather case and looked over the 38 long, metal picks. I took out a thin piece of curved metal, called a "tension wrench," and used it to apply pressure to the lock. I took out a pick with a squiggly tip, called a "snake pick," and began to pick the lock. Most lock-pickers need to use a variety of picks, but I had developed a method of picking pin and tumbler locks with only a snake pick.

Picking a lock isn't hard if you know what to do. I had to use my snake pick to poke inside the lock and push seven pins into the correct position, then the lock would open. I rubbed the snake pick against the pins and heard two of them move into the proper position. I needed to move five more pins into the proper place and then I could get inside Hickson warehouse.

I could hear a noise nearby. It made me nervous. The mysterious man had been a statue, but it had made me doubt myself and the accuracy of my equations. What if I had been wrong and someone was coming to disturb me, two minutes early? I couldn't stop looking behind me. I didn't see anything, but the noises were making me shake with anxiety and I kept looking nervously over my shoulder. The area around the back of Hickson warehouse was dark and smelly, with a lot of garbage on the ground. The only light came from a dirty, yellow lamp.

I heard the two pins in the lock move out of the correct place. I had not been concentrating on my lock-picking and now I needed to start again. Frustration was building up inside me, and it made my hands shake even more. Now, I had even less time to pick the lock. I looked at the clock on my wrist TV.

"One minute and twenty seconds left!" I said.

A loud noise made me drop my snake pick. The metal pick made a loud clatter as it hit the ground and I saw something moving behind me. I was seized by panic and screamed. I turned around and saw a black and white cat run from out of the garbage. I watched its white tail as it disappeared into the shadows. I was now so thoroughly nervous, I felt nauseous.

I picked up my snake pick and tried to resume picking the lock. My fingers kept shaking and it was hard for me to handle the pick. I kept missing the lock and hitting the metal beside it. Soon the lock was covered in small, shiny scratches.

"No!" I said. "Scratches! Now someone might realize I was picking the lock. A lock-picker should never leave scratches!"

I tried to wipe the scratches away with my fingers, but it didn't work. I tried to wipe the scratches away with my coat's sleeve, but it only left black stains on my sleeve. I looked at my dirtied sleeve and felt my heart pounding. It was easy to pick a lock in my granddad's garage, but it was harder to pick a lock in stressful situations. I hadn't expected to be so tense.

"I wish I would stop shaking!" I said.

I pushed the snake pick into the lock, but I must have pushed it in too hard, because it made a loud scraping sound and got stuck in the lock. I couldn't remove it. This had never happened to me before and I panicked. My stomach was tight from tension and I felt like I'd be sick. I crawled over to the garbage and hid behind a garbage can, not sure if I would vomit.

"2, 3, 5, 7…" I said, remembering how much prime numbers helped me to relax.

I could smell sour milk and discarded coffee among the garbage and my knees were resting in something wet. But soon I had forgotten my uncomfortable surroundings. The crisp, indivisible images of the prime numbers formed in my mind, and I felt my stomach loosen and my hands stop shaking.

"11, 13, 17, 19…" I said.

I heard a sound and stopped counting. Someone was walking towards me. I looked at the clock on my wrist TV.

"My time's done," I said to myself. "Someone's coming!"

I hid my face behind my hands and peeked between my fingers. A man in a gray trench coat was approaching from out of the shadows. He wore black sunglasses and a wide hat. But I was too terrified to notice any more details. He walked towards me with loud, confident steps and I was sure he'd push the garbage cans aside, find me cowering in the corner and do something horrible to me. He walked briskly, as if he had a purpose. In my horrified state, I was certain that purpose was to pull me out of my hiding place and punish me severely.

I closed my eyes and began to think of prime numbers again. I tried to forget about my situation, but it was hard for me to concentrate. Every moment, I expected to hear the sound of garbage cans being pushed over and feel the strong, ruthless fists of this mysterious stranger, pulling me from my hiding place. But after a few dozen prime numbers, nothing happened.

I opened my eyes and cautiously peeked out from behind the garbage can. The mysterious man was gone, and my snake pick was no longer jammed in the door's lock. No one was around. I used my wrist TV to determine when I would next be disturbed. It told me that no one, except for me, would be in this back lane for the next 28 minutes and 15 seconds. I emerged from my smelly hiding place and examined the warehouse door.

It was partly open. A brick had been used to prop the door open. My snake pick had vanished. I was incredibly confused about why someone would come, take my snake pick and then leave the door open for me. But I felt lucky that I was able to get into the warehouse. I thought I had failed so badly that I would need to cancel the mission. I looked at the item on my checklist, "pick lock of the back door of Hickson warehouse."

"I actually did pick the lock," I said, "although I didn't successfully open it. The stranger opened it. But I did pick it for a while. So, I think I can cross it off my checklist."

I crossed it off, opened the back door as gently and silently as I could and entered Hickson warehouse.

Inside, the warehouse was large, with ceilings approximately three stories high and lined with big, bright lights. Everything was metal and glass and the sound of metal hitting metal echoed through the building. It smelled like burning electrical wires. I could hear people talking somewhere. This warehouse was obviously occupied, but I was not worried, because I had prepared for that possibility.

I went to a dark corner of the warehouse, which had a table and chair. I took a small box from my pocket. Inside the box were a few machines that Dr. Rozzozzo had invented for me.

I had designed them specifically for this occasion and I was eager to discover if they worked.

"Trueman!"

I jumped from the shock of hearing my name. In a few moments I realized the voice was coming from my wrist.

"Trueman, are you there?" asked Nora.

I looked at my wrist TV and saw Nora's face. She seemed to be somewhere very dark, because I could hardly see her. Only the blue light of the wrist TV's screen illuminated her face.

"Yes, Nora," I said. "I'm here. Is it 10:05 pm already?"

"Yeah, it is," said Nora. "I made it into the building and I'm trying to get into apartment 5A, where your equation said the diamond-cutting crime occurred. How are you doing?"

"I'm about to use my TET," I said.

"TET?" she asked.

"Yes, that's what I call it," I said. "A Triangulating Evidence Tracker. Dr. Rozzozzo made it for me. Using my new Ulam spiral equation, which can locate evidence, I made a device that can lead me to it. It actually points me in the correct direction. All I need to do is follow the arrows."

"Oh, really?" she asked. "You've got a machine to lead you to the evidence? Shouldn't I have one of those too?"

"Just wait, Nora," I said. "Didn't you read the checklist plan? When we are both inside the possible crime scenes, I use my TET to look for evidence of counterfeiting. If I find something, then we know that Malcolm and Eddie were counterfeiting, so that means they weren't diamond-cutting. In that case, you can leave the apartment building. But if I find no evidence, that means Malcolm and Eddie were probably diamond-cutting. In that case I will use the TET to lead you to the evidence, which would be somewhere in the apartment building that you are currently inside. Do you understand the plan?"

"Yes, Trueman," she said. "How did everything go, so far? Did you see anyone? You picked the lock okay?"

"Good, yes and yes," I said.

"What?" she asked.

"I answered your three questions," I said. "I was able to successfully cross off three items on the list. I saw a mysterious man, but I was able to get into the warehouse on time. I am glad that so far our plan has been a success."

"Wow!" she said. "You picked a lock in two minutes? I'm impressed, Trueman. I couldn't do that to save my life! You'll have to teach me that someday."

"I'll gladly teach you," I said. "It's not so hard."

"You know, I'm really impressed with you, Trueman," she said. "I'm sorry I ever worried you couldn't handle this on your own. You definitely know how to take care of yourself."

My face turned red from pleasure. Although Nora didn't know about the many mistakes I had made, I was still proud and happy to impress her. Her kind encouragement made me feel confident again. I felt like an expert detective in the middle of a successful mission. I could hardly wait to start up my TET and find that evidence. I could imagine how much Nora and everyone else would be impressed when I located the evidence.

"Thank you, Nora," I said. "Now, I should start using my TET and locate that evidence! Please write 'receive call from Trueman at 10:15 pm' onto your checklist."

"Okay, Trueman!" said Nora. "Good luck! But I know you don't need it. I know you'll succeed. You and that great mind of yours will find the evidence, if there's any there to find!"

"Thanks," I said.

I started laughing.

"What's so funny?" asked Nora.

"Oh," I said, "I just thought of something funny. I said I should start 'using my TET' to find the evidence."

"So?" she asked.

"Well, don't you understand?" I asked. "TET sounds like the French word 'tête,' which means 'head.' So, it's like I said that I should start 'using my head' to find the evidence!"

I laughed at the amusing language joke I'd created.

"Oh, yeah," she said.

I couldn't hear Nora laughing and so I looked at her face on the TV screen. It was too dark to see her expression clearly. I couldn't decide if her face expressed amusement or annoyance. Before I could interpret her face, I heard voices.

"Something's happening, Nora," I said. "I must go!"

"Okay, Trueman," she said. "Good luck! Call me if something bad happens. Like an emergency or something, okay?"

"Yes, bye," I said.

I switched off my wrist TV and switched on my TET. It was approximately the size of an egg and fit perfectly into my palm. It was designed to lead me directly to the evidence, based on data I had previously inputted into it. A compass and an arrow appeared on the screen, pointing towards a metal staircase that led to the second floor. The voices that had disturbed me were getting louder, and it sounded like a pair of men were approaching my area of the warehouse. I moved as quickly and as quietly as I could towards the stairwell. Soon I was on a large, metal platform on the second floor. From this height, I could see everything that was happening in the warehouse.

About a dozen men were visible below, carrying heavy objects and dropping them into what looked like vats of boiling water. The smell like burning electrical wires was stronger here. It was accompanied by a pungent odor, which I couldn't identify. The smell caused the image of a toilet to appear in my mind. I had once watched my granddad cleaning a toilet bowl with hydrochloric acid. This odor was similar to hydrochloric acid. Perhaps it was the smell of another type of mineral acid compound? Were they dissolving something in acid? I was curious, but I didn't investigate.

I was on a mission for evidence, and I tried to concentrate on my immediate goal. The metal platform split into two paths. I had the choice of proceeding in two different directions. One direction went along the east wall of the warehouse and the other went over a bridge. This bridge spanned over the area where the men were working. To my horror, the arrow on my TET pointed towards the bridge. The evidence, if there was any, was located over that bridge. I would need to cross immediately over the working men and breathe in the fumes from their acid.

I sat down against the wall, and thought of a solution to this problem. If I had to cross that narrow bridge, I might be visible to the men below. I also might suffer from the effects of breathing acid fumes. I took my yellow scarf and wrapped it around my face. My sunglasses protected my eyes, so I was safe from acid. Now, I needed to think of a way to remain unseen.

Luckily, I had included my jerk magic equation into the TET. It automatically calculated the chances of my being seen, if I went in a particular direction, at any specific time. Right now, the TET said I had an 82 percent chance of being seen if I crossed the bridge. But it was changing every twenty seconds. Soon it said there was a 58 percent chance of being seen. I would sit and wait for it to say there was a 0 percent chance.

I sat against the wall, anticipating the percentage changes. Every time it seemed to go down, it would then go back up to a high percentage. I whispered the percentages aloud.

"50 percent... 21 percent... 26 percent... 32 percent... 90 percent."

The corrugated metal beneath me was beginning to dig into my flesh and make me uncomfortable. My feet were getting numb from squatting for so long. The percentage did not go below 10 percent. I was starting to feel panic again.

"Hey!"

The loud, angry voice made me fall down to the floor and hide under my trench coat. I thought I had been discovered.

"Who left the back door open?"

I peeked out from under my trench coat and saw a thick, powerful-looking man walking among the men below. He was shouting and waving a heavy wrench at them.

"You idiots!" he said. "You want someone to just waltz in here and catch us doin' this? Who did it? Huh? Someone better come forward and admit to this. Right now!"

All the men were silent and the angry man threw his wrench against the concrete floor. He seemed ready to kill someone.

"Well, if no one opened it, then some stranger might be inside!" said the man. "So, we're all gonna have to stop what we're doing and search this place. You understand what I'm saying? Go ahead, you idiots! I said, get searching!"

The men stopped working and started searching through the warehouse. I was horrified. Soon, someone would decide to search up here on this platform and I would be discovered! And the TET wasn't giving me any good percentages! I felt trapped.

For a few moments, panic seized me and I wanted to call Nora and plead for help. But then I remembered the pride I felt when she expressed her confidence in me. She was certain I would succeed and I didn't want to disappoint her.

"Please, TET!" I said. "Please give me a good percentage!"

As if the TET heard me and obeyed my command, a good percentage appeared on the TET screen.

"Two percent chance of being seen!" I said.

I decided that was a safe percentage and started moving as fast as I could over the bridge. I bent low, so I wouldn't be seen. But then I realized the TET made its predictions based on the assumption that I use a normal walking speed and posture. I stopped crouching and walked normally. I looked at my surroundings as I walked. Sometimes I saw men walking nearby. I felt the urge to run, but I resisted the temptation.

It seemed like a long time before I reached the opposite end of the bridge. As I stepped off the bridge, I felt incredibly relieved. Looking behind me, I could see that men were now climbing the stairs to the second floor platform. I had barely managed to escape being discovered. I realized the TET's low percentage had probably come because most of the men had left the area under the bridge and gone separate ways.

I looked at my TET and saw the arrow pointing towards a large, metal door, behind me. I ran to the door, praying it wasn't locked. I didn't want to experience another failed lock-picking attempt. I sighed from relief when I discovered it was unlocked. I hastened to open the door and stepped through it.

I felt a blast of cool air and recognized the smell of the Hudson River. I was outside of Hickson warehouse, under a yellow lamp. I was standing on the top landing of a staircase that led down to the ground. The area below was surrounded by high, barbed-wire fence. There was industrial garbage everywhere and a few old cars. The arrow on my TET was pointing down towards the body of a wrecked 1967 Chevrolet Impala. The car looked like it hadn't been operational for a very long time. A small circle on the directional arrow of the TET indicated the evidence was located in the ruined Impala car.

I heard my wrist TV make a crackling noise and looked to see the face of Nora on my wrist TV.

"Trueman?" asked Nora. "You're late! Is everything okay? You're never late."

"Sorry," I said. "I had a serious problem."

"What?" she asked. "You okay? Should we come get you?"

"No, no," I said. "I'm fine. In fact, I've found the evidence. It seems that Malcolm and Eddie are counterfeiters."

As I thought about this development, several facts seemed to fall into place. The ink on Malcolm and Eddie's knees could well have come from the counterfeiters' ink; the distinctive cuts on both of their eyes could have come from that unique type of monocular microscope used by jewellers. Malcolm and Eddie may well have been using such a device to examine counterfeit dollar bills. The explanations for all twenty-five similarities began to form in my mind. But before they could do so, I was interrupted from my thoughts by the sound of men's voices in the warehouse. I decided to start climbing down the stairs and searching the Impala for evidence.

"Trueman?" asked Nora. "If they're counterfeiters, that means they couldn't be diamond-cutters, right? I can leave this apartment now?"

"Yes," I said.

"I'm so proud of you, Trueman!" she said. "You found the evidence! Now we can nail that jerk Malcolm!"

"Nail him?" I asked.

"Sorry, that's another expression," she said. "It means we can give him what he deserves. That jerk deserves jail!"

I walked through the messy yard, through the debris of car parts and oil barrels. Soon I was beside the Impala car.

"Yes," I said. "Malcolm will get what he deserves."

I jumped over the front hood of the Impala, trying to get to the driver's side window, which was open. I landed on something soft and cold. It was hard to see it in the dark.

"Just a minute, Nora," I said. "I need my flashlight."

I switched on the tiny flashlight that was installed into my wrist TV.

"Malcolm!" I said.

"Yes!" said Nora. "We'll give him what he deserves!"

"No!" I said. "I mean Malcolm's here!"

"What?" she asked. "Where?"

"Under my feet!" I said.

"What?" she asked.

I had landed on Malcolm's body, which was stuck between the Impala car and an old refrigerator. His face was blue and he was staring at me with cold, dead eyes. I felt nauseous and panicky. I'd never seen a corpse and I started screaming.

"Trueman!" shouted Nora. "What's happening?"

Just when I felt I couldn't be any more terrified, I heard a sound that made my skin turn cold from fright. The door leading into the warehouse opened and the mysterious man in the gray trench coat appeared. He must have heard my screams, because he looked at me and immediately started running down the stairs towards me. I jumped into the ruined Impala car and desperately searched for a place to hide. I found a tattered old coat in the back seat and hid myself underneath it. I was certain the mystery man would find me, but I couldn't think of any other solution. I could still hear Nora shouting.

"Trueman!" shouted Nora. "Please say something!"

I switched off the wrist TV, so I wouldn't be heard.

"Yeah, Trueman," said a voice. "Say something."

I didn't want to acknowledge this horrifying situation, so I tried to pretend I didn't hear the voice and thought of prime numbers instead. I whispered the numbers to myself.

"29, 31, 37…"

I felt two strong hands grab me and pull me out of the car window. I smelled a familiar aroma and the image of Detective Buckley formed in my mind. It was the smell of lavender, anise and vanilla. I opened my eyes and looked at the face of this mysterious man. I recognized the constellation of Orion on his cheek and realized that he was Detective Buckley.

"Say something, Trueman!" said Buckley, "Something like, what the hell you think you're doing here!"

"Stop it!" I said. "You're standing on him!"

"What?" he said. "Make sense, Trueman!"

"You're standing on Malcolm Vrie!" I said.

"I'm what?" he asked.

Buckley looked down at his feet and dropped me. He took a flashlight out of his pocket and examined the corpse. He took a handkerchief out of his pocket and covered his nose. I had been so excited and shocked, I had failed to notice how much Malcolm's corpse stank. I covered my nose with my scarf.

"Trueman," said Buckley, "you better come with me."

The door of the warehouse opened and a uniformed police officer appeared.

"Detective Buckley, sir," said the cop.

"Yeah!" said Buckley.

"We've got all of them in custody now," said the cop. "It looks like they were trying to dissolve some silicon counterfeiting plates with what looks like fluoroboric acid."

"Okay," said Buckley. "There's a dead man down here!"

"A dead man, sir?" asked the cop.

"Yeah, that's what I said!" said Buckley. "Get Detective Costas out here to take care of it, will ya? I've got to take this fella down to the station with me!"

"Yes, sir!" said the cop.

"Trueman?" asked Buckley.

"Yes?" I asked.

"Let's get outta here," said Buckley.

THE MYSTERY OF
THE ZEROES

A dozen police officers stood all around me. I was sitting in an office at the police station. The office was adorned with venetian blinds, fluorescent lights, cork billboards and the scent of stale coffee. I would have been delighted to be in an office that looked exactly like my granddad's old office, but I was too tense. We had just entered the office of Chief Stokowski. The Chief, who I had met at the detectives' convention, stared at me in a way that made me nervous.

I sat on a chair and Buckley stood beside me. He was leaning on a desk and staring at his mobile phone.

"Now, Trueman…" said Buckley, "would you care to explain to us what you were doing at the Hickson warehouse tonight?"

"I was looking for evidence," I said.

"Evidence of what?" asked Buckley.

"I suspected Malcolm Vrie was involved in illegal counterfeiting," I said. "And I thought the evidence would be found at Hickson warehouse."

"You say you knew this?" asked Stokowski. "How did you know this?"

"I used my crime-fighting equation," I said.

"What?" asked Stokowski. "What did he say, Buckley?"

"He said he used an equation," said Buckley. "What the hell are you talking about, Trueman? Just what kind of equation are you talking about?"

"It's a crime-fighting equation," I said. "It's a mathematical equation I invented that can solve crimes."

"You don't say?" asked Buckley.

"Yes, I do say," I said. "Remember the time we were driving in your taxicab and you said it would be good if there was an equation for solving crime? Well, I invented one!"

Buckley sighed and looked at his mobile phone.

"Is he nuts?" asked Stokowski. "Listen, kid. You better stop lying to us. You're in serious trouble. You're a suspect in the murder of Malcolm Vrie! He was a good friend of mine, you know. If you killed him, I'm gonna see to it that you get nailed for it. I swear, if you killed him, I'll string you up!"

"I didn't kill him!" I said. "He was dead already!"

"Oh, yeah?" asked Stokowski. "Says who?"

"Says Detective Costas," said Buckley.

"What?" asked Stokowski.

Buckley put his phone in his pocket and looked at me.

"I just got a text message from Detective Costas," said Buckley. "He says a doctor confirmed that Vrie's been dead for more than twenty-four hours. So Trueman, here, is telling the truth. He was already dead when Trueman found him. He's in the clear."

"In the clear?" I asked.

"Yeah," said Buckley. "It means you're innocent."

"That's what I told you!" I said to Stokowski.

Stokowski's eyes narrowed and I thought I recognized an intensely negative emotion in his eyes. It was either hatred, anger or a desire to punch me in the face. Whatever it was, it made me nervous and I had to stop looking at him.

"Just who is this guy, anyways?" asked Stokowski.

"Trueman Bradley," said Buckley. "A private detective."

"You're a private detective?" asked Stokowski.

"Yes," I said.

"Yeah," said Buckley. "He owns and operates a detective agency here in Manhattan."

"Owns an agency?" asked Stokowski. "You've got to be joking me! This kid? How old are you kid, seventeen?"

Before I could answer him, my wrist TV made a beeping sound. I looked at it and realized Nora was sending me a text message on her wrist TV.

"Turn that thing off, will ya, Trueman," said Buckley.

"What's he got there?" asked Stokowski.

"It's a wrist TV," said Buckley.

"A what?" asked Stokowski.

"A wrist TV!" I said. "Like Dick Tracy uses."

"The kid thinks he's Dick Tracy now?" asked Stokowski.

Buckley shook his head and sighed.

"So it would seem," said Buckley.

"I don't think I'm Dick Tracy!" I said. "Not really! I'm just pretending to be him, because it helps me concentrate on being a good detective. That's all. I know I'm not really him, but if I use a wrist TV and wear a yellow trench coat, I can imagine I'm him and it helps me imitate his detective powers."

Stokowski scowled at me.

"What's wrong?" I asked. "Don't you like comic books?"

"No, I don't like comic books!" said Stokowski. "And, what's more, if you think being a detective is like the comic books, then you're crazy! Take my word for it, a police detective can't learn a thing from reading comic books!"

Stokowski looked at my trench coat and scarf, which I had taken off and hung on a coat rack, near the door. He grabbed my scarf and started examining it.

"Did you say your trench coat was yellow?" asked Stokowski.

"Yes," I said. "And my hat and scarf are yellow, too."

"You call this yellow?" asked Stokowski.

My scarf and coat had become white. There were a few yellow spots remaining on my trench coat but, except for that, there was nothing to prove they had ever been yellow.

"Well, I guess the acid fumes bleached them," I said.

Stokowski put down the scarf and glared at me.

"You may not've killed Malcolm," said Stokowski, "but you were trespassing! You think you've got the perfect right to break into Hickson warehouse and traipse around? Acting as if it's your own private property? You'll do jail time for that!"

"I didn't break in!" I said.

"Oh yeah?" asked Stokowski. "Then how'd you get inside?"

Buckley coughed.

"Well…" said Buckley. "Trueman didn't exactly break in."

"He didn't, huh?" asked Stokowski. "Then what happened?"

"Well, I think he was planning to break in," said Buckley. "But he didn't get a chance."

Buckley turned and started talking to me.

"You see, Trueman," he said. "It was like this. After I learned you'd started an agency, I was kind of worried you'd get in over your head."

"Over my head?" I asked.

"Oh, right," he said. "You don't like expressions, huh? I meant, I thought you might get into trouble and so I followed you. Any free time I had, I'd follow you around, just to make sure you were alright, you know? Well, I was following you. I followed you into the parkland beside Hickson warehouse, but I couldn't find you. I didn't know where you were. It was like you vanished into thin air."

"Oh, I was probably hiding behind the tree," I said. "That's why you couldn't see me."

"Hiding?" he asked. "Why? You knew I was following you?"

"Oh no," I said. "I was hiding from the statue."

I could recognize confusion on Buckley's face.

"Hiding from a statue?" he asked. "Okay, whatever. Never mind. The point is, I lost you. I must've walked every inch of that park looking for you! Then, when I walked behind Hickson warehouse, I saw a lock pick stuck in the back door lock."

"That was my lock pick," I said. "My snake pick."

Buckley took a long, shiny object out of his pocket and handed it to me. It was my missing snake pick.

"Thanks," I said. "It's my favorite lock pick."

"You're nothing but a lock-picking thief!" said Stokowski. "So, you did pick that lock? That's unlawful entry, buddy! You'll do jail time for that!"

"No, sir," said Buckley, "Trueman didn't pick the lock. Trueman must have heard me coming and hid somewhere."

"I hid behind the garbage can," I said.

"Yeah," said Buckley. "But when I saw the lock pick I figured Trueman broke into the warehouse and so I followed him."

"How did you get in?" I asked.

"I picked the lock," said Buckley. "Using your pick."

"I didn't know you can pick locks too," I said.

"Yeah, it's a handy skill for a detective," he said.

"That's what my granddad said too," I said.

"Anyways," said Buckley, "the door was locked when I found it. But as you might know, that kind of door locks automatically after you close it. So I imagined you'd picked the lock and then closed the door. I picked the lock and used a brick to keep the door open. You must have followed me."

Stokowski hit his hand against his desk. His eyes were wide open and he was sweating. I couldn't interpret his face, but he was getting excited about something.

"You morons!" said Stokowski. "What on earth are you doing picking locks and trespassing? Trueman! I should throw you in jail this very moment! And Buckley! I oughta fire you right now! What right have you got to break in without a warrant?"

"I'm not a moron!" I said. "And I didn't trespass! Trespassing in the third degree only applies to unlawfully entering private property. Hickson warehouse isn't private."

"What?" asked Stokowski.

"When Hickson warehouse was built," I said, "it blocked all access to a small piece of public parkland on the Hudson River."

"So?" asked Stokowski.

"So," I said, "according to my research, Jefferson Hickson, the original owner of Hickson warehouse, signed a public easement agreement with the city of New York."

Stokowski and Buckley looked at each other.

"What does that mean, Trueman?" asked Buckley.

"Don't you read law books?" I asked. "A public easement agreement means the owner of that land allows the public to walk through its property. In this case, he allows the public to walk through his land to get to that small piece of public parkland. Do you understand? It means I have a right to walk through his land. All of New York City has this right."

"So, walk through his property to get to the park," said Stokowski. "But don't pick the lock and break in!"

"How can I walk through the property?" I asked. "He has fences with barbed wire everywhere! Walking through the building is the only way to get through the property. So, you see, I'm not breaking the law. Actually, he is breaking the law because he makes it hard for people to walk through his land, which is their right according to the law. Of course, I don't blame him, the easement agreement is from 1952. He just forgot about it. But I didn't forget. I memorized most of the legal cases in New York City history, from 1951 till the present."

Stokowski glared at me, but didn't say anything.

"I'm afraid he's right, boss," said Buckley. "Legally, anyone has a right to enter Hickson warehouse. The owner probably doesn't realize that. He probably did forget about the easement agreement. Trueman, here, didn't break any laws."

"I wouldn't break the law!" I said. "I'm a detective, not a criminal! I detect and punish criminals. My granddad always said never to pick a lock to enter private property, so I wouldn't pick the Hickson warehouse's lock if it was illegal."

"I'm still not convinced," said Stokowski. "I'm gonna get our lawyers to check into that. I think I can still nail you for trespassing in the third degree."

Buckley coughed.

"Chief," said Buckley, "with all due respect, I'm not sure Trueman, here, did anything illegal. In fact, if I hadn't entered that warehouse and called for backup, we never would've known about these counterfeiters. He helped us out, you could say. Although, I grant you, he didn't know what he was doing."

Stokowski looked at me for a long time. The silent staring made me nervous and I wanted to hide my face behind my hands.

"How did you know about all that?" asked Stokowski.

"All what?" I asked.

"The counterfeiting!" said Stokowski.

"I told you!" I said. "I used my crime-fighting equation! And I wasn't certain if Malcolm Vrie was counterfeiting. He could also have been cutting stolen diamonds illegally. My crime-fighting equation doesn't always give an exact answer."

"Crime-fighting equation?" asked Stokowski. "What the hell are you talking about?! Equations can't solve crimes!"

"Yes they can!" I said. "I saw signs and clues on Malcolm and Eddie, and I used my equation to determine what crime they committed and it pointed me towards Hickson warehouse! It was correct, you see? Equations can solve crimes!"

"That's nuts!" said Stokowski. "This kid's crazy!"

"I'm not!" I said. "I solved more than one case with my equations. I also solved the case of Erik Lendaleinen. I even was able to predict Malcolm Vrie's death! I predicted his death weeks before I even entered Hickson warehouse!"

"You did?" asked Buckley. "You never told me that."

"Actually," I said, "I didn't realize until just now. In my equation, Malcolm and Eddie resulted in zero. I was confused by that, because my equations had never before given a variable resulting in zero. But now that I know Malcolm is dead, I understand what zero means. Zero means the person in the equation has died. Probably it means they were murdered."

"Poppycock," said Stokowski.

"What?" I asked.

"Wait, Trueman…" said Buckley, "you said that both Malcolm and Eddie resulted in zeroes, and resulting in zero means the person's dead? Murdered?"

"Yes, I think so," I said.

"Then Eddie's dead too?" asked Buckley.

I had only recently realized what a zero result meant. I hadn't yet thought that it might mean Eddie was dead. I was so surprised by this possibility that I didn't answer Buckley.

"If Eddie's dead, there's no need for me to investigate this anymore," I said. "I guess my first case is over."

"No!" said Stokowski. "There's no need for you to investigate anything anymore! You're not gonna run around playing detective anymore if I can help it! I'm gonna shut down that agency of yours, if I can! You're just some nutso kid and you got no right pretending to solve crimes!"

"You're wrong!" I said.

"No, I'm not!" said Stokowski. "I'm the chief of police, that's what I am! And I've got the power to shut you down, mark my words! What's more…"

Stokowski picked up the telephone and dialed a number.

"…I'm gonna prove to you that you're wrong."

Stokowski waited for a minute, listening to the phone.

"Hello?" asked Stokowski, talking into the phone. "Is this Detective Costas? Yeah, you and Malcolm brought Eddie Sipple into custody, right? Okay. He's alive and well, right?"

Stokowski's face changed. It twisted and contorted into a shape I'd never seen before. He rubbed his eyes and sighed.

"How come I didn't hear about it, Costas?" asked Stokowski.

The room was silent and Stokowski looked at me. I could recognize anger in his eyes and some other emotion I couldn't identify. Whatever it was, it made me want to flee in panic.

"Yeah," said Stokowski, into the phone.

Stokowski put down the phone and stood up.

"Buckley?" asked Stokowski.

"Yes, Chief," said Buckley.

"Arrest Mr. Bradley," said Stokowski.

"For what?" I asked.

"For the murder of Eddie Sipple," said Stokowski.

"What?" I asked.

"I've just heard that Eddie was killed," said Stokowski. "He was released from custody because of lack of evidence. A few hours later, he was found murdered at La Guardia airport."

"But, that's good!" I said. "It proves my equation was correct. My equation correctly predicted Eddie's death!"

"No," said Stokowski. "All it proves is that you knew Eddie was murdered before that information was released to the public. I didn't even know Eddie was killed yet and I'm the chief here! So how comes it that you know about it, huh? I'll tell you how you know it, because you killed him, right?"

"No!" I said.

"Chief!" said Buckley. "I was following Trueman for days! If he killed someone I would've seen it! Besides, Trueman's just not capable of murder! I really object to this arrest!"

"What you object to doesn't matter!" said Stokowski. "I'm the boss, not you. Maybe this doesn't prove you killed Eddie, but the fact you knew about it is mighty suspicious and that's good enough for me. That's probable cause in my book. Now, if you'll excuse me, I've got something I've gotta take care of."

Stokowski walked out of the room and most of the police officers followed him. I was left alone with Buckley.

"Trueman," said Buckley, "I hate to do this. But I'll have to arrest you for the murder of Eddie Sipple. You have the right to remain silent. Anything you say can and will be used against you in a court of law…"

As Buckley read me my Miranda rights, the true horror of my situation became clear. I did not want to believe that I was being arrested for murder. I didn't want to accept this reality. I closed my eyes and started counting prime numbers.

"2, 3, 5, 7…"

*

"10,627… 10,631… 10,639… 10,651…"

"Why do you keep counting like that?" asked Buckley.

"It relaxes me," I said.

"Well, stop it, will ya?" he asked. "You're driving me crazy with that. Besides, you got no reason to be tense."

"Why not?" I asked. "I'm under arrest for murder."

"Yeah, but you'll go free. Don't worry," he said. "Now, let's concentrate on this, please. I've got to ask you a few more questions for my paperwork. Pay attention, okay?"

It had been twenty-three hours since I first entered the police station, and I had been imprisoned in this holding cell for most of that time. Most of the time, a scowling and unfriendly police officer guarded me. But Buckley had come and sent the police officer away. He'd been questioning me for ten minutes. I was glad to see Buckley, but I was getting sick from this stuffy room, which smelled of sweat and metal polish and had no windows for sunlight to get in.

"Now…" said Buckley, looking at a clipboard that held his paperwork, "I think I've actually asked you all I need to know. But, personally, there's a few questions I'd like to ask you…"

"What do you want to know?" I asked.

Buckley moved closer to the bars of my cell. He smiled and spoke to me in a low whisper.

"Off the record…" he said, "how did you know Eddie was dead? I mean, really? Did you witness the crime or what?"

"No!" I said. "I used my crime-fighting equation!"

"Come on!" he said. "Do you really expect me to believe that story? A mathematical equation cannot solve a crime."

"It can!" I said. "I used New York City crime statistics from 1951 until the present. I inserted them as variables into a very long and complicated equation and applied a path integral structure to them. At first, I wasn't sure if it worked. Even a very short time ago, I was doubting my equations. But now that I realize how accurately I predicted the murders of Malcolm Vrie and Eddie Sipple, I'm convinced my equations work!"

Buckley looked at me for a long time.

"Okay," he said. "I can tell a lot about a person just from looking at them. Nineteen years of detective work'll do that to you. I don't think you're lying to me. But it's still kinda hard to believe, you know? A part of me thinks you're crazy, I admit it. But another part of me thinks that, if this is true, your equations could be a real breakthrough."

"A breakthrough?" I asked.

"Yeah," he said. "It means your equations could improve the lives of police everywhere. It's a long shot, but I'm willing to give you a chance to prove it to me."

"I don't understand," I said.

"I mean," he said, "I'll let you prove to me that your equations work. How would you like to work on a case with me?"

"Really?" I asked. "Me? Work on a real police case?"

"Yeah," he said.

I was so happy, I felt like jumping around the jail cell.

"Yes!" I said. "I'd like that very much!"

I was tempted to dance, I was so happy. But my joy was soon ended, when I realized that I couldn't help Buckley.

"But I can't help you!" I said. "How can I help you solve a case if I'm imprisoned? I'm suspected of murdering Eddie."

"Like I said, don't worry about it," he said. "You'll be let free. The police can only hold you in jail for twenty-four hours. Unless we find some serious evidence to prove you killed Eddie, Stokowski has to let you free after twenty-four hours. Understand?"

I looked at the clock on my wrist TV.

"I'm free to go in ten minutes and five seconds!" I said.

"Yeah," he said. "There's no way they could get any evidence to prove to the court you killed Eddie. Because during the time Eddie was killed, I was in a car watching you! You and that chauffeur of yours were sitting in an Italian restaurant at the exact moment Eddie is believed to have been killed."

"I see," I said. "So that proves I'm innocent."

"It sure does!" he said. "There's no way you could've done it! And you and me are gonna find out who did kill Eddie."

"Is that the case you want me to help you with?" I asked.

"Yeah," he said. "I'm investigating Eddie's death. So far, I've got nothing. If your equations work the way you say they do, then I'd appreciate your help in this matter."

"Of course I'll help!" I said.

"Good," he said.

The telephone rang and Buckley answered it.

"Yeah?" he asked, into the phone. "Okay, sure."

Buckley put the phone down and put on his trench coat.

"You've got visitors, Trueman," he said. "Seems like your friends from the agency are here to come get you. Just sit tight, I gotta go let them in, okay? Don't you go anywhere."

Buckley walked out the door and I stood with my hands grasping the prison bars.

"How could I go anywhere?" I asked. "I'm in jail."

I looked at the ground and started counting the cracks in the concrete. I had already counted them fifteen times since I arrived in this holding cell, but I was curious if another one might have formed since the last time I counted.

"1, 2, 3, 4..." I said.

"What are you doing?"

I looked up from the cracked concrete and saw the large face of Chief Stokowski. He had a strange look in his eyes, which I'd never seen before. It was similar to fear, but also similar to the way a dog looked when it wanted to attack.

"I was counting the cracks," I said.

"Yeah, sure," he said. "You were counting cracks. Now, listen. I've got a few questions I'd like to ask you."

"What questions?" I asked.

"How come you knew about the counterfeiting at Hickson warehouse?" he asked. "And don't say it was because of your magic equations! I don't buy that cock and bull story."

"Cock and bull?" I asked. "You mean the animals?"

"What?" he asked. "Shut up and answer me!"

"Don't be so rude to me!" I said.

"Listen," he said. "I'm asking you one simple question. What do you know about the counterfeiting? Just how much do you know, huh? Someone told you about it? Is that it?"

"I don't know what you mean!" I said. "No one told me anything! Like I said, I used my crime-fighting equation."

Stokowski sighed and grabbed the bars of my cell with his big hands. It seemed to me like he wanted to pull the bars apart and strangle me. I moved a few steps away from him.

"Fine," he said. "But let me ask you something. Do you like whiskey? Maybe you'd like a little taste of this?"

Stokowski pulled a small bottle out of his pocket and showed it to me. It was full of a brown liquid and had a label that said "Orkafend's Blend Whiskey." I noticed the bottle was not opened, it was shaped like a lopsided oval and the ink on the label was so faded that it was hard to read.

"No thanks," I said. "I don't drink alcohol. It makes no sense to drink something that is toxic to the body and kills brain cells. I need my brain functional for detective work."

Stokowski stared at me and slowly moved the bottle of whiskey back into his pocket. He was examining me very closely.

"Yeah…" he said, "it kills brain cells."

Someone opened the door. It was opened so forcefully that it swung and hit the wall. The loud bang caused Stokowski to jump and knock the whiskey bottle out of his pocket. It smashed on the floor and soon the entire room smelled like whiskey. Nora, Mrs. Levi and Sal had walked into the room and Buckley arrived soon after them. Buckley walked to Stokowski and looked down at the broken bottle of whiskey.

"You drop something, Chief?" asked Buckley.

Stokowski's wide face became as red as a beet and his embarrassment was so obvious, I could interpret it instantly. He rubbed his face and sighed, looking down at his own feet.

"Yeah…" said Stokowski, "I was holding that for someone. It was evidence. Well, I guess it's no good now, though, huh?"

I was not the best at interpreting emotions or subtle body language, but even I could discern the fact that Stokowski was lying. The whiskey wasn't evidence. It seemed to me Stokowski was embarrassed because his smashed alcohol bottle made him seem like an alcoholic. Stokowski sighed again and left the room.

"Evidence, huh?" asked Buckley. "Detectives are usually pretty good liars. Chief Stokowski isn't your usual detective."

Buckley fetched a mop and started cleaning the whiskey and broken glass from the floor. He bent down to pick up the glass.

"Trueman! I'm so glad to see you!" said Nora.

Nora hugged me tightly.

"Yes, dear," said Mrs. Levi. "We're glad you're alright! And I made your favorite dessert! Raspberry lemon cake!"

Mrs. Levi was carrying a small cake. My mouth watered at the scent and I realized I hadn't eaten very much since I had been arrested.

"A cake, huh?" asked Buckley. "Doesn't have a file in it, I hope? Or I just might have to confiscate it."

Buckley laughed. No one else did.

"I don't understand," I said. "Do you mean a paper file?"

"No," said Buckley. "You know, that old movie or book or whatever... this guy's in jail and his wife bakes him a cake with a metal file hidden inside it? Then the guy in jail uses the metal file to saw the bars of his cell and he escapes?"

"Oh," I said. "I've never heard of that before."

The room was silent for a minute. Buckley coughed.

"Well, never mind," said Buckley. "I'll call you tomorrow, Trueman. We'll talk about the case, yeah?"

"Oh, yes!" I said. "I'll be waiting for your call!"

I followed Nora, Sal and Mrs. Levi out of the police station and out onto the street. Our Lincoln car was waiting for us.

"It's good to have you back, Mr. Bradley!" said Sal, as he started the car and began driving us back home, to Reade Street.

"Thank you, Sal," I said. "I'm happy to see you all."

Nora hugged me.

"By the way…" said Mrs. Levi, "what did the detective mean? He said he'd talk to you about a case? What case?"

"Oh, I'm working on a police case!" I said.

"Are you kidding?" asked Nora. "A real police case?"

Everyone in the car began making excited noises. I could read enough of the emotion in their words to know they were happy about this new case. I was happy too; this was only our agency's second case and we were already doing police cases.

"Good for you, Mr. Bradley!" said Sal. "You go into the station a murder suspect and you come out with a police case!"

"Yeah!" said Nora. "I'm so impressed with you, Trueman!"

Nora's adoration made my face turn red with pleasure. I wanted to impress her, but I didn't want her to know how much I wanted it. I had learned from my granddad that nobody likes a person who brags, so I decided to sound as humble as I could.

"Oh, it was nothing special," I said. "It was just a few equations. I didn't really solve the case, after all. Buckley helped me. And he's the one who arrested the counterfeiters."

"That's not what the newspapers are saying!" said Nora.

"What?" I asked.

"Sal, throw that paper here, will you?" asked Nora.

Sal picked up a newspaper that was on his lap and threw it towards us. Nora picked it up and started reading.

"Private detective uses mathematical equation to expose counterfeiters," she read, aloud. "Manhattan private investigator, Mr. Trueman Bradley, reportedly exposed the activities of a gang of counterfeiters whose existence was previously unknown to police. Preliminary reports indicate that Bradley is a mathematical genius who divined the activities of the criminals by way of a mathematical equation of his own design."

"How do you like that!" said Nora. "You're not only a free man, you're famous! Our agency is famous! We'll get all kinds of cases now!"

I sat in my chair, feeling numb. When I woke up this morning, I had expected to be convicted of murder. Instead, I had been given my liberty and I would soon be working on a real police case. And, in addition to all that, I was famous. I was a "mathematical genius." Nora hugged me closer. I felt such bliss and contentment that I couldn't speak a word. I never wanted to leave Nora's arms. I never wanted to leave this perfect moment, where everything was just how I'd wanted it.

I sat for a long time, staring out the window and savoring the moment. I was trying to think if I could somehow make time stop, so I wouldn't need to go into the future, where everything might change and become imperfect again. The future was unpredictable and I wanted to stay where everything was perfect.

"Here we are, boss," said Sal.

We parked outside our agency on Reade Street. Sal turned around and looked at me. I realized that everyone was looking at me as if they expected me to say something.

"Well?" asked Sal. "What do we do now, boss?"

I looked at the faces of my friends and realized they relied on me to lead them and manage the successful resolution of our cases. I realized I had to be brave and face the future, no matter how unpredictable. My friends were relying on me.

"We'll work all night!" I said. "I need to make a complete chart of La Guardia airport! Sal, go get Dr. Rozzozzo for me. I need her advice… and Mrs. Levi… we'll need a lot of tea! Well? Open the door, Nora! We've got a lot of work to do!"

A TRUE MAN
EXPOSES TRUTH

It was a bright, cloudless day. The sky was visible through the windows of the Trueman Bradley Detective Agency. The windows were open and a warm wind moved through the room.

I caught a paper that was about to fly off my desk.

"Please close that window, Mrs. Levi," I said.

"Why, of course, dear!" she said.

Mrs. Levi moved to the window that was beside my desk and tried to close it. It seemed to be stuck and I watched her as she struggled to close it. Her arms shook and her shoulders heaved.

But I didn't have time to continue watching her. I had made an exact schedule about what I would do today. I had every minute planned with precision and, this time, I didn't intend to deviate from my checklist. Everything would be done perfectly.

Mrs. Levi had been answering the telephone all day and had scheduled appointments for people to meet me. After my name had appeared in the newspapers, many people started calling our agency or knocking on our front door. Everybody was interested in me: newspaper reporters, television stations, college students doing research papers, police agencies, other private detectives and hundreds of hopeful people, believing I could solve their case with my seemingly magical equations.

We had to turn away hundreds of people, telling them to call again later. But I devised a method of scheduling eighty meetings in four hours, by strictly organizing them and limiting each meeting to three minutes exactly. I had an antique clock timer used for chess games. Sal had found it for me at an antiques shop. I wasn't sure what year it was made, but a few Russian Cyrillic letters on the side indicated where it had been manufactured. I used the Russian antique chess clock to limit my meetings to exactly 180 seconds.

I looked at my checklist. My recent successes had inspired me to improve my checklist system. Instead of writing a list of things for me to do in a day, I created a diagram. I have a better memory for images than I do for words. So I created a big circle that represents my day, and inserted symbols at the degrees of the circle that represent certain times of day or night. The symbols represented what I must do. With this improved, visual checklist, I was able to see the perfection and symmetry of my daily plan more easily. Also, I could quickly and easily remember what I had to do next.

I was working my way through today's meetings and was nearly at the end.

"Next," I said, "I must meet with Mr. Dermot Kelly, from the neighborhood of Windsor Terrace, in Brooklyn."

I looked at the other side of the office, which served as our waiting room. Sal and Nora had escorted the people into a line and ensured they were ready for their meeting. I hit the starter button on the chess timer and Nora led an elderly man to my desk. He wore a red and white checkered hat and walked with an oak cane.

"Mr. Trueman Bradley?" asked the elderly man.

"Yes," I said. "That's me. What do you want from me?"

Mrs. Levi sorted through some papers.

"This man is Dermot Kelly," she said. "He wants you to solve the case of his missing grand-daughter."

"That's right, sir!" said Mr. Kelly. "The police have been no help! No, none at all! I read about your miraculous powers, sir. I was hoping you were the miracle I'd been waiting for. If only you could use your powers to save my grand-daughter and bring peace to my mind again, I'd be willing to pay you everything I have! You can't imagine how painful it is, losing my little grand-daughter. She's all I have in the world…"

I felt sympathy for the old man, but I knew there were only 137 seconds remaining before our meeting was over and I'd be busy with Buckley's case for at least two days. I needed to help him quickly, or I wouldn't be able to help for a long time.

"Quick!" I said. "Tell me the following details of your grand-daughter's disappearance. The time, the date, the exact location and how old she was."

"Oh…" he said, "well, if memory serves me correct, sir, I do believe it was right about the time I lost my wallet on the subway. I was changing trains, you see, at Broadway Junction, when this young fella came up behind me…"

"Please!" I said. "I only have 90 seconds to solve this case! I want you to tell me the details I asked for!"

"Oh, I'm sorry…" he said. "Of course, the details, yes. Well, just a moment, let me think now…"

"Oh, hold on a minute, dear!" said Mrs. Levi. "I got that information from Mr. Kelly when we talked on the telephone. I wrote it down. Mr. Kelly's grand-daughter, Katherine Kelly, vanished fifteen days ago at approximately midnight. She was last seen on the corner of Remsen Street and Clinton Street."

"And how old is she?" I asked.

Mrs. Levi examined her papers.

"Katherine is nineteen years old," said Mr. Kelly.

"Okay," I said. "Wait, please."

I closed my eyes and put my earphones into my ears, so I would not be distracted. I inserted these variables into my crime-fighting equation and quickly calculated a solution.

"Katherine Kelly ran away from home," I said. "She probably ran away with her boyfriend, who is probably older than her and lives in Brooklyn. If you visit the apartment building at 80 Clymer Street, east of the Brooklyn Navy Yard, I think you will discover Katherine and her boyfriend are living there."

I hit the stop button on the antique chess clock.

"Three minutes!" I said.

Mr. Kelly's face had changed. He didn't appear to be sad. Now he had a look on his face I could recognize as anger.

"Ran away, did she?" he asked. "With a man? That little brat! I'll go get her and bring her home, you mark my words!"

"Please!" I said. "Your time is done. Next!"

"Wait, sir!" he said. "I didn't pay you!"

"I have no time for that!" I said. "Next!"

Nora grabbed Mr. Kelly and pulled him away. Sal approached, leading a gray-haired lady. She was dressed in a green suit.

"Mrs. Tabitha Sparks?" I asked. "Freelance reporter?"

"Yes, dear," said Mrs. Levi. "She's your next appointment."

"Mr. Bradley!" said Mrs. Sparks. "What a pleasure to meet you! I was wondering if you'd be so good as to grant me an interview? You've become quite a sensation in New York and I understand you haven't given any interviews to the press?"

"You understand correctly," I said.

"Fabulous!" she said. "Aren't I lucky to have been the first to catch you, then? You don't mind if I conduct a short interview, do you? It'll be in all the newspapers, I'm sure. You're big news, Mr. Bradley! You don't mind, do you?"

"No," I said.

Mrs. Sparks smiled and pulled a small digital sound recorder from her pocket, as well as a notebook and pen.

"Can we start then?" she asked.

"Okay," I said.

"First, let me tell you again what a pleasure it is to meet you, Trueman!" she said. "Do you mind if I call you Trueman?"

"No," I said. "Why would I mind? That's my name. What else would you call me?"

"Oh!" she said. "Ha-ha! Funny! Yes, of course. Why would I call you any name but the one you were born with, right? And, please, feel free to call me Tabitha."

"I wasn't born with the name Trueman," I said.

"You weren't?" she asked. "Do tell!"

"My name was originally spelled T-R-U-M-A-N," I said. "That was the name my mother gave me after I was born. I changed it to T-R-U-E-M-A-N when I decided to become a detective."

"Oh, really?" she asked. "Why did you change it?"

"Because," I said, "I thought that's a good name for a detective. Because detectives try to solve mysteries and expose the true details of what happened. So I am a 'true man,' because I am a man who exposes the truth for people who are seeking the truth. A 'true man' exposes truth and exposing truth is my job, so my name should be Trueman. This makes logical sense. Do you understand what I'm saying?"

Mrs. Sparks scratched her head with her pen and I could not interpret her expression. She wrote something in her notebook.

"Okay," she said. "Let's move on to the next question. Since you've been in the newspapers, your name's become well known. It's even been reported that powerful and prestigious people have become interested in your equations. I've read the Federal Bureau of Investigation is interested! Is that true? I also read the Associated Licensed Detectives of New York

State want you to give a seminar, explaining your equations. Are you planning to accept that invitation? I hear you've been flooded with hundreds of phone calls from around the world. Everyone wants you to solve their cases. People think you're something like a magician and that your equations are a kind of magic that can solve every mystery. So, given all this media attention and all these different people asking for your attention and assistance, what exactly are you planning to do?"

I couldn't speak a word. I had realized that I was getting attention because of the newspaper stories about me, but so far, I had been able to confront it all in simple, understandable, three-minute chunks. Mrs. Sparks revealed to me how big and intimidating this attention really was. I can only comfortably confront a problem if it is given to me in small pieces.

I was also confused because she had asked me three questions and I wasn't sure which one I should answer. Mrs. Sparks' questions were too confusing and I was getting nervous.

"Well…" I said. "I don't know."

She looked at me for a few seconds, in silence.

"You don't know what do about it?" she asked.

I stared at her, unable to talk. How could I tell her what I planned to do about it, if I had no idea what to do or exactly what "it" was. I had just now realized I was required to do something and had no answer yet. I looked at the chess timer.

"Three minutes!" I said.

I hit the stop button on the timer.

"Next, please!" I said.

"What?" asked Mrs. Sparks. "Next? But we just started the interview! I have fifteen more questions to ask you!"

I made a hand motion to Sal and he understood my wishes. Sal came and pulled Mrs. Sparks away from me. She continued to protest loudly as Sal forced her to leave the building. I was glad to see her go, because her questions made me nervous.

"Next!" I said. "Who's next, Mrs. Levi?"

"Me, Trueman!" said Buckley.

I saw that a group of police officers were the only people remaining in the waiting area. Detective Buckley was standing in the middle of the group. He looked at his wristwatch.

"We were scheduled to meet you at 11:00 am," said Buckley. "Here we are, exactly on time. You run a tight ship, Trueman."

"Hello Detective," I said. "I'm glad to see you! Does this mean we're finished the eighty appointments?"

"Yes, dear," said Mrs. Levi. "Detective Buckley is your last appointment for today."

"Great!" I said. "Then we can begin talking about our mission! I'll get out my chart of La Guardia airport and we'll begin. But I'm confused about your statement, Detective."

"What statement?" he asked.

"I run a tight ship?" I asked. "I don't know what you mean. Are you talking about boats or shipments?"

"Forget it, Trueman," he said. "Just an expression."

"Okay," I said. "Could everyone come here, please? Please come watch me! We'll discuss the plan for today's mission!"

Nora, Sal, Mrs. Levi, Buckley and the six policemen that accompanied him all stood around my desk and gave me their full attention. I unfolded my chart of La Guardia airport. I had written hundreds of mathematical equations on the chart and made geometric diagrams with my compass and protractor. Because of my additions, it looked more like an engineer's blueprint than a map of La Guardia airport. I picked up a small pointing stick and started explaining my plans for executing this mission.

"As you can see," I said, "La Guardia airport has four separate sections. The first section is called the Central Terminal, the second is called the US Airways Terminal, the third is called the Delta Terminal and the fourth is called the Marine Air

Terminal. Now, what we're going to do is… Nora, Sal, Mrs. Levi and I will each wait in one of the four terminals. When the suspect arrives, we'll call the police and they'll come arrest the criminal. Then we can begin the search for evidence."

Everyone was silent.

"Do you understand my plan?" I asked.

"No," said Buckley. "Why are you guys waiting in four terminals? I don't even know who it is we're looking for."

I hadn't realized that Buckley and the others were unaware of the purpose of our mission. I had not told them the results of my equations, but somehow I had assumed they already knew.

"Did I forget to tell you?" I asked. "I didn't tell you how I solved the murder of Eddie Sipple, did I?"

"No," said Buckley. "You neglected to mention that."

"I guess I did," I said. "Well, I used my crime-fighting equation to determine the true details of Eddie's murder. I tried to locate the murderer, but I couldn't."

"I thought your equation is supposed to solve crimes," said Buckley. "Now you're telling me it just didn't work?"

"No, you don't understand!" I said. "My crime-fighting equation does work! But it is designed to work in New York City. It doesn't work anywhere else. The murderer of Eddie Sipple left New York City. So, I have no way of knowing where he is! My equation only works in New York City. Do you understand what I'm saying?"

"Yeah, okay," said Buckley. "I understand you. But if that's the case, then why are we looking for the murderer at La Guardia? You said you have no idea where he is, right?"

"Correct," I said. "My equation doesn't know where he went. But it can tell me when he'll return to New York City. I know he will be returning today. My equation told me he will be in La Guardia airport at noon. So, that means he must be arriving in a plane. Do you understand my plan now?"

"Okay!" said Buckley. "Now I understand you! You don't know which terminal he's arriving at, right? That's why each of you are waiting in the four terminals to see if he arrives."

"Correct!" I said.

"Okay, I get it," said Buckley.

"Guys," he said to his men, "I want one of you to join each of these people and keep an eye on them, okay? Except Trueman. I'll be his partner. He's the man with the plan, guys. So, let's all take care of Trueman, okay? All you guys listen to whatever he says, okay. If he tells you to do something, obey him as if he was me. Trueman's the boss today."

The police officers nodded their obedient assent and looked at me expectantly. Nora was smiling and I could recognize that she was pleased with me. I wasn't sure if it was pride or affection she was feeling, but either way, it made me happy.

"Well, boss," said Buckley, to me, "you ready to go?"

I looked at the expectant faces that surrounded me and felt proud to have somehow inspired the confidence of all these people. Not only were my friends confident in my ability to lead them and solve this case, even the police were impressed with me and willing to let me determine their course of action.

I looked up at the Dick Tracy comics that were displayed on the walls of my office. I was now as famous and respected as Dick Tracy and I wanted to lead this mission with all the manly, self-assured confidence that Dick Tracy would if he were in my position. I concentrated as intensely as I could and imagined I was Dick Tracy. I looked at the new, yellow trench coat I had bought to replace the one that had been bleached by acid. I put it on slowly, imagining I was Dick Tracy. I grabbed my yellow hat from the coat rack and put it on my head.

"Alright," I said, in a manly voice. "Let's go."

I walked confidently through the crowd, planning to lead them out of the building. My feet hit a chair and I fell down to the ground, knocking down half the chairs in the waiting room. I screamed in terror and landed on my back in the middle of the waiting room floor. Nora screamed and ran towards me.

"Trueman!" she shouted. "Are you alright?"

Nora picked me up.

"Yeah," I said. "I think I'm okay."

I looked at the police officers and noticed some of them were smiling. I wasn't sure what that meant, but I knew my clumsy fall was not something Dick Tracy would have done. I felt embarrassed by my clumsiness. I've always been physically awkward and have often lost my balance like this and fallen down to the ground. Nora took my arm and led me towards the exit. We walked out onto the street.

"Don't be embarrassed," whispered Nora. "Everyone trips sometimes. It's happened to me lots of times. There's nothing wrong with that. That is, there's nothing wrong with you."

"No," I said. "There is something wrong with me. I'm clumsy. I've always been physically awkward."

"Well," she said, "then I'll be your partner for this mission, okay? I'll do anything that takes a lot of… balance, or physical work, okay? We can be a team, okay?"

"No," I said.

"Why not?" she asked.

"I don't need help," I said. "I won't be clumsy for much longer. I've found a cure."

"You found a cure for clumsiness?" she asked.

"Yes," I said.

"Well, what's the cure for clumsiness, then?" she asked.

"Shh! It's a secret," I said. "I'll tell you later."

We stopped on the sidewalk, where crowds of pedestrians were beginning to appear, enjoying their lunch hour in the summer sun. The police officers turned to face me and I felt

I had a second chance to look professional in front of these cops.

"Detective! Officers!" I said. "Please get into your cars and follow our Lincoln car to La Guardia airport."

I looked at the faces of the police officers and saw no indication of laughter or mirth. They seemed to be taking me seriously, as if I were an actual police detective, like Buckley or Dick Tracy. That particular tone of voice, manly and confident, seemed to work very well. I made an effort to remember to use that tone of voice in the future.

"That is all!" I said, in the same manly tone.

I walked quickly towards the Lincoln car and sat in the back seat. I was in a hurry to leave the company of the police, before I could trip or do something else to make myself look ridiculous. Sal, Nora and Mrs. Levi got into the car and we were soon driving through the heavy late-morning traffic.

I took my chart of La Guardia airport and began marking a circle on it with my compass. I needed to determine the likely number of people that would be at Marine Air Terminal today at 2:00 pm. If I would be visiting there, I didn't want to be paralyzed because of unexpected crowds. I needed to know what to expect. I took my protractor and made a thirty degree angle.

"What are you doing?" asked Nora.

"Oh, just a simple geometric probability diagram," I said.

Nora said nothing and I could recognize her confusion.

"It's not important," I said. "I can do it later. Now, everyone, please listen to me. I will tell each of you what your task is. We each have a task in this important mission."

"We're listening, boss!" said Sal.

I moved my chart to the front seat, so everyone could see it and I circled locations on the map to indicate where each of us would be positioned for this mission.

"Sal," I said, "you will go to the Central Terminal of the airport and wait on the Arrivals Level."

"Sure thing, boss!" said Sal. "Only, what do I wait for?"

"Oh, yeah," I said. "I forgot to tell you what you're waiting for. You're waiting for a young man, between the ages of eighteen and twenty-five. Okay?"

Nobody replied. I looked at everyone's faces and couldn't interpret their emotions. They stared ahead, like mannequins.

"Do you understand who we're looking for?" I asked.

"Trueman, dear…" said Mrs. Levi.

"Yes?" I asked.

"You do know there are probably hundreds of young men in the airport who are that age, right?" she asked.

"Please, don't tell me that is all you know about this murderer!" said Sal. "If all these police discover you brought them out to look for a man like that they'll be plenty mad!"

"What?" I asked. "Why mad?"

"Because, Trueman!" said Nora. "A young man aged eighteen to twenty-five? That could be anyone! We thought you knew exactly who this man would be, not just a vague, general idea like that!"

They were silent and I could interpret the disappointment on their faces. They had expected me to create mathematical miracles and solve this case, but now they were disappointed to think I really had no idea, exactly, who the murderer was.

"No!" I said.

"What?" asked Nora.

"No, you're wrong!" I said. "This vague description is not all I have! It is true there are hundreds of young men in the airport between the ages of eighteen and twenty-five years old. But we can easily identify which one is the murderer!"

"How?" asked Nora.

"It is simple," I said. "Sal will wait in the Central Terminal and watch everyone who arrives on a plane. If he sees a man like the one I described, he will use his wrist TV to execute my crime-fighting equation! Do you understand what I'm saying? My equation will indicate who the true murderer is."

"Ah!" said Sal. "Now I understand!"

"Good!" I said. "You, Mrs. Levi, will wait in the Delta Terminal of the airport. You will wait on the Arrivals Level and look for such a young man as I described."

"Yes, dear," said Mrs. Levi. "Then, I use your little equation there on my wrist TV to tell if he's the murderer?"

"Yes," I said.

"And what about me, Trueman?" asked Nora.

"Well," I said, "you wait in the US Airways Terminal of the airport. Wait on the Arrivals Level and look for…"

"I know what to do, Trueman," said Nora. "But I'd rather wait with you. I'd feel a lot better if we could be a team."

"No," I said. "That's not on the plan! I am waiting in the Marine Air Terminal. I am to wait there with Buckley."

"But why can't I join you?" asked Nora. "You can send Buckley to wait in the US Airways Terminal…"

"No!" I said. "He can't do it! He has no wrist TV! What if the criminal arrives at US Airways Terminal? None of us will test him with the crime-fighting equation. He'll escape!"

"Okay, fine…" said Nora. I could recognize by the look in her eyes that she was disappointed.

"I'm sorry," I said, trying to comfort her. "But I chose the Marine Air Terminal for myself because my equation says the murderer is 20 percent more likely to arrive at the Marine Air Terminal than at the other three terminals. I should wait at this terminal because I can do the equations faster than everyone else, because I can do the equation in my head. I don't need the wrist TV to help me. Also, I need to be alone. I can't be distracted. The Marine Air Terminal is the most important one."

"Yeah, Trueman," said Nora. "I understand already."

I looked at Nora, but I still saw no indications that she was comforted. I couldn't interpret her emotional state, but I knew it was not any of the good emotions I could recognize.

"I think we're just about ready for our mission, Trueman dear," said Mrs. Levi. "You really are a born leader! The way you line us up and give us our orders so clearly, like a general with his troops... you really have become quite the detective!"

I felt my face become warm from pleasure.

"I'm glad you think so, Mrs. Levi," I said.

"Even your voice sounds different!" she said.

"Oh really?" I asked, in a manly tone of voice.

"Yes," she said. "But, you forgot one thing."

"I did?" I asked.

"Yes," she said. "None of us have any idea how to use the computers in our wrist TVs!"

"That's right, boss!" said Sal. "How are we going to use your crime-fighting equation to find this murderer if we have no idea how to use the equation or the wrist TVs?"

"Oh, yes," I said. "I forgot about that."

I threw my chart onto the back seat and displayed my own wrist TV. As the sun shone over us, and cars honked around us, I described the method of inputting data into the wrist TV and how to use the crime-fighting equation.

By the time I had finished the lesson, we had arrived at La Guardia airport. I could see the massive air traffic control tower and hear the sound of plane engines roaring in the skies.

"Alright, my friends," I said. "Now, we start the mission. If we follow the plan exactly, then I'm sure we will succeed."

LA GUARDIA AIRPORT

I was holding a cup of tea and trying to watch the crowds of people in the Arrivals area of the Marine Air Terminal. But the noise of the crowds and the airplanes made my head hurt. To avoid the discomfort caused by the noise, I had to put my earphones into my ears. I wore my special sunglasses to avoid any visual distractions and stared at the clock on my wrist TV.

Something touched my shoulder and surprised me. I jumped and the cup of tea fell from my hand and spilled on my lap. I screamed and fell backwards, off my chair.

"I'm sorry!" shouted Nora.

I could see Nora standing over me. She took my arm and helped me get up. She led me to my chair and wiped the tea from my clothes, with napkins she'd gotten from a napkin dispenser.

"I was only touching you because you weren't answering me!" she said. "I wanted to tell you that a plane just arrived! It's almost 2:00 pm. So, this is the murderer's plane, right?"

I sighed and tried to relax. The airport was starting to get busier and noisier and I tried not to look around me. I had already been nervous, but after being scalded with hot tea and falling to the ground, I was even more nervous.

"I wish you hadn't insisted on joining me!" I said.

"Why?" she asked. "You don't like my company?"

"I like your company!" I said. "But it wasn't part of my plan. It makes me nervous if we don't follow my plans exactly! Because I was nervous about changing my plans, now the crowds are making me nervous and my reactions, also, are more nervous."

"That's why you jumped when I touched you?" she asked.

"Yes," I said.

"You're saying I'm responsible for making you nervous?" she asked. "Because I'm the one who made you change your plans?"

"Yes," I said.

"Well, Trueman," she said. "If that's what you think, then just think about this. What if you got nervous and I wasn't here to pick you up and put you back in your chair? What if something else went wrong and you got nervous, and I wasn't here to help you? You don't like crowds when you're nervous."

"That's correct," I said. "Crowds are unpredictable."

"Well, then," she said. "If that's the case, then how would you be able to complete this mission without my help? How could you find the murderer in the crowd if you're too nervous to even look at the crowd? You need me to help you, Trueman!"

I realized Nora was right. This was the same logic she had used to convince me she should come with me to the Marine Air Terminal. It was true I might need someone to help me in this crowded place, in case the crowd caused me problems and rendered me helpless. Because this was the terminal where the murderer was most likely to arrive, I didn't want to risk any problems.

"Besides," said Nora, smiling, "we had an agreement!"

"Agreement?" I asked.

"Yeah!" she said. "Remember 545 East 13th Street?"

"Yes," I said.

"Well, when we were there, I promised I'd teach you how to be a detective, remember?" she asked. "We've only had one lesson, so far. Maybe we'll have our second lesson today. Lesson two can be called 'how to apprehend a suspect.' You said the murderer's likely to arrive here, right? Well, then we'll probably need to chase and arrest him. I'll teach you how to do that. It's not so hard, really. Just watch what I do, okay?"

"Okay," I said.

A loud crackling noise filled the room and I put my earphones into my ears. Nora's hands appeared in front of my face. She was writing something on a piece of paper. I realized she probably didn't want to make me nervous by touching me again, so she was writing her messages on a piece of paper.

"People are coming," she wrote. "People arriving. Murderer probably in this group? Should we start now?"

I nodded my head to indicate I was ready. I increased the volume of my portable music player. The sound of Mozart's Symphony #41 in C major helped me to concentrate on my equation. Earlier, Nora and I had discussed the most efficient method for us to identify the murderer in the crowds. Nora would look for men who appeared to be between the ages of eighteen and twenty-five and would note down the exact time of their arrival, as well as a few other physical details I could use in my equation. I could then use my crime-fighting equation to determine which of these men was the true murderer. This was the most efficient method because Nora had no problems enduring noises or looking at crowds, like I did. And, using this method, I could wear my earphones and sunglasses and fully concentrate on my equations.

I concentrated on Nora's hand and saw her writing times and details. She wrote quickly and so I knew that people were probably arriving in large crowds.

"12:01:30," I read. "Brown hair, 200 pounds, Caucasian."

I used my equation to determine if this was the murderer.

"No," I said. "That's not him."

I crossed off that suspect's details from Nora's list. Soon we had noted the details of five men and seven minutes had passed. Nora's hand wrote slower now and I realized the crowds were probably getting smaller and most of the passengers had already arrived. I started to wonder if we'd missed the murderer. Maybe Nora hadn't noticed him in the crowd?

"12:08:15," I read. "Black hair, 130 pounds, Caucasian."

I closed my eyes and inserted this information into my crime-fighting equation. I felt something touch my shoulder and I jumped. Luckily, I had no more tea to spill into my lap and Nora grabbed me tightly, so I wouldn't fall down.

"What?" I asked. "What's happening?"

"It's him!" she said. "We found the murderer!"

"What?" I asked. "Him?"

I closed my eyes and finished executing the equation.

"You're right!" I said. "The result of my equation is positive! It's the black-haired, 130 pound Caucasian man! But how did you know? Do you also have a crime-fighting equation?"

"What?" she asked. "No! I was talking about Buckley! Detective Buckley found him!"

"Buckley found the murderer?" I asked.

"Yes!" she said. "He just called me on my mobile phone! Remember, you gave Buckley my wrist TV and sent him to US Airways Terminal to watch the arrivals? Well, he used your equation, used my wrist TV, and he found the guy!"

"No!" I said.

"What?" she asked. "Aren't you happy? We found him!"

"But something's wrong!" I said. "I just found the murderer! He's that black-haired man whose details you wrote on the paper! There can't be two murderers! There's a mistake!"

Nora looked at the crowds and pointed at a small man with black hair who was waiting at the luggage carousel.

"That's the murderer?" she asked.

"If he's the man whose details you most recently wrote on the paper, then yes!" I said.

"Then," she said, "who did Buckley find? Did Buckley find the murderer or is it this guy? What should we do?"

"I don't know!" I shouted.

I grabbed my head. This was unexpected and confusing. I couldn't deal with it. I wanted to fall to the floor and hide under my coat. Nora grabbed me and spoke in a soothing voice.

"Relax, Trueman," she said. "I know you're nervous, but we can do this. Since we don't know which of these two people is the real murderer, I suggest you go meet Buckley and discover what's happening. Maybe Buckley didn't use your equation correctly, right? It could happen. So, you go find Buckley and I'll stay here and follow this black-haired guy, understand?"

I nodded my head to indicate I understood what she was saying. Nora put her arm around me and pointed to a staircase.

"Go down those stairs to the exit," she said. "There are taxicabs parked out there. Take one to US Airways Terminal and call me when you figure out what happened, okay?"

I was too confused to do anything but obey. I ran towards the stairwell and out the heavy metal door marked "EXIT." I looked around, but saw no taxicabs.

"Nora said there'd be taxicabs!" I said.

I couldn't deal with any more unexpected surprises like this. I leaned against the building and fell to the ground. I was tempted to count prime numbers and forget about the mission.

My wrist TV crackled and I waited a minute before responding to it. I was deciding if I should risk looking at my wrist TV or if I should hide from reality by counting prime numbers. The wrist TV may give me more unexpected surprises.

I decided to look at my wrist TV and saw Buckley's face. He appeared to be in a crowded room and he seemed to be running.

"Trueman!" said Buckley. "You haven't been responding to my messages. I've been trying to get in touch! We've been following this guy! I just wanted you to confirm it for me."

"Confirm?" I asked. "What do you mean confirm?"

"I mean," he said, "my little wrist TV here told me this guy's the murderer! Does that mean he really is? Should we arrest him? You're the guy who invented this thing, so I just wanted to ask your permission before we nail this guy!"

"Well, I'm not sure…" I said.

"Not sure?" he said. "Come on, Trueman, we've got to arrest him before he takes off! We need to hurry here! Now, why is it you're not sure? Don't these equations of yours work?"

"Yes, of course they work!" I said.

I didn't want Buckley to lose confidence in me and start thinking my equations didn't work. But I was confused about my equations. I knew something was wrong, because there could not be two murderers. I was starting to doubt my equations again, and I needed to discover why they hadn't worked. But I needed to discover this in a way so Buckley wouldn't know I was doubting my equations.

"Yes, it works!" I said. "I confirm it! Yes, of course, you can arrest him. I'm glad you caught him, Detective."

"Yeah, me too!" said Buckley. "If this proves to be a successful mission, you'll be a real hero, Trueman! I mean, all the cops in the world will want one of these wrist things! Having the solution to a crime at my fingertips, like this… it's just amazing, Trueman. I'm over the moon about this!"

I didn't understand his reference to the moon, but his joy made me even more nervous, because I didn't want to reveal my doubts to him and ruin his good opinion of my equations. I thought of a plan to secretly determine what had gone wrong.

"Are you arresting him?" I asked.

"Yeah," said Buckley. "They're arresting him, now."

"Can I watch the arrest, please?" I asked.

"You wanna watch?" he asked. "How exactly are you gonna watch the arrest from across the airport, Trueman?"

"Just point your wrist TV at the arrest," I said, "and I will be able to see it. The wrist TV has a camera inside it."

"Oh yeah," he said. "That shoulda been obvious, huh? As you can see, I'm still not quite used to these wrist things."

Buckley pointed his wrist TV at the scene of the murderer being arrested. I saw a large man with black hair, probably 250 pounds and seemingly of the Latino race. I quickly examined the memory of my wrist TV's computer. I had designed these wrist TVs so that I could examine everything that had ever been inputted into them. I could not only view the input history of my own wrist TV, I could also view the input history of all the other wrist TVs. I looked for the information that Buckley had inputted about this man and checked its accuracy, compared to the information I had observed. Buckley appeared to have inputted the information correctly. I did not know exactly what time the Latino man had entered the building, but this was a minor variable, and so I assumed the equation was correct.

Buckley had inputted the information correctly and the crime-fighting equation said this Latino man was the murderer. I sighed with relief. I had verified the accuracy of Buckley's equation and if this man was the murderer than I must have made a mistake with my equation. There was simply no other logical explanation to explain the situation.

"Maybe I made a mistake," I said, "because Nora interrupted me in the middle of executing the equation."

"What did you say?" asked Buckley.

"Oh, nothing," I said. "I was talking to myself. I need to go now. I need to tell Nora that you found the murderer."

"Sure thing, Trueman," said Buckley. "We'll meet you in the parking lot, okay? Just wait there for us."

I ran back into the Marine Air Terminal and thought about how to locate Nora. I had forgotten that she had no wrist TV.

"I know," I said. "I'll call her mobile phone."

My wrist made a crackling sound and started talking.

"I tell you, I didn't do anything!" said a voice. "I've never even been to New York City before!"

I looked at my wrist TV and could recognize the blue navy pants worn by the Latino man. Buckley had forgotten to switch off his wrist TV. I could see the airport from the perspective of Buckley's wrist. I had heard the voice of the Latino man.

"How could I be under arrest for a murder in this city?" asked the Latino man. "I said I'd never even been here before!"

I switched off my wrist TV and found a public pay phone. I called the number of Nora's mobile phone.

"Trueman?" asked Nora, through the telephone.

"Yes," I said. "Buckley found the true murderer."

"Oh, okay," she said. "Then I don't have to follow this guy anymore?"

"No," I said. "He's not the murderer. Please come and meet me on the first floor of the round building."

"That's funny," she said.

"What?" I asked. "Why is it funny?"

"Well, I've been following this guy," she said. "And that's exactly where he's going. He's going to the first floor of the round building. So, if you're there, you should see him any second now. We're almost there. I'm hanging up, okay?"

I put down the telephone and looked for Nora and the black-haired man. As I waited, I was continuously distracted by a persistent thought. The Latino man had said he never entered New York City before. I was distracted by the thought that I could probably confirm or disprove that fact by using my crime-fighting equation. This thought was so distracting that I decided to quickly use my equation to determine if the Latino man was lying. I closed my eyes and inserted the variables into my crime-fighting equation. Executing the equation, it told me the Latino man had definitely not been to New York City before.

"That can't be!" I said to myself. "If he wasn't in New York City, how could he have killed Eddie?"

I was so disturbed by this thought that I decided to use my mind to confirm the Latino man was truly the murderer. I executed the equation in my mind. The result was shocking.

"The Latino man isn't the murderer!" I shouted. "But if he isn't the murderer, why did the wrist TV computer say he was?"

I started to wonder if maybe there was a mistake in the design of the wrist TVs. Maybe the wrist TVs just didn't work. The wrist TV had given a different result than my mind, and I knew my mind worked correctly, so the wrist TV must be wrong.

As I was thinking this, a man passed in front of me, followed by a woman who grabbed my shoulder. I emerged from my concentrated thought and realized it was Nora. She smiled at me and pointed at the man who had walked in front of me.

"There he is," she said. "See?"

I recognized him as the black-haired man Nora had been following. At that moment, a horrible thought entered my head. We had made a big mistake and I was watching the true murderer as he walked towards the exit. I couldn't allow him to escape.

"Stop him!" I shouted.

I ran in front of the black-haired man and blocked him from exiting the building. I recognized the shock on his face.

"Nora!" I shouted. "He's the one! Let's grab him!"

Everyone in the building stopped what they were doing and stared at us. The black-haired man also stopped and stared, his face expressing the recognizable signs of shock and fear. Then, as fast as a rabbit, he turned around and ran up a stairwell.

Nora ran to me and grabbed my shoulders.

"Trueman!" she said. "Here's lesson two of being a detective. If you suspect someone of being a murderer, you don't run up to them and shout 'He's the one!' You understand? He's sure to run away! Now, you already told me Buckley found the murderer! Now you're saying this guy's the one? Make a decision, please! Which one of these guys is the murderer?"

"That guy who ran up the stairwell!" I said.

"Okay, then, follow me!" she said.

Nora ran towards the stairwell and I tried my best to follow her quickly. Nora was extremely athletic and I was not accustomed to moving this fast. We climbed stairs and ran through long hallways. As we ran, I was worried I may do something clumsy and fall to the ground. But I was able to concentrate on my actions and avoid falling.

We came into a big round room on the second floor. It had a domed skylight in the ceiling, with a miniature airplane hanging from it. There were murals painted on the upper walls and I was distracted by the beauty of the architecture.

"This is a wonderful example of 'Art Deco' style architecture," I said. "I've memorized architecture books."

"What?" asked Nora. "Trueman, please! Not now! We need to know where that guy went! I lost him! Help me, Trueman!"

The black-haired man was nowhere to be seen. Looking around, I noticed there were four doors. The murderer could have run through any of these doors. The first door had the word "Departures" above it. The second door had the word "Restaurant" above it. The third was marked "Keep Out— Staff Only." And the fourth had no label, but seemed to lead outside, because sunlight was visible through it. I tried to think of a method to determine which door the murderer had gone through.

"Come on, Trueman!" said Nora. "Every second counts!"

I didn't understand the expression she was using, but her reference to "counting seconds" reminded me of the time I was in the Hickson warehouse, counting the seconds on my TET and waiting for the ideal time to go across the bridge, over the acid vats. I was reminded of that, because this was a similarly stressful situation. It gave me a wonderful idea, and I wondered if that is what Nora had meant by her strange comment.

"Aha!" I said. "Good idea, Nora! The TET!"

"What?" she asked.

I took the TET out of my pocket and removed it from its holding container. I put it in my palm and began inputting all the necessary information about our mission.

"What's that?" asked Nora. "What are you doing?"

"It's my TET," I said. "It finds evidence. Last time I used it, the evidence was either very near to the criminal, who was Malcolm Vrie, or else maybe the evidence had been in his clothing? I was just thinking, if the black-haired man is the murderer, maybe he's also carrying the evidence in his clothes."

"And if he is?" she asked.

"Then the TET will find him," I said.

I finished inputting data and saw the compass and arrow appear on the TET's computer screen. It pointed towards the door that had a sign on it reading "Keep Out—Staff Only." I ran towards the door and tried the handle. It was unlocked.

"This way, Nora!" I said.

Nora and I entered the forbidden room and climbed up a poorly lit stairwell. There was a battered, metal door at the top of the stairs, with light shining from underneath it.

We opened the door and ran out onto thick gravel, which made crunching noises under my feet. It did not take long for me to realize that we were on the roof. There were vents and skylights and many pipes that pointed to the sky. It smelled like tar and the coolants used in air conditioning systems.

"There he is!" whispered Nora.

She pointed towards my left and I saw the black-haired man. He was pulling on a rope, which he had tied to the casing of an air conditioning unit. He seemed not to have noticed us, because he didn't look at us and made no attempt to run away.

"You're a genius, Trueman!" said Nora. "We got him!"

"What do we do now?" I asked.

Nora pulled a gun from a holster she had hidden under her jacket. I had noticed the type of gun she had used before, when she was pointing it at Eddie in the hallway of 545 East 13th Street, but didn't have a chance to ask her about it then.

"That is a Colt model 1903 pocket, hammerless, semi-automatic pistol," I said.

"Uh, yeah," she said. "That's right. Let me guess, you memorized gun catalogs?"

"Yes, my granddad was a cop," I said, "so he had a lot of gun catalogs. That's an old one. They only manufactured them with grips like that before 1924. Your gun was made before 1924. It looks like it's in bad condition. Does it work?"

"If it didn't work, I wouldn't have it in my hands right now," she said. "As for its condition… as I told you once before, I don't have much money. I'm on a budget, here. Now, stay close behind me, okay? I'm going to go and confront him."

Nora gripped her gun with both hands and pointed it towards the murderer. She stepped cautiously in his direction and I followed her, trying not to make much noise.

"Freeze!" shouted Nora. "Don't move or I'll shoot!"

I could see the black-haired man's reaction, but couldn't interpret his thoughts or feelings. He flew over the edge of the building and the rope he had prepared was pulled tight.

"He's climbing down the wall with the rope!" said Nora.

Nora ran towards the edge of the building and jumped over. I expected to hear her screaming and the sound of her body hitting the ground, but when I reached the edge of the building and looked down, I saw her climbing down the rope.

She descended the rope so quickly that she reminded me of the monkeys I'd seen at the zoo. I knew Nora was athletic, but I had not realized the full power of her athleticism until then.

I could see the black-haired man. He had lowered himself onto the roof of the first floor and was now climbing down a tree. If he succeeded, he would reach the street below. Nora landed on the first floor roof-top and turned to look at me.

"Trueman!" she said. "Can you climb down?"

I looked down and felt sick. I wasn't sure if I could climb down. I often tripped and hurt myself walking down the street. If I tried to climb down the outside of a two-storey building, I might kill myself. I felt fear and confusion, and it made me dizzy. I grasped the edge of the building.

"Trueman!" said Nora. "You can't do it! You might trip and fall! You said you were clumsy, remember? So don't even try it! Just stay up there! Just wait for me there, okay?"

I felt dizzy. I could not see Nora clearly, but her words reminded me of something I had entirely forgotten.

"Aha!" I said. "Wait for me, Nora! I'm coming!"

"No!" she said. "Trueman, don't! You'll kill yourself!"

"No, I won't!" I said.

I took a small box out of my coat and opened it. Inside was an invention Dr. Rozzozzo had made for me. It was called the "Clumsiness Compensating Console" or "CCC." I had designed it to cure my clumsiness. Just like the TET was able to predict the ideal moment for me to walk somewhere without being seen, the CCC was able to tell me the ideal moment for me to perform a particular athletic action without tripping, getting hurt or dying. All I needed to do was input the details of what athletic action I was trying to accomplish.

"Trueman!" said Nora. "He's getting away! The murderer's escaping! I have to go! Just, please, stay up there, okay?"

The CCC was square, with a leather belt attached to it, and I was able to strap it securely to my forearm. I inputted the necessary data into the CCC and looked at its small computer screen. Every ten seconds, it displayed the likelihood of avoiding injury or death, if I tried to climb down the rope.

"Fifty-eight percent chance of avoiding injury or death," I read, aloud. "Not good enough!"

I was standing on the edge of the building, ready to jump. It was windy and I could see the blue water of nearby Bowery Bay. I saw the black-haired man. He had reached the street and was running away, but Nora was still below me, staring at me.

"Trueman!" said Nora. "I said stay there!"

"Twelve percent chance," I read. "That's not even close to good!"

"Trueman!" said Nora. "You're making him escape! We're gonna lose him! Why won't you listen to me and stay put?!"

"Ninety-seven percent chance," I read.

I realized the technology was assuming I jumped the instant I read the number and so I didn't stop to think if 97 percent was an acceptable level of safety. I grabbed the rope and jumped over the edge of the building. As I descended, I hugged the rope tightly. I felt as if I was floating for a few seconds, and then my weight caused the rope to pull against my arms with painful force. My view of the world was changing so quickly that I couldn't interpret anything I saw. I felt a sudden, paralyzing confusion and heard Nora's voice screaming loudly.

I was so paralyzed that I could do nothing but grip the rope tightly and close my eyes. I could feel myself swinging on the rope. I wondered how I would ever get down safely if I continued to swing like this. I was in a paralyzed, shocked state, so how would I be able to free myself? It seemed to me that I would swing like this forever.

I started to spin. It made me violently ill. I became so ill that I lost the ability to grip the rope. I released the rope and felt myself flying through the air. For a brief, horrible second, I wondered if the CCC was imperfect. The wrist TV had failed to correctly identify the murderer of Eddie, so maybe the CCC had incorrectly estimated my chances of survival and I was falling to my death.

I felt a sudden impact against my back.

"Trueman!" shouted Nora.

I opened my eyes in response to Nora's yell. I could see the sky. I sat up and discovered that I was sitting on top of a moving bus. I must have fallen off the roof and somehow landed on the top of a bus. I could see Nora above me, leaning over the edge of the first floor roof and screaming at me.

Before I could interpret the meaning of all this, the bus made a sudden stop, which caused me to slide over the roof until I fell off the front of the bus. I saw a flower garden, with fresh, unpacked earth. I felt the earth impact my body.

I was laying in the flower garden, surrounded by a black, wrought-iron fence. I looked up at the sky and waited. I was not certain if I was safe yet, or if something else, unexpected and horrifying, would happen to me. I waited for what seemed like a long time, but nothing happened.

"Trueman!" shouted Nora.

I sat up and looked at the geraniums and tulips that surrounded me. My body had crushed some white tulips. Outside the fence, I could see a bus driver staring at me. Nora appeared, jumped over the fence and held my hands tightly.

"Are you okay?" she asked. "Are you hurt?"

I tried to identify any pain, but I couldn't.

"I'm not hurt," I said. "I guess the CCC works."

Nora picked me up and led me out of the garden.

"We'll call Sal!" she said. "We can't go on with the mission! You must be in shock after a fall like that!"

"But we need to apprehend the criminal!" I said. "Where has the black-haired man gone? We can't let him escape!"

"He already escaped!" she said. "I think we'd just be wasting our time, trying to find him. You must be in shock! You just fell off a two-storey building! You sure you're okay?"

"Yes," I said.

I felt a sensation in my fingers and toes. It was a tingling, burning sensation that travelled up my arms and legs until it covered my whole body. I was suddenly consumed with a horrible anxiety that came so quickly and suddenly that it felt like someone had beaten my head with a stick. My mind was filled with fearful, nervous thoughts and I began to realize that I was not okay. I had been deeply disturbed by my fall.

The CCC had correctly predicted that I would not be physically injured or killed, but it couldn't predict how upsetting this dizzying fall would be to my mind. After so many unexpected shocks, I was in a state of psychological collapse. I could not endure it any longer. I fell down on the street.

"Trueman!" shouted Nora.

I could only see black, but I heard Nora's voice. Soon I could not hear anything. My mind shut down and I felt nothing.

*

Our office on Reade Street was dark and humid. It was evening and the dark gray skies of New York City were visible outside my window. It was raining, but my window was open, because I needed fresh air. Water soaked the floor beneath the window and Mrs. Levi would mop it up every couple of minutes.

"Such weather!" said Mrs. Levi. "Just awful!"

I lay on my back on the settee that served as my bed. I had collapsed and become unconscious at the Marine Air Terminal. When the ambulance arrived, however, they had easily revived me. Apparently, I had fainted. Unexpected events are hard for me to endure, but all the unpredictable mishaps of our mission at La Guardia airport were completely impossible for me to endure. It had been so traumatic for me that I fainted.

I still felt dizzy sometimes, so I was laying down among soft blankets and pillows, while Nora and Mrs. Levi nursed me to health. I was starting to feel better. But feeling physically better was not entirely good. The healthier I felt, the more clearly I could remember what had happened at Marine Air Terminal. And the more I remembered about what happened, the more sad and humiliated I felt. Our mission had been a failure.

There was a sound of someone knocking on our front door.

"Ah, that must be Dr. Rozzozzo," said Sal. "I'll get it."

Sal went to open the front door and I tried to get up.

"Keep down!" said Nora. "You're still too weak to get up. Remember what the doctor said?"

"No, I don't remember," I said. "I was unconscious!"

"Oh, right," said Nora. "Well, I was conscious, and I remember what the doctor said. He said you should stay in bed until tomorrow morning. So, you can bet I'm not going to let you get up until tomorrow morning. Got that, mister?"

"But I need to talk to Dr. Rozzozzo," I said. "I asked her to come here because I need to tell her the wrist TV computers don't work! I have to yell at her and get my money back."

"Yell at her?" asked Mrs. Levi. "Why yell at her, dear?"

"Why?" I asked. "Well, because that's what my granddad would do if he bought something and it didn't work. He'd go back to the store and yell and then ask for his money back."

"Well, Trueman," said Nora, "I respect your granddad, but most of the time yelling just makes things worse."

"Yeah," said Mrs. Levi. "Yelling's not a good idea most of the time. Better to just keep it civilized, if you can help it. Unless, of course, you're dealing with a real yutz who really gets on your nerves. But, most of the time, you should try not to yell at people, Trueman dear. It doesn't help anything."

"But her wrist TVs don't work!" I said. "When Buckley used it to determine the murderer of Eddie, it said the Latino man was the murderer! That was just wrong! So, what can that mean? It can only mean that her wrist TVs don't work properly!"

"Well, how do you know it wasn't correct?" asked Nora.

"Because..." I said.

I stopped talking because I realized that I might not want Nora and Mrs. Levi to know the truth. Buckley's wrist TV had said the Latino was the murderer and when I used my mind to use the crime-fighting equation, it said the black-haired man was the murderer. Either the wrist TV didn't work correctly or my mind didn't work correctly. Or maybe my crime-fighting equation didn't work? I didn't know what the answer was, but I preferred to believe the wrist TV didn't work. Because if it did work, then there was something wrong with my mind or with my equation.

"Nothing," I said. "Never mind."

I decided not to talk about it until I knew for certain what wasn't working. I was scared they'd discover there was a problem with my mind or equations, and they'd stop admiring me.

The doors opened and Sal walked in, followed by the unmistakable figure of Dr. Lucretia Rozzozzo. She was dressed in a yellow laboratory coat, which she customized with many pockets and belts. A variety of small contraptions were strapped to her body, and continually made mechanical noises. She had a strange odor that was not unpleasant, but was impossible to identify. She wore a hat made of leather belts and topped with a metal ball. Her gray hair poked out from between the belts and stuck up in the air, making her head look like a peacock's tail. I had intended to yell at her, but her dark, intense eyes expressed power. Her eyes always intimidated me, and I couldn't say anything. I lay on my settee and stared at her.

"Hello Trueman," said Rozzozzo. "Why are you lying down? If you want to go to sleep, why'd you ask me to come here? I'm busy, you know. I've got over eighteen inventions I'm working on."

Her tone of voice was also powerful and intense, and I was still too intimidated to talk. I continued to stare silently.

"What's wrong with him?" asked Rozzozzo.

"He's not feeling too good," said Mrs. Levi.

"Yeah," said Nora. "He had an accident and fell off a building. He has to lie down until tomorrow morning."

"Fell?" asked Rozzozzo. "You should have used the CCC! Then you wouldn't have fallen. Now, what do you want, Trueman?"

"Um…" I said. "It's about the wrist TVs."

"What about them?" asked Rozzozzo.

"Well, I'm not criticizing you…" I said, "but I was just curious about something. Although I'm not criticizing… um…"

"Come on, Trueman!" said Rozzozzo. "Spit it out!"

I lifted my hand and felt if there was anything on my lips.

"Spit what out?" I asked. "There's nothing in my mouth."

"Oh, right," said Rozzozzo. "You don't like expressions? Well, 'spit it out' means stop hesitating and speak."

"Oh," I said. "Well, the thing that confuses me is this. Earlier today, Detective Buckley and I were searching for a murderer at La Guardia airport. We were in two different terminals and using my crime-fighting equation to find the murderer. And we both found two separate murderers."

"So?" asked Rozzozzo. "Congratulations catching two murderers. That's even better than catching one, isn't it?"

"No!" I said. "You don't understand! There was only one murderer! The equation could not possibly have identified two murderers! I tested the equations many times and I know there was only one murderer of Eddie Sipple!"

"Fine," said Rozzozzo. "How does this concern me?"

"Well, there can only be one murderer," I said. "So, either I was wrong or Detective Buckley was wrong. I got my result from executing the equation in my mind. Buckley got his result from executing the equation on the wrist TV."

"So, you think the wrist TV's computer doesn't work?" asked Rozzozzo. "What if the detective inputted the data wrong?"

"No!" I said. "I checked that. He did it correctly. Now, my brain probably works fine, so the only explanation is that your wrist TV computers don't work! When I bought them, you told me they'd work! I want my money back! Immediately!"

I slammed my fist against the nearby table. I was mimicking the way my granddad would protest, when he was demanding his money back for defective merchandise. I had forgotten all about Rozzozzo and had become concentrated on my memory of how my granddad would yell and demand his money back. After I hit my fist on the table, I looked at Rozzozzo and immediately regretted my protestations. She was looking at me with her eyes narrowed. I couldn't interpret her emotions, but she looked more intense than ever, and I hoped she wasn't angry.

"Is that what you think, Trueman?" asked Rozzozzo.

I didn't answer. I was so intimidated by the way she had asked that question that I was paralyzed from terror. This powerful woman was walking closer to me, and it seemed to me she'd descend on me, like a hawk or an eagle, and tear me to pieces. I lifted my arms and hid my face underneath them.

"I'm sorry!" I said. "Don't hurt me!"

"What?" asked Rozzozzo. "What nonsense! Who said I was going to hurt you? Just let me see that wrist TV of yours!"

Rozzozzo grabbed my arm and removed my wrist TV. She walked to a nearby table and sat down. She removed some kind of bizarre tool from her belt and started examining the wrist TV.

For a few minutes, everything was silent, apart from Rozzozzo's loud breathing and the symphony of electrical noises that always accompanied her. This woman emanated such an aura of power and intensity that no one dared speak, for fear of disturbing her concentration.

"Okay," said Rozzozzo. "I think I can guess what went wrong. There's a zero in your equation. This zero makes all the results equal one. So, it must be a mistake."

"All answers equal one?" I asked. "So, that means it would always give an affirmative answer?"

"Yes," said Rozzozzo. "Everyone is the murderer."

"So, there is a problem!" I said. "It doesn't work!"

"Yes," said Rozzozzo. "I must have made a mistake. I thought this was a zero. What is supposed to be there?"

Rozzozzo held up the wrist TV so I could see it. I recognized a part of my crime-fighting equation displayed on the TV screen. There was definitely a zero that was not supposed to be there.

"That should be an infinity symbol," I said. "Not a zero."

"Aha!" said Rozzozzo. "Now I see what went wrong. I always hate not knowing what my mistake was. You can't solve your problems unless you know what they are first, right?"

"Oh, I agree," I said. "So, now that you know what the problem is, you can fix it, right? The wrist TVs will work?"

"No," said Rozzozzo. "I'm afraid I can't fix it."

"But why not?" I asked. "You said you can't fix a problem unless you know what the problem is! Now you know—so fix it!"

"I just can't," said Rozzozzo. "You see, computers don't have an infinity symbol. Infinity isn't a number! I didn't even know you could use infinity in a mathematical equation."

"You didn't?" I asked. "How could you not? It's an important mathematical concept. It was used in ancient Greece!"

"Well, I'm an inventor, not a mathematician," said Rozzozzo. "Sorry, but until you make a new equation without any of those infinities in it, or until society invents a computer that can understand infinity, I'm afraid you'll have to forget about putting that equation of yours onto a wrist TV."

I was disappointed to realize that my equation was not transferrable to computers. I remembered the excitement I recognized on Buckley's face when he imagined he could solve any crime with his wrist TV. He said I would be a hero. Now, I wouldn't be a hero. Instead, I'd be ridiculed. Because it didn't work on the wrist TV, everyone would think my equations simply don't work. I hid my face behind my hands and sighed.

"Don't be sad, Trueman," said Nora. "It's not that bad. Maybe you can make a new equation without infinities in it? At least you can be proud knowing you're smarter than a computer!"

I was too upset to give full attention to Nora. But her words made me think of something. I may not be able to give Buckley the power to solve crimes by himself, but my equations still worked. The only condition was, they needed to be executed by human minds. Maybe if I called Buckley and explained that, he wouldn't be disappointed in my equations.

"Quick!" I said. "Nora! Give me your phone, please!"

Nora grabbed her mobile phone and gave it to me.

"Who are you gonna call?" asked Nora.

"Buckley," I said. "If I hurry, I can talk to him before he realizes the Latino man is innocent. Then he won't be disappointed in my equations and I can still be a hero."

Rozzozzo coughed loudly.

"You might want to look at this, before you make that call," said Rozzozzo. "I think you might be too late."

Rozzozzo took a newspaper from under her coat and began reading it aloud.

"Mathematical genius botches police case," she read, aloud.

"What does 'botches' mean?" I asked.

"It means you failed to solve the case," said Rozzozzo.

I hid my face behind my hands. I was terrified and my stomach began feeling tight. I wondered if I might faint again.

"Trueman Bradley," read Rozzozzo, "the Reade Street genius who has recently become New York City's latest celebrity, reportedly caused the police to arrest an innocent man. It is reported that Mr. Bradley's famous 'crime-fighting' equation gave an incorrect answer and seems to indicate that his equations are not as perfect as previously reported. Detective Buckley, of the NYPD, who made the arrest, refused to comment pending…"

"Stop it!" I shouted. "Just stop it!"

"Stop reading!" said Nora. "Can't you see he's upset?"

"Sorry," said Rozzozzo. "I didn't realize."

I held my face as tightly as I could and tried to escape reality. My worst fears were coming true; everyone thought my equations didn't work. The public wouldn't acclaim me anymore, Buckley wouldn't respect me anymore, Nora wouldn't love me anymore. This horrible situation made me moan with misery.

"No!" I shouted. "I just can't endure this!"

The doors of the agency office opened and I was shocked to see Detective Buckley. He stopped in the waiting room and looked at me. The look on his face resembled the look I'd seen on the face of mourners at a funeral. This made me think that he would say something horrible. My skin turned cold from fear. I knew he would tell me how disappointed he was in me. I didn't want to hear it. I didn't want to live in this reality.

I closed my eyes and counted.

"2, 3, 5, 7…"

THE COURT CASE

I could feel someone grabbing my shoulders and shaking me. I kept my eyes closed and counted louder. I didn't want to acknowledge this person who was shaking me and wanted to tell me how completely I had failed. I put my earphones into my ears and pressed them tightly, so they wouldn't fall out.

"Trueman!" said Buckley. "Did you hear what I said?"

The music from my earphones had stopped and I could hear Buckley shouting at me. I looked down at my portable music player and noticed my earphones were no longer plugged into anything. Buckley had unplugged my earphones and held my portable music player in his hand.

"Trueman!" said Buckley. "You hear me? I said, that's it! I'm done! And you're about to get yourself nailed!"

I looked at Buckley in fear. I didn't entirely understand what he was saying. But Nora had told me that "nailed" was an expression that meant giving someone what they deserved, so it seemed to me that Buckley would punish me for botching the police case—maybe even arrest me.

"No!" I said. "Leave me alone! Don't arrest me!"

I lifted my arms up, to protect myself.

"What the…" said Buckley. "I'm not going to arrest you!"

"But…" I said. "You said you're going to 'nail' me. That means you're going to punish me!"

"No!" said Buckley. "That's not what I meant. I'm not the one who is gonna nail you, Trueman. It's the police!"

"But you are a policeman!" I said.

"No, I'm not!" said Buckley.

I was confused. I knew Buckley was a detective, but he was telling me he wasn't. People so often said things that didn't make sense to me. I wondered if he was using an expression.

"I knew it!" said Buckley. "You weren't listening to a word I was saying. Trueman, I told you three times already, I'm not a cop anymore! Understand? I left! I'm done with the NYPD. You understand what I'm saying here?"

I understood what he said, and the thought horrified me.

"I got you fired?" I asked. "Because of my failure I made you arrest an innocent man! And now you've been fired! I'm sorry, Detective Buckley! I'm sorry that I'm so stupid!"

"Trueman!" said Buckley. "Stop saying that, okay? You're not stupid! And besides, I didn't get fired. Didn't you hear a word I've been telling you? I left because of this!"

Buckley pulled some papers out of his coat pocket and thrust them into my hands. I looked at the untidy bunch of papers. I was too scared to unfold them and look at them. I didn't know what they were, but I was sure it was more bad news.

"What are those?" asked Sal. "Are those legal papers?"

"Yeah," said Buckley, "I guess you could say that."

Sal took the papers out of my hands and examined them.

"This is a subpoena, Mr. Bradley," said Sal.

I stared in silence.

"Oh, I used to do all my own legal work," said Sal. "That's why I know a lot about law. Yeah, I always wanted to be a lawyer, in fact... that and a detective."

"What does it mean?" I asked.

"A subpoena means you're being summoned to appear in court," said Buckley. "Chief Stokowski is charging you..."

"What?" I asked. "Is he charging me with murdering Eddie? I thought you said they had no evidence against me!"

"He's not charging you with murdering Eddie," said Buckley. "He's charging you with lying on your application form to get a detective's license. According to this subpoena, Stokowski says you shouldn't have been permitted to get a detective's license because you have Asperger's Syndrome."

"What?" asked Nora. Nora ran to Buckley and started screaming at him. I could recognize the rage in her eyes.

"How dare he!" shouted Nora. "Does he think Trueman's mentally handicapped or something? I could kill that chief!"

"Stop that!" said Buckley. "You shouldn't say stuff like that, you understand? Now, I know you're real angry and not serious about wanting to kill him, but if a judge or a cop hears you saying that, they'll think you're seriously threatening him. You can get in a lot of trouble by uttering threats to a cop."

Nora made an effort to control her emotions and became calmer. But I could still recognize the rage in her eyes.

"Hey!" said Buckley. "I'm angry too! I know how you feel! Stokowski says people with 'mental problems' shouldn't be allowed to get a detective's license. He's saying your Asperger's means that you've got some kind of mental sickness and should be locked up in a sanitarium! I tell you, when Stokowski told me he was charging you, I got so mad I spat right in his face and walked out of the station. I quit! Right then and there. The last thing I'm ever going to do for Stokowski is deliver this subpoena to you. It says you've got to appear before a hearing officer of the State Department in a week. You see what I'm saying, Trueman? You've got to meet this officer and he'll decide if your Asperger's means you're mentally incompetent. If he decides you're not competent, they could revoke your license. They could shut down the agency, Trueman."

"Just because he has Asperger's?" asked Nora.

"That's discrimination!" said Mrs. Levi. "It's not fair!"

I looked at the papers. I knew they would be bad news. I had been so successful, until recently, that I had almost forgotten I had Asperger's. I had friends who didn't mind that I thought differently; the newspapers called me a genius; police and detectives trusted me. I had felt so accepted and valued that I felt like a new Trueman Bradley. But now, I felt like the old Trueman Bradley. The one who had lived in Heartville and was called "different" and "strange" by everyone, except his granddad. I was, once again, being discriminated against for having Asperger's and it stung me like a cut from a knife.

"I'm stupid!" I said. "Because of my stupidity, you lost your job and now I'm in trouble with the State Department!"

I was filled with frustration and self-hatred. I looked at the wrist TV I'd invented and felt a powerful hatred for it. I threw it down on the ground as hard as I could. It made a loud crackling sound and broke into pieces.

"What are you doing?" asked Rozzozzo.

"Stupid!" I shouted. "I'm stupid! My inventions don't work! My equations don't work! Stokowski's right, I have mental problems! I'm just weird! I should have listened to you and shouldn't have even tried to be a detective! I'm too stupid to be a detective! I'll just go back to Heartville…"

"Will you stop that!" said Buckley. "For the love of God, stop putting yourself down like that! Look, Trueman. Sorry, I can see you're upset, but can't you see why I quit the police? I quit because I don't think you're stupid! I was so mad about Stokowski calling you stupid, that I quit! I'll be damned if I'm gonna work for a prejudiced guy like Stokowski. What's more, Trueman, I'm gonna help you. I'm gonna go with you to that court hearing and I'm gonna defend you! I know you're smart! You're smart as hell! Smarter than me! And I'm gonna prove it to that idiot Stokowski, and the court. Before we're through, Trueman, everyone's gonna know Asperger's doesn't mean you're stupid. Before we're done, this whole city will know!"

"But how can you think I'm smart?" I asked. "My equation didn't work at La Guardia airport. You arrested the wrong man."

"Well, sure," said Buckley. "But I know your equations work. Probably, I just used that wrist thingy wrong or something. I said, I'm not too good with technology! I probably inputted the data wrong or something. Whatever happened, I'm 100 percent sure it wasn't your mistake. Because you've got a real eye for details. I never seen you make a mistake."

"It's true," I said. "It was not my mistake. Dr. Rozzozzo did not put the correct equation into the computer of the wrist TV. She put a zero where an infinity sign should be."

Rozzozzo was picking the pieces of my broken wrist TV off the floor. She looked at Buckley and shrugged her shoulders.

"Computers can't do everything," said Rozzozzo. "The wrist TV can't execute Trueman's equation because computers don't understand mathematical infinity. Not even an experienced inventor, such as myself, could make a computer understand infinity. You'll have to use Trueman's brain, instead."

"There!" said Buckley. "You see? It wasn't your fault! I knew it all along. And you're smarter than a computer? That's something! I wish I could say the same about myself. See, Trueman? You're smart as hell. There's the proof right there. Now all we got to do is convince that hearing officer how smart you are. Don't worry about it, I'll think of a way."

"Me too!" said Nora. "I'm a licensed detective! I'll let those jerks know how good a detective Trueman is! With two detectives testifying for him, we're sure to win the court case. Don't worry about it, Trueman, Buckley and me are here to help."

"Me too!" said Sal. "I know the law! I'll serve as your legal representative. We won't let them hurt you, boss!"

"I'll help too!" said Mrs. Levi. "After all, I was the one who didn't mention your Asperger's on the application form. I'm the one who deserves to be punished, not Trueman! Don't you worry, dear. Your friends are here to help you through this!"

I looked around the room and felt lucky to have such loyal and supportive friends. I smiled at them in the hope they would understand how much I appreciated their friendship. I was comforted to know I was not facing Stokowski and the State Department alone. But although I was comforted, I was still worried. Even if the future was not as scary as I had first imagined, my plans had gone horribly wrong. I thought about my visual checklist of today's activities and how many mistakes had been made. What happened today was so different from what I had planned that I felt sick with confusion and worry.

I watched as Rozzozzo crawled on the floor. She picked pieces of broken wrist TV and made grumbling noises. As I watched her, I wished I could invent a machine that could warn me if something unexpected was going to happen. Then I could avoid unpredictable, disturbing days like this. If I could make inventions that told me the likelihood of falling, then I could also invent a machine that told me the likelihood of something unpredictable happening. I felt so comforted by the thought of having such an invention that I couldn't stop thinking of it and forgot about the presence of my friends.

"If I had an invention like that," I said to myself, "I would never need to endure an unexpected surprise. This job would be easier. I would never be shocked like this again."

"What?" asked Buckley.

"Oh, nothing," I said. "I was talking to myself."

It became windy outside and cool, wet air blew into my office. Mrs. Levi ran to close the window. I could see my big blackboard reflected in the darkened glass of the window. The sight of the blackboard inspired me to do math. I started to get up from the settee.

"Trueman!" said Nora. "The doctor said you should lie down until tomorrow!"

"I know," I said, "but I need to do something very important. Would you mind leaving me alone? I need to make a new equation. This equation could solve all of our problems."

"But Trueman, you'll get sick again!" said Nora.

"No," I said. "I must invent this equation so that I will never faint again. I got sick because unexpected things happened to me. Surprises make me ill. This equation I'm going to invent will predict all surprises and so I will never get sick again. So, you see, I must get up and work on the equation. Because it will ensure I'll never get sick again."

Everyone was quiet. I didn't know if they were quiet because of the logic of my argument or because they were confused by my argument.

"I need to be alone to work on it," I said.

They seemed to understand me, because everyone started to leave the room. Nora walked towards me and touched my arm.

"Call me if you need anything," she said.

"I will," I said.

Nora left the room and I was alone with my blackboard. I turned on my music player and lit a candle, to create the proper "bubble" of concentration. Now I was ready to invent an equation. I grabbed a piece of chalk and began scratching numbers on the blackboard. Outside, I could see lightning flashes. At first, they distracted me, and I wanted to close the curtains. But then I had a thought that inspired me.

"Lightning is unpredictable," I said. "It is like a symbol for the surprises that I can't endure. I think the lightning is protesting because I am inventing the equation that will protect me from unpredictable things. This equation will be my shield from any future shocks. I just need to invent it…"

My legs felt weak and the lightning flashes addled my senses, but I continued writing and concentrating on the logic of my thought patterns. I was confident I'd find an answer.

"Everything can be summed up into an equation," I said.

*

I sat in a chair, surrounded by fluttering papers. The wind was blowing through the agency office and making all the papers on the nearby desks rustle. All around me, my friends were running around and busily working. But I was not paying very much attention to my surroundings. I was sitting and sipping a cup of tea. I sat in a big, comfortable chair that Sal had bought for the office. Nora had wrapped me in warm blankets and Mrs. Levi had made me tea and raspberry lemon cake. I was feeling very tense and they sat me here to help relax me.

I had read that Asperger's was related to a condition called "autism." People with autism have difficulty communicating with the outside world. They are sometimes unaware of other people. Asperger's is supposed to be similar to autism, but with less extreme symptoms. I was never certain if this is true, because I am very aware of other people, and some other people I have known who had autism were also very aware of other people. It seemed to me the label of "autism" was full of unfair and illogical generalizations that amounted to a prejudice. And so, I never identified myself as autistic.

But sometimes, when I was especially nervous or afraid of something, I would hide in myself, like a turtle hiding in its shell. I called this type of hiding "becoming autistic." When I had explained this to Nora, she assured me that most people would hide in themselves if they became afraid of the world, and so it was not something only autistics did. But I liked to call this state of hiding "becoming autistic" because this is how I imagined it would feel like to be unaware of the world. According to the assumptions of society, this is how people with autism felt at all times. I knew it was false, but remaining in this "autistic" state helped me to feel safe and secure.

We were leaving to meet the hearing officer soon. Even though I knew I had good friends to defend me, I was still terrified at the thought of going to a court and being accused of something. I feared the negative attention; I feared the aggressive Stokowski; I feared the unpredictable events that surely would happen. I sat in the comfortable chair and "felt autistic." I didn't want to deal with reality or the world around me, so I convinced myself there was no world outside me.

"Trueman?" asked Buckley. "Hey! Anybody home?"

Buckley waved his hand in front of my face.

"Boss!" said Sal. "We got to go now, boss!"

I understood that we would be going to the court house to meet the hearing officer, but I felt too "autistic" to reply. I didn't want to go. It had been a week since I had first learned about the charges against me, but I still didn't feel ready to go to court. I wanted to sit in my chair and be "autistic."

Sal and Buckley looked at each other and seemed to be talking about how to make me move. Sal noticed the thick postal letter that was in my hands and he took it from me.

"What's this, boss?" asked Sal. "Mail? Ah, yes. I see this letter is addressed to Dr. Rozzozzo. My eccentric friend! Do you want me to put postage stamps on it and send it to her?"

"Yes," I said.

Remembering the letter to Rozzozzo caused me to come out of my "autistic" state. During this last week, I had designed an invention that could warn me of anything unpredictable. The thought of having such an invention comforted me so much that I felt a new sense of bravery. This invention would stop the world from being unpredictable and shocking. And so, going to court and meeting the hearing officer would be the last truly shocking and unpredictable experience of my career. Knowing this would probably be the last such experience, I felt brave enough to come out of my "autistic" state. I rose from the chair and Nora unwrapped the blankets from my body.

"Ready to go, boss?" asked Sal.

I nodded my head to indicate I was ready and Nora led me to the front door. As she was helping me to put on my coat, a flash of light blinded me. I screamed and fell to the floor.

"Get out of here!" shouted Nora.

"I'll get him! The damned jerk!" said Buckley.

I was temporarily blinded and confused. I thought Buckley and Nora were talking to me. I was terrified by how quickly the unexpected and shocking events were happening. Did Buckley and Nora just blind me and threaten me?

"Leave me alone!" I shouted.

"Trueman, relax!" said Nora.

My vision returned to normal and I felt Nora's hands stroking my hair. She was comforting me. Outside the glass of the front door, I could see Buckley. He was swinging his fists at a man and shouting something. I realized what had happened.

"There are a lot of newspaper reporters outside," I said.

"Yeah!" said Nora. "They took a picture of you."

"That was a camera flash?" I asked.

"Yes," she said. "Now, get up, Trueman. Everybody? Let's all form a circle around Trueman and protect him. We're going to go out to the Lincoln car, okay Trueman? We'll stay in a protective circle around you, okay? Just keep calm."

Nora, Sal and Mrs. Levi formed a triangle of protection around me and we walked out onto the street. I heard a lot of reporters yelling and saw cameras flashing. I closed my eyes and tried to stay in the triangle of protection.

"I'm safe in the triangle of friendship," I said.

"That's right, Trueman," said Nora. "Now, just stay calm. We're almost at the car."

I kept my eyes closed, so I wouldn't be surprised by another blinding flash. I felt the hands of my friends, pushing and pulling on my trench coat. Soon I felt soft leather against my hands and recognized the feel of the Lincoln car's seats.

I opened my eyes and saw the inside of the car. Sal was in the driver's seat, Buckley sat next to him. I sat in the back of the car, protected on both sides by Nora and Mrs. Levi. Outside, reporters were looking in at me and pointing their cameras. Nora and Mrs. Levi shielded me from the flashes by using their coats to cover the windows.

Sal started the car and we were soon free of the pushy, unpredictable journalists. We drove down Reade Street and I watched the pedestrians, too disturbed in my mind to observe them and take note of their numbers. I was tense, but tried to take comfort in the knowledge that Rozzozzo would soon make an invention that could shield me from such things, and this was possibly the last time I'd ever be so shocked and disturbed.

"Turn this way, Sal," said Buckley. "We're going to the Manhattan criminal court house."

"Criminal?" I asked. "Why am I going to a criminal court? Am I being charged with a serious crime? I thought I was only charged with applying for my license incorrectly?"

"Relax, Trueman!" said Buckley. "The State Department decides where the hearing happens. They decided to have the hearing in a courtroom at the Manhattan criminal court building. I guess one of the courtrooms was free, so that's why they chose it for the hearing. It doesn't mean you're being charged with any kind of criminal offense. So, relax."

"Oh, good," I said.

"In fact, it just might be a good thing," said Buckley. "Because there aren't any cameras or anything allowed in the Manhattan criminal court building, so all those reporters can't follow us in there. Those jerks are still following us, huh?"

I looked out the window and saw a car pass us. In the window was a reporter pointing a camera at me. I hid my face, so as to avoid being blinded again. I tried to comfort myself by imagining my new invention.

"I think I'll call it the 'surprise revealer,'" I said.

"What?" asked Nora.

"I was just talking to myself," I said. "Sal? Did you send that postal letter to Dr. Rozzozzo yet?"

"Oh, no I didn't," said Sal. "Look, there's a mailbox. We'll just stop here for a second and I'll send this letter."

Sal stopped the car and stepped out onto the street. After we stopped, reporters parked beside us and started crowding around our Lincoln car like a swarm of bees around a flower. I saw flashes of light and closed my eyes. I hid my face behind my hands. I comforted myself by thinking of my new invention.

"Sal sent the letter," I said. "I'll have the new surprise revealer. This is the last unpredictable day I need to endure."

*

The Manhattan criminal court building is built in a similar architectural style to the Marine Air Terminal. Entering the building, we had continued to be harassed by reporters. But I could ignore the noise and commotion by concentrating on the beautiful "art deco" design of the criminal court building.

Now inside the courtroom, Sal, Buckley, Nora, Mrs. Levi and I sat at a table in front of the judge's bench. Chief Stokowski sat at another table to our right. He stared at me in a way that made me nervous and I hid my face behind my hands. But no matter how completely I covered my eyes and ears, I could still hear the voices of the dozens of reporters in the room.

Detective Buckley had been wrong when he said the reporters would leave us alone after we entered the court house. It was true that cameras and recording devices were not allowed in the court house, but most of the reporters decided to leave their cameras outside and followed us into the courtroom anyway. Dozens of them sat in the back and talked loudly to each other. Each of them carried a notebook and pen, ready to write down anything that was said or anything that happened.

The noise of the journalists, who threatened to write down everything I did and tell the world; the frightening stare of Stokowski; the possibility that I might be declared "mentally incompetent" and be discriminated against: all of this made me feel tense and my hands were shaking. In my confusion, I had forgotten my portable music player at the agency office and so I could not escape the noise. I covered my ears, but could still hear. Every time I heard a loud, unexpected noise, I would wince, believing it was a sign that something bad was happening.

"Alright, everyone settle down!"

A tall, gray-haired man had entered the courtroom. He wore a neatly pressed suit with pinstripes and a matching tie. He carried a big, black briefcase and the intensity of his eyes intimidated me. He climbed up to the judge's bench and sat there. With horror, I realized that he was the hearing officer. This intimidating man who spoke in a merciless, commanding voice was the man who would decide if I was capable of being a detective or if my Asperger's meant that I was mentally incompetent. I was sure this hard man would condemn me.

"My name is Sidney Saul Tritch," he said. "I'm the hearing officer and I'm in charge of these proceedings. Now, can someone tell me why there are so many people in here? Who are all these people?"

"The media!" said Stokowski. He looked back at the crowd of reporters in a way I interpreted as threatening. The reporters responded by writing busily in their notebooks.

"And, frankly," said Stokowski, "I think you'd be doing your duty if you asked all these journalists to bug off!"

Tritch stared silently at Stokowski.

"You think so, do you?" asked Tritch. "And who are you?"

"I'm with the NYPD," said Stokowski. "I'm the chief of police. Now, can you get rid of these reporters, please?"

"Tell me, Chief," said Tritch, "do you think because you're chief of the NYPD that you're also chief of the State Department, chief of this hearing and chief of me?"

"No," said Stokowski.

"Then shut up!" said Tritch. "I'm in charge here and I'll decide what's my duty and what isn't! I was just asking who they were. I didn't say I wouldn't allow the media to witness this hearing. As long as they're quiet, they can stay here."

Stokowski's eyes were wide open and his face reminded me of a little boy I'd once seen, who had just realized his bicycle had been stolen. I guessed he was shocked and didn't know what to say. Some of the media started to laugh and Stokowski's face became red. I couldn't be sure if he was angry or embarrassed.

Buckley leaned towards me and whispered into my ear.

"That's lucky!" said Buckley. "It seems like the hearing officer doesn't like Stokowski much. That should help us!"

I looked at Tritch and noticed he was frowning at Stokowski. Even with my poor ability to interpret emotion I knew that he hated the Chief. Tritch was writing something on a piece of paper, and I guessed he was writing something bad about Stokowski. My mood improved as I started to hope that maybe if Tritch hated Stokowski, he might like us and let me keep my license. I began to hope that we might win this case.

"Stokowski," said Tritch, "you're the one who is charging Mr. Trueman Bradley of making a 'material misstatement' on his application for a detective agency license, is that right?"

"Yeah," said Stokowski. "And so, Mr. Trueman Bradley should have his license revoked and shouldn't be allowed to do any kind of detective work because he's mentally incompetent!"

"Shut up, you idiot!" shouted Nora.

The courtroom was filled with shocked gasps and some of the reporters began to laugh.

"Asperger's isn't a mental problem!" said Nora. "It's not like he's stupid! You're just a prejudiced son of a…"

"Order!" said Tritch. "Be quiet!"

Buckley grabbed Nora's shoulders and she stopped shouting. But I could recognize that she was still angry.

"Now," said Tritch, "one more disturbance like that and I'll have you kicked out of this hearing, understood?"

"Yes, sir," said Nora.

"I hope everyone understands that," said Tritch. "I don't tolerate interruptions. Now, Chief Stokowski, I understand you are claiming Mr. Bradley lied on his application because he didn't mention he has Asperger's Syndrome, right?"

"Yeah," said Stokowski. "He's got a serious mental problem! So, he's mentally incompetent and shouldn't be a detective!"

"That's for me to decide!" said Tritch. "I asked you a 'yes or no' question. I didn't ask for your opinion. Now, that is the second time you tried to tell me what I should do. If you don't behave, Chief Stokowski, I'll dismiss your case and Mr. Trueman Bradley gets to keep his license, understood?"

Stokowski's eyes widened again. This time, I couldn't interpret his emotions. But I was amazed at how he had changed. His usual bossy, pushy way of speaking was replaced with a meek and gentle voice. He lowered his head and spoke softly.

"Yes, sir," said Stokowski.

The reporters in the back began laughing.

"Quiet, now," said Tritch.

Tritch took some papers out of his briefcase and examined them. He seemed to be getting ready for the hearing and organizing his thoughts. The courtroom was silent, except for the hushed conversations of the reporters in the back. Although they spoke quietly, I could hear parts of their conversation.

"Stokowski…" said a reporter, in a whisper.

Stokowski must have also been able to hear because he turned around and stared at the reporters.

"Stokowski's prejudiced against Asperger's…" said a reporter. "If we print that, the public will feel sorry for Trueman. Stokowski's a bully and a jerk… everyone will hate him. This will make a good story."

"What did you say?" asked Stokowski. "I'm a what?"

Stokowski stood up and seemed like he was about to go to the reporters and start beating them. Tritch also stood up. He crumpled up a piece of paper and threw it at the Chief.

"Sit down!" shouted Tritch. "Honestly! You're a chief? You act like a child! Now sit down or I'll dismiss your case!"

Stokowski hastened to obey Tritch and I could interpret the fear on his face. I imagined he was afraid of Tritch's threat that he would dismiss his charges against me and I would be allowed to keep my license. I started hoping that Stokowski would get angry again and do something else that Tritch didn't like. Tritch would dismiss the charges and I could go home.

The reporters in the back were laughing.

"Ha-ha!" said a reporter. "Let's make that a headline in the paper! 'Hearing officer called Chief Stokowski a child!'"

I looked at Stokowski, hoping he would hear the reporters and get angry again, but he seemed to be ignoring them.

"Stokowski!" said Tritch.

Stokowski jumped and hastened to answer.

"Yes, sir?" asked Stokowski.

"Come up here and tell us why you think Mr. Trueman Bradley should not be a detective," said Tritch. "And please, try not to do anything childish. This is not a kindergarten playground. It's a State Department hearing. Try to act professionally."

The reporters started laughing and Stokowski's face became red. I could recognize his embarrassment. I was gratified to realize that not only did Tritch dislike Stokowski, it seemed the reporters didn't like him either and were making fun of him. Stokowski stood up and walked towards the judge's bench. He turned to face the crowd and coughed. His eyes had none of the confidence and arrogance they previously had. He looked like a shy schoolboy, forced to speak in front of his class.

"Mr. Trueman Bradley…" said Stokowski. "Mr. Bradley lied on his application form. When he applied to open a detective agency he didn't mention he has Asperger's Syndrome. Now, that's a mental problem and so it's a serious condition. The fact that he didn't mention it qualifies as a 'material misstatement.' Meaning, he neglected to give important information on his form. Now, I do believe the punishment for making a 'material misstatement' on an application form is revocation of his agency license, is that right, Mr. Tritch?"

"Yes, that's right," said Tritch.

"Well then," said Stokowski, "I think there's no question about it. He should have his license revoked immediately."

Sal stood up and spoke to the hearing officer.

"Can I ask the Chief some questions, Mr. Tritch?"

"Please don't interrupt," said Tritch.

"Yeah," said Stokowski. "Shut up! In case you didn't notice, I was talking! Now, will you let me finish, buddy?"

Tritch glared at Stokowski and I thought I could recognize annoyance on his face. Something about the way Stokowski spoke seemed to irritate Tritch.

"On second thoughts," said Tritch, "go ahead and ask the Chief all the questions you want."

"But, sir!" said Stokowski. "I'm not done talking!"

"Quiet!" said Tritch. "I'm in charge here, not you! How many times do I have to tell you that before you understand? You just think you're the boss of everyone, don't you? Now, you listen, Chief! I am not a fan of pushy people like you. Now, I'm going to try not to let that affect my decision, because it would be unprofessional to let my personal feelings decide this case. But let me just tell you that it's not a good idea to make me hate you any more than I already do, understand?"

The reporters laughed and I felt like laughing too, because I thought that Stokowski had finally annoyed Tritch enough for him to dismiss the charges. I couldn't recognize Stokowski's emotions, but he seemed to shrink a few inches. Tritch looked at Stokowski with a stern look that seemed to paralyze him. But, despite his annoyance, Tritch didn't dismiss the case.

"Go ahead and ask your questions," said Tritch.

"Thank you, Mr. Tritch," said Sal. "Now, Detective Stokowski. You said that Asperger's Syndrome is a 'mental problem' and a 'serious condition.' Why do you say that? Do you have any proof of that or is it just your opinion?"

Stokowski didn't answer immediately. When he did, his voice sounded very uncertain.

"Well…" said Stokowski. "He doesn't think like you and me, does he? That means there's something wrong with him."

"Prejudice!" said a reporter.

All the reporters started writing in their notebooks and Stokowski looked at them nervously.

"No!" said Stokowski. "It's not prejudice!"

"Then, where did you get that information?" asked Sal. "Why do you think Asperger's is a serious mental problem?"

Stokowski was silent and sweat started to form on his forehead. He began to remind me of a deer I had once seen when driving with my granddad at night. It stood there, stunned by the headlights of our car and didn't move.

"Answer the question," said Tritch.

"I don't know why I think that," said Stokowski. "I don't have an exact answer for that. But it isn't discrimination."

Tritch looked at Stokowski with a hard, merciless stare. He wrote something on a piece of paper.

"I'll decide that," said Tritch. "Now, is there someone present who can explain Asperger's Syndrome to me? I admit I know very little about it. If someone can define it for me, I can decide for myself if the Chief, here, is guilty of discrimination. If you can prove to me that Asperger's is not a disabling mental condition, then I'll suggest that you file a complaint against Chief Stokowski in civil court. I'll recommend he be charged with the violation of Mr. Trueman Bradley's basic human rights."

"What?" asked Stokowski.

"Yes, Chief," said Tritch. "Discrimination against a person based on a non-disabling mental condition is a serious violation. I would think a police chief would know that."

I could hear the reporters gasping and writing frantically in their notebooks. Stokowski's face was even sweatier than before and I could easily recognize the shock on his face. He was so shocked, his face was becoming as white as a cloud.

"But, sir!" said Stokowski.

"I didn't ask you to talk!" said Tritch. "Sit down!"

"But, sir!" said Stokowski. "You don't understand…"

"Sit down!" shouted the reporters.

Stokowski retreated to his table and sat down. He was as white as a ghost and seemed like he was about to cry. I felt incredibly relieved. I didn't know exactly what was happening, but I could tell by Stokowski's face that we were winning.

Nora stood up and spoke to the hearing officer.

"Sir?" she asked. "If you will allow it, I've brought with me some notes explaining Asperger's Syndrome."

"You have?" asked Tritch. "Well, that's perfect! Would you kindly stand up and read your notes for the court?"

"Yes, sir," said Nora.

Nora walked towards the witness box, where witnesses usually sat during criminal trials. She sat in the box and adjusted the nearby microphone. She took some papers out of her coat and sat in silence, organizing them. The reporters sat on the edge of their seats, their pens positioned to write into their notebooks everything that Nora would say. I noticed Stokowski peeking at the reporters, as if afraid of their pens; afraid maybe they would write more negative things about him.

"Ladies and gentlemen," said Nora, "Asperger's Syndrome is a condition related to autism. Autistic people have trouble relating to the world around them. They can become unaware of other people and their environment. Autism is considered to be a 'disabling' condition, because autistic people sometimes have trouble interacting with the outside world. But I grew up with a cousin who had Asperger's Syndrome. So I know, from experience, that it is not quite the same as autism. As far as I know, there's not a single medical or psychiatric organization that calls Asperger's Syndrome a 'disabling' condition. That label came out of the Chief's prejudiced mind! Anyone who has ever known a person with Asperger's will tell you that they don't have a 'mental problem,' they just think in a different way. They're intelligent, sensitive people who just have a few problems communicating like the rest of us and who look at the world a little bit differently from the way we do. In fact, many people with autism are also intelligent, sensitive people and should not be discriminated against, just because they think or communicate differently. Thinking differently is no excuse for discriminating against someone! So, in spite of what the chief of police thinks, thinking differently isn't a crime or disease. And he has no right to persecute Trueman because of it!"

The reporters applauded and voiced their agreement with Nora's statement. Their applause grew loud, but Tritch did not seem to mind. He wrote on a piece of paper and smiled at Nora.

"Well said," said Tritch. "I will need to verify some of that, but a firsthand account from someone who has a relative with Asperger's is valuable, in my eyes. But, explain it a bit more, will you? If Asperger's is not like autism, what are the symptoms of Asperger's? Are they aware of other people?"

"Yes," said Nora. "Trueman for example… I've gotten to know him pretty well. He's very aware of other people and his environment. Maybe he phases out and ignores the world if life starts getting difficult, but we all do that, right?"

"I would say so," said Tritch. "But please explain what problems he has. What are the symptoms of his Asperger's?"

"Well…" said Nora, "he has some trouble understanding expressions and figures of speech. For instance, if you say you're going to 'nail a criminal' he doesn't understand what that means. Because he takes it literally, he thinks you're talking about actual nails, like the kind you hit with hammers. It's hard for him to understand that to 'nail a criminal' actually means to catch a criminal. Expressions like that make no logical sense, and his mind is logical. In fact, his mind is more logical than a normal person's mind. So, he finds it hard to accept illogical expressions, even if he knows what they're supposed to mean."

"So, he's more logical than a normal person?" asked Tritch, giving Chief Stokowski a disapproving look. "That's what you call a 'mental problem,' Chief?" he asked. "Trueman's more logical than most people and he should get his license revoked for that? Maybe if you were more logical, Chief, then you'd know how to behave in my court!"

The reporters laughed and Stokowski's face turned red.

"Okay, quiet everyone," said Tritch. "What other symptoms does Mr. Trueman Bradley have?"

"Well," said Nora, "he is aware of people and he understands emotions. But he sometimes has a bit of trouble interpreting other people's emotions. He can't always look at someone's face and instantly know what they're feeling, the way most of us can. But that doesn't mean he doesn't have feelings. He wants to love and be loved like the rest of us. He feels empathy and kindness and has feelings. He's a very sensitive man. He just doesn't know how to express his emotions as well as we do. He doesn't have the skills. But that doesn't mean he doesn't have the desire. Trueman's a good and kind man."

"So, you're saying he does empathize with people," said Tritch. "This doesn't sound like a disabling condition so far. Does he have a disorder classified as 'disabling'?"

"No," said Nora. "According to my notes, Asperger's cannot be labeled as 'disabling' because its definition is too loose and a lot of people diagnosed with Asperger's Syndrome are capable of living relatively normal lives. They may have a few problems learning to socialize like the rest of us, but that's all. They're smart, loving, kind people who are misunderstood."

"And discriminated against," said Tritch, staring at Stokowski. Stokowski hid his face behind his hands and sighed.

"In fact," said Nora, "if you don't mind, sir. I have some personal observations about people with Asperger's. I'd like to share them with the court, if I may?"

"I don't mind," said Tritch. "Go ahead."

"Well," said Nora, "from my experience with my cousin and especially with Trueman... because they don't understand the subtleties of social interaction, they also know nothing about the devious little games we 'normal' people play with each other. Trueman is honest, sincere. I can trust him with my whole heart. I never have to worry that he's lying to me and playing some kind of subtle game with me. Because he isn't even aware of those things. Like expressions, he doesn't understand the subtleties of insincerity or social manipulation. They say sociopaths are dangerous because they know the subtleties of social interaction better than most people and they use this knowledge to use and exploit people. Well, it seems to me people with Asperger's are the opposite of sociopaths. Trueman's sensitive and kind and doesn't even know how to be a jerk. All he asks is a little love and understanding and he'll give you the world. He can't be a jerk, because to be a jerk you need to be insincere and socially manipulative. I doubt Trueman could be those things, even if he wanted to be. Maybe it's because of his Asperger's that he's like this. I don't know. But I wish there were more men in the world like Trueman. If Asperger's is what makes him like he is, then I wish all men had Asperger's. Because this would be a safer and truer world."

The courtroom was silent and I tried not to disturb the silence. But it was hard for me to be quiet, because I felt I would start crying. Nora had never told me how she felt about me and her words made me so happy, I felt like sobbing. It was so comforting to know she understood me and accepted me, in spite of my different way of thinking. I wanted to run towards her and embrace her, but I didn't want to disturb the court. Everything seemed to be proceeding well and I didn't want to risk angering the hearing officer by making a disturbance. I hid my face and discreetly wiped the tears from my eyes.

"Thank you," said Tritch. "I think I speak for everyone here when I say your words in defense of Mr. Trueman Bradley were moving. I think I begin to understand Asperger's Syndrome. And I don't see any reason to call Mr. Bradley's symptoms disabling. If anything, I'd be willing to classify the symptoms you describe as a genetic improvement! After all, if Asperger's makes a person more logical, then maybe it's Asperger's that made Mr. Bradley invent these 'miracle equations' we've all been reading about in the newspapers. If Asperger's makes people mathematical geniuses, then maybe it's an improved way of…"

"No, sir," interrupted Nora. "I'm sorry to interrupt, but my cousin, who I grew up with and had Asperger's, wasn't a mathematical genius. He just thought differently from how I do and you do. He thought similarly to Trueman... but he wasn't a mathematical genius. Trueman just happens to be a mathematical genius, but that doesn't mean all people with Asperger's are. All it proves is that people with Asperger's can be geniuses too! People with Asperger's can be anything we can! They are people just like us who have the same human needs and the same human potential. With all due respect, Mr. Tritch, the point isn't whether Asperger's people are good at math or even in any way better or worse than the rest of us! The point is simply that no one should be discriminated against for thinking in a different way. Whether they are Asperger's, autistic or what!"

Tritch glared at Stokowski.

"I certainly agree," said Tritch. "Although, mathematical geniuses or not, I still wonder if people with Asperger's Syndrome might have an improved way of thinking, especially when I compare Mr. Bradley to so-called 'normal' individuals like our Chief Stokowski here! May I ask you, Chief, why you brought this charge against Mr. Bradley, if Asperger's Syndrome is not a 'disabling' mental condition? You had no right to do that! I am now certain your charges were motivated by your own prejudices and I will be recommending you be charged with violation of Mr. Trueman Bradley's basic civil rights!"

"Please, sir!" said Stokowski. "Just let me speak!"

Tritch stared at Stokowski severely.

"I'll let you speak," said Tritch, "but only because I'm certain that whatever you have to say will probably only serve to further convince me of your guilt."

Stokowski coughed nervously and stood up. He took a handkerchief from his shirt pocket and wiped his sweaty brow.

"Now, sir," said Stokowski, "if you'll examine the charges I laid against Mr. Trueman Bradley, you'll notice that I didn't only charge him with 'material misstatement.' I also charged that Mr. Bradley should lose his license because he has 'proven himself incompetent.' Now, isn't it true that if Mr. Bradley has proven himself incompetent as a detective, the punishment is to revoke his license? Isn't that the law?"

Tritch picked up the paper that outlined the charges against me and nodded his head.

"That's true," said Tritch. "If you can prove that he has proven himself incompetent, then his license could be revoked."

"Well, sir," said Stokowski, "Mr. Trueman Bradley used a faulty equation to make one of my detectives arrest the wrong man. Those supposedly 'magical' equations of Mr. Bradley's don't work! So he's proven himself to be incompetent, right?"

The court was silent. I felt like I was frozen with fear. I thought we were winning, but now Stokowski was mentioning my failures. All my old fears of being seen as a failure returned to me. I covered my head with my hands and tried not to listen.

"Isn't it true?" asked Stokowski. "Didn't he tell the NYPD he had a magical equation that could solve crime? And then when one of my detectives tried to use his equation, he got the wrong man! I tell you, isn't that nuts? There could never be an equation to solve a crime! I mean, that right there shows he's not all right in the head, right? He doesn't understand real detective work! He thinks it's a little mathematical game! In my eyes, that means he's proven himself incompetent, right?"

The court was silent. Tritch's face was still and severe.

"Perhaps," said Tritch.

Buckley stood up and spoke to the hearing officer.

"Mr. Tritch, sir," he said, "if you'll allow me, I was the detective who used Trueman's equation. I haven't made any comment about it to the media yet. But this seems like a good opportunity to explain what happened to both the court and the media. Do you mind if I stand up and explain what happened?"

"By all means," said Tritch. "Please tell us."

"Thank you, sir," said Buckley.

Buckley stood up and started pacing back and forth across the courtroom floor. He would stop and talk to every person in the room, but he was actually addressing us all. I could guess from Buckley's convincing way of speaking that he was accustomed to giving speeches in front of crowds.

"Now, Mr. Tritch," said Buckley, "and ladies and gentlemen of the press. I've been a homicide detective for nineteen years. In fact, it would be my twenty-year anniversary next month if not for the fact that I quit recently. You see, I used to work under Chief Stokowski here. But I objected so strongly to the charges that he laid against Mr. Trueman Bradley, that I quit my job!"

The reporters hissed and shouted their disapproval of Stokowski. The Chief looked back at the reporters and I could recognize how much he hated them. In response to the hissing, Buckley smiled and raised his hand.

"Okay, quiet please," said Buckley. "Now, the fact that I quit should tell you something about my opinion of Mr. Trueman Bradley. Believe me, I know how ridiculous this sounds. Who would ever believe that someone could invent an equation that solves crimes in New York City? Lord knows it's hard enough for us who put in our time at the academy and a good few decades of hard hours. When I first heard about Trueman's equations, I was doubtful too. But, now that I've seen them in action, I can say without hesitation... as crazy as it sounds, Trueman's equations do work and Trueman himself is a mathematical genius."

A male reporter lifted his hand and spoke.

"Mr. Tritch? Do you mind if I ask a question?"

"Hm…" said Tritch. "I suppose not. Go ahead."

Stokowski jumped from his chair and shouted.

"I object! The media has no right to ask questions at an official hearing!"

Tritch looked at Stokowski as if he'd kill him.

"Shut up!" shouted Tritch.

Stokowski sat down and hid his face behind his hands.

"Go ahead and ask your question," said Tritch.

"Thank you," said the reporter. "Detective Buckley. If Trueman's equations work, then why is it you arrested the wrong man? You did arrest the wrong man, didn't you?"

"Yeah," said Buckley, "but that wasn't Trueman's fault. You see, we tried to put Trueman's equations onto a little computer that straps to your wrist. But there was a problem with the computer. So, you see, it was just because of a computer glitch. There's nothing wrong with Trueman's equations. The fact is, Trueman's equations are so complicated, computers can't do them. The computer made me arrest the wrong guy. Understand? Trueman's got to do the equation in his own head or it won't work, because Trueman's smarter than a computer."

The media gasped and started writing in their notebooks.

"Smarter than a computer…" said Tritch.

Tritch gave Stokowski another severe look.

"Smarter than a computer, and the Chief here says he's incompetent?" asked Tritch. "I wouldn't doubt it, knowing what a devious sort this Chief seems to be. But I'm afraid I will require proof. You say he's smarter than a computer, Detective. But can you prove it to me?"

Buckley lifted up a finger.

"Yes!" said Buckley. "I thought you might ask me that. So, I arranged proof. I've been in contact with a mathematics professor at New York University, named Eldrich Larsen. I've sent him Trueman's equations and he can verify that they work."

"He can?" asked Tritch. "Well, then please ask him to come up and speak to the court."

"Um, about that..." said Buckley, "he couldn't be here today because he has a class to teach. But he said if you want to get verification from him, he can give you an appointment next Thursday..."

"Detective!" said Tritch. "I don't have time for that! This hearing is only scheduled for this one day. We must come to a decision today, not next Thursday! If you didn't bring your proof to the hearing then you have no proof that Mr. Bradley's equations work."

Buckley held up his finger again.

"Yes, I do, Mr. Tritch," said Buckley. "Yes, I do. I thought this might happen, so I brought some extra proof. Sal, could you take out the projector? Somebody get the lights."

Sal took a small video projector out of a bag and put it on the table. Buckley pulled down a projector screen and somebody switched off the lights in the courtroom. Soon we were watching a video on the projector screen. To my surprise, it was a video of the Marine Air Terminal.

It showed me standing on the roof of the Marine Air Terminal with my CCC device in my hand. This must have been a video that was filmed of me when I was getting ready to jump off the roof. I didn't know there had been a camera recording me, and I wondered what was the purpose of showing this to the court.

I watched the video of me grabbing the rope and swinging. The rope swung for a few seconds and then began to break. The weaves and knots of the rope began to unravel and I watched myself spinning in circles as the rope unraveled. As the rope unraveled, it became longer and soon I was on the roof of the first floor. Nora tried to catch me, but I swung off the edge and landed on top of a bus that had "M60" on the front of it. The bus drove for a short time before stopping abruptly. I watched as I slid off the roof and landed in a flower garden.

The reporters cheered and applauded. When the video ended and the lights were switched back on I realized that they were applauding me. Every face in the room was looking at me and smiling, except for Stokowski's. Even Tritch looked at me in a pleasant way and clapped his hands.

"Impressive acrobatics, Mr. Bradley," said Tritch. "But I don't see how this proves that he's a mathematical genius."

"I'll tell you how," said Buckley. "Mr. Trueman Bradley designed a device that uses a mathematical formula to determine when and how he could jump off that building without being hurt. This footage was recorded by a security camera, and as you see, Trueman fell off a two-storey building without a scratch."

Tritch's face contorted and I could recognize that he was either confused or didn't believe what Buckley was saying.

"Okay, Detective," said Tritch. "I'm afraid I find that a little hard to believe. Such an invention is not possible."

"Don't take my word for it, Mr. Tritch!" said Buckley. "If you don't believe me, ask the media! They're here, ask them!"

"The media knows about this?" asked Tritch.

"Sure, I released this video to the media the day before this hearing started," said Buckley.

"That's why all these reporters are here?" asked Tritch.

"Yeah," said Buckley.

"Why did you release this to the media?" asked Tritch.

"Because I wanted them to research the story, so they could confirm what I say is true," said Buckley. "The media always makes a lot of phone calls to confirm if a story's true before they report on it, right? Well, this way, I have all these reporters in the room who can verify what I say is true."

Tritch looked at the crowd of reporters.

"Is what he says true?" asked Tritch.

A young, blonde reporter stood up and answered.

"Yes, Mr. Tritch. My name is Gwen Tone, and I researched this story. I got in touch with a research scientist and inventor named Dr. Lucretia Rozzozzo. She confirmed that Trueman commissioned such an invention. We also got testimonials from the various scientists that helped her develop it. They're all well-respected research scientists. Apparently, there's been so much talk about Trueman's inventions in the academic community that every university in the state wants Trueman to come speak with them about his equations and his inventions."

The whole room was silent. Tritch started to laugh. He shook his head and wrote something on a piece of paper.

"Stokowski!" said Tritch. "How many university professors want to talk to you about your mathematical ideas, huh? You dare to call Mr. Bradley incompetent and stupid? My official ruling is that he's infinitely smarter than you! Now, if you have nothing else to add, I will be dismissing this case!"

"Wait!" said Stokowski.

Tritch looked at him severely. Stokowski stood and nervously licked his lips. He put one hand on the table and looked down at the floor. He spoke quietly and slowly, like someone who was very close to losing his patience.

"You can't let him be a detective," said Stokowski.

"Why not?" asked Tritch.

"Because," said Stokowski, "he is a murder suspect. That's right. He is a suspect in the murder of Eddie Sipple at La Guardia last week. Isn't it the law that a detective's license will be revoked if he's charged with a serious crime?"

"Yes," said Tritch. "Is he charged with the crime?"

"No, he's not!" shouted Buckley.

"Don't shout!" said Tritch.

"Sorry, sir," said Buckley, "but I know because I was the one investigating that case before I quit. We held Trueman under suspicion, but there was no evidence to prove he killed

Eddie! In fact, I was following Trueman around at the time. During the time Eddie was murdered, Trueman was in an Italian restaurant! There's no evidence. I have no idea why the Chief is making up all this stuff and trying to get rid of Trueman!"

"Nonsense," said Stokowski. "I'm not trying anything. And there is proof. I didn't use it before, because we just found the evidence yesterday. That's right. We found a white scarf belonging to Mr. Trueman Bradley at the murder scene. That means, of course, Mr. Trueman Bradley was at the murder scene."

Buckley shouted and ran towards Stokowski.

"What?" asked Buckley. "White scarf? There wasn't a white scarf at the scene! I investigated that case!"

"Keep calm, Detective!" said Tritch.

Buckley stopped and pointed his finger at Stokowski.

"Wait a minute," said Buckley. "Trueman has a yellow scarf. His scarf turned white because of exposure to acid fumes, but that was after Eddie was already dead! How could Trueman's white scarf be found at the murder scene if his scarf didn't even become white until after Eddie was murdered?"

Stokowski's face turned as white as my scarf. I could recognize that he was suddenly very afraid.

"Well, okay," said Stokowski. "His scarf wasn't at the murder scene. I didn't mean to say that. Just listen…"

"Wait," said Buckley. "I know what's going on here. I remember that day when we took Trueman in for questioning. I remember you asked about his scarf. Trueman told you it turned white because of the acid fumes. A dozen cops heard him say that! They can all confirm that Trueman's scarf wasn't white when Eddie was murdered! You scum you, you're losing the case, so you panicked and now you're trying to fabricate fake evidence against Trueman, so you can get his license revoked!"

The reporters gasped and Tritch looked at Stokowski.

"What?" asked Tritch. "I'm not sure what you're talking about, but if you're trying to fabricate evidence to get Trueman's license revoked, I'm going to report this to the proper authorities! I mean, you're a police chief, for Pete's sake! I'm going to lodge a complaint with the criminal court!"

Stokowski's eyes looked very wild and animated. His body shook and it seemed to me that he was getting very panicky. Gwen Tone stood up and spoke to the hearing officer.

"Mr. Tritch? Can I ask Chief Stokowski a question?"

"Yes," said Tritch.

"Thank you," she said. "I'm a little bit confused. Did you just claim that you found Mr. Bradley's scarf at a murder scene? And then you claimed you didn't find his scarf? Did you just contradict yourself? If so, were you lying about the scarf being at the murder scene? If so, did you just attempt to fabricate evidence against Mr. Bradley to make it seem like he was guilty of a murder he didn't commit?"

The room was silent. Stokowski didn't answer. He moved his shaky hands up to his face and wiped the sweat off his face.

"Listen…" said Stokowski.

The whole room was silent and the reporters' pens were positioned to write down every word Stokowski said.

"…I have to use the bathroom," said Stokowski.

Stokowski ran out of the courtroom.

"Stop!" said Tritch. "Stop him! I didn't give you permission to leave! Stokowski!"

Stokowski's footsteps could be heard down the corridor of the building, running out of the building.

"I don't think he's coming back," said Buckley.

Tritch was standing and shaking. The anger and indignation on his face was so intense that it was easy to interpret.

"How dare he leave my court without permission!" said Tritch. "I'll get him nailed for violation of human rights! I'll get him nailed in criminal court for lying to an officer of the State Department! And I'll see he gets convicted too!"

The reporters were writing energetically in their notebooks and talking to each other excitedly. Tritch sat and started writing something on a piece of paper. Occasionally, he would look with stern disapproval towards where Stokowski had run out of the courtroom. Finally, he stopped writing and stared directly at me.

"Mr. Trueman Bradley," said Tritch. "Please stand up."

I stood up and bowed my head.

"Given the evidence presented before me," said Tritch, "I find no basis to uphold the charges against you. I dismiss all the charges laid against you by Chief Stokowski. You keep your agency license."

Everyone cheered and applauded. I felt so relieved that I was unable to speak or react in any way. I stood, dazed, and could only manage to smile slightly. Nora ran from the witness box and threw her arms around me in a tight embrace.

"Quiet everyone," said Tritch. "I would like to add, Mr. Bradley, that I find the behavior and motivations of Chief Stokowski very suspicious and I will be asking that his activities be investigated. I feel you were unjustly discriminated against and persecuted, and I will use what powers I have to see that Chief Stokowski does not get away with this. I will consider the recommendation of lodging complaints against him in both civil and criminal court."

A male reporter stood up and spoke to the hearing officer.

"Pardon me, Mr. Tritch? I was wondering if we are allowed to report on this? What I mean is, can we put in the newspaper that Stokowski is charged with violating Trueman's human rights and possibly of attempting to frame him for murder?"

"Yes, you can!" said Tritch. "In fact, I want you to report on it! I said I won't let him get away with this. I want everyone to know. So please, put it in the newspaper!"

Gwen Tone stood up and spoke.

"Can I ask a question?"

"I suppose," said Tritch.

"Well," said Gwen, "we've gotten so many good stories out of this hearing! Trueman's equations do work... Chief Stokowski is suspected of several crimes... Trueman's amazing new inventions. These are great stories! But, I think I speak for every reporter here when I ask the following question..."

Gwen turned to face us and spoke to Nora.

"You're Ms. Nora Lucca, right?" asked Gwen.

"Yes," said Nora.

"Well," said Gwen, "we're just curious what you meant when you said, and I quote: 'I wish there were more men in the world like Trueman.' Did you mean that you're in love with Trueman? Are you two a couple or romantically involved in any way?"

Nora stopped hugging me and walked a few feet away. Nora's face was becoming red and I guessed that she was embarrassed.

The reporters all started laughing and writing in their notebooks. I could hear them whispering about Nora and me.

"I knew it," whispered Gwen. "They are a couple!"

Nora turned to look at the hearing officer.

"Do I have to answer these questions?" asked Nora.

Tritch laughed and started organizing his papers.

"No," said Tritch. "These questions are starting to get a little bit off topic. Ladies and gentlemen of the press, if you have any more questions for these people, please go ask them outside; this hearing is over! Let's all get out of here. A criminal case will be happening here in only an hour's time!"

Tritch hastily packed his papers into his briefcase and walked out of the courtroom. Buckley grabbed my shoulder and led me out of the building, keeping reporters away from me with a protective hand.

Outside the building, the day was sunny and bright; the air was cool and pleasant-smelling. I had never seen a more beautiful day in New York City. We walked towards the Lincoln car and I began to realize the day seemed so beautiful to me because I was so happy and relieved. Not only had I avoided having my license revoked, Stokowski, my enemy, had been disgraced; the media once again thought I was a genius and Nora had even shown some signs of loving me more than I'd dared to hope she would. I was so full of bliss I felt like I was floating over the sidewalk. Even the noise of the media and the flashes of their cameras didn't upset me. I stopped walking, right in front of our Lincoln car and even let the media take my photo. I smiled and waved for the cameras.

"Trueman!" said Gwen, who was approaching me with an audio tape recorder. "Can I ask you a question?"

"Sure!" I said.

"Are you and Nora a couple?" asked Gwen.

"No, I'm single," I said.

Gwen smiled at me and touched my shoulder.

"I don't believe it!" said Gwen. "A handsome guy like you, still single?"

Nora moved between Gwen and me and pushed her back.

"Leave Trueman alone!" said Nora. "He's had a hard day and he's in no condition to answer questions!"

"Ah, jealous are you?" asked Gwen. "See, guys, I told you she was in love with him!"

Nora's face became red and she helped me get into the car.

As we drove away, the sun shone through the window and onto my face. I closed my eyes and savored the warmth. After many worrying surprises, everything had become perfect again. I wanted to stop my life and stay in this perfect moment forever. I thought about my new invention and realized, with joy, that I would never need to enter an unpredictable situation again.

"The surprise revealer will keep these situations away," I whispered to myself. "This is the last unexpected situation I'll ever need to endure. I've endured my last big surprise."

ONE MORE BIG SURPRISE

It was a rainy afternoon on Reade Street, and we were all seated around a table, playing poker. I thought about the past, when this office was dirty and empty; I thought about the first poker game I played here, with my friends. Mrs. Levi, Nora, Buckley and I had been sitting here for hours. We had locked the front door and turned off all the telephones, so we wouldn't be disturbed by clients, visitors or media people. After all these days of activity and conflict, it was nice for me to sit down with my friends and have a relaxing time, playing cards.

Buckley put his cards on the table.

"Four kings!" said Buckley. "Beat that."

I looked at my cards. I had another royal flush, the best hand in poker. My hand beat Buckley's hand, again. I had already beaten him fifteen times, and I wondered if I should pretend he beat me, so he wouldn't get depressed. But I remembered the advice of my granddad.

"I'm sorry, Detective," I said. "My granddad told me never to tell a lie. So, I have to admit... I beat you again."

I put my cards on the table and Buckley groaned.

"You've had twelve royal flushes!" said Buckley.

"Yes," I said.

Buckley sighed.

"I don't know how you do it," he said.

Sal, who had gone out to buy a newspaper, appeared at the door and walked towards us. He had an excited look on his face.

"Trueman!" said Sal. "Look at this! Another story about you in the newspaper! This time you're on the front page!"

I looked at the front page and saw a story about me printed in a little box at the bottom of the page.

"Genius detective, Trueman Bradley," I read aloud, "works on his latest equation: Trueman + Nora = Love?"

Everyone laughed and Nora's face became red. She grabbed the newspaper from me and read it.

"What does that mean?" I asked.

"It means Mrs. Nora is in love with Mr. Trueman!" said Sal.

"Quiet, Sal!" said Nora. "This is written by that annoying reporter, Gwen Tone! How can she get away with writing gossip like that? I'm gonna write the editor and complain!"

Mrs. Levi started giggling. Nora looked at her, with a look I couldn't interpret. Soon, everyone except Nora was giggling. I wasn't sure what was funny, but I looked at Nora and smiled.

"I don't see what's so funny about it," said Nora.

Although she said this, the smile on her face told me otherwise. I could recognize signs of amusement on her face.

"Another royal flush!" said Buckley.

"Yes," I said. "I win again."

"Thirteen royal flushes!" said Buckley. "How do you do that?"

"It's not very hard to win at poker," I said. "There are really very few variables. A simple equation is sufficient."

"Well, at least none of us ever have to worry about our retirement!" said Buckley.

"Retirement?" I asked. "What do you mean?"

"Well, we don't have to worry about having money when we're really old!" said Buckley. "We'll just take you to the casino and we'll make enough money to last the rest of our lives! You could probably make a million dollars in one hour at a casino."

"Hm, I didn't think of that," I said. "I can make an equation, or create a machine to win at gambling. I'll call it the 'retirement machine'!"

Everyone laughed.

"I'll take one of those!" said Sal. "I should have retired last year! Me and Mrs. Levi can take a holiday to Hawaii!"

"I'm not that old, Sal!" said Mrs. Levi.

"You don't look a day over thirty-five, Mrs. Levi," said Buckley.

"Oh, thank you, Detective," said Mrs. Levi. "Here, have another piece of cake."

Mrs. Levi passed Buckley a piece of cake and he thanked her warmly. I felt very peaceful, knowing that my friends were all friendly with each other and were having a good time together. I could easily interpret the happiness on their faces.

"Detective," said Mrs. Levi, "you said 'we' don't have to worry about our retirement. Does that mean you're planning on staying with us for a while?"

Buckley's face changed and I couldn't interpret his emotions. It was similar to the face made by people who were in pain. My granddad used to make that face after eating hot peppers. He said it was caused by the pain of his heartburn.

"Do you want a pill?" I asked.

"What?" asked Buckley.

"We have pills in the bathroom if you want," I said. "For your heartburn. We have pills that cure heartburn."

"Heartburn?" asked Buckley.

"Don't you know what heartburn is?" I asked. "It is also called 'acid reflux.' It is caused by stomach acids accidently burning the esophagus. Sometimes caused by eating hot foods…"

"Trueman!" said Buckley. "I know what heartburn is. But I don't have heartburn, okay? I was just thinking about something. There's something I've been hesitating to say."

"Oh…" I said. I tried to remember this, for future reference, that people made that particular face when they had heartburn and also when they were hesitating to say something.

"Hesitating?" I asked. "Well then, spit it out!" I said, using the expression I had learned from Dr. Rozzozzo.

"Okay," said Buckley. "Well, I was thinking. Since I've got no job, at present, and since I'm pretty sure your agency could use the help of an experienced detective…"

"Oh, my God!" said Nora. "You want to work for us?"

I had no idea how Nora had guessed this, but the thought of Buckley working for our agency was so exciting, it caused me to drop my cup and my tea spilled all over the table. My tea cup rolled off the table and hit the ground.

"Oh, I'm sorry!" I shouted.

Everyone collected the cards off the table, so they wouldn't get wet, and Mrs. Levi wiped the table dry.

"Detective, I'm so happy to hear that!" said Mrs. Levi.

"Yes, sir!" said Sal. "This is great news!"

I went down on the floor to find my tea cup, which had not been broken. I examined it closely, but there were no cracks in it. My granddad had told me a superstition: if you drop a tea cup and it doesn't break, it means good luck with whatever you will be doing in the near future.

"This is good luck!" I said, holding up the cup. "I'm happy you're joining us, Detective Buckley! Thank you!"

"My pleasure, Trueman," said Buckley. "I know you guys could use my help. I can teach you all about what real detective work is all about. And you guys could probably teach me a few things too. Trueman, I know, can teach me a lot! In the short time I've known you people, I have to say I'm enjoying working with you. I have a feeling I'm gonna like it here."

Nora and Mrs. Levi embraced Buckley and Sal gave him a pat on the back. I was smiling widely and I hoped that was enough for Buckley to know how appreciative I was for his support and his friendship. Not only did I succeed in my attempt to become a detective, I got a real-life police detective as my partner! I was so grateful to him, I decided to let him win at poker. I didn't need to lie about winning. The next time we played a round of poker, I purposely tried to get only the worst cards.

"I'm grateful to you," I said.

"Who, me?" asked Buckley. "Forget about it, Trueman."

"I'm glad to have a real policeman as my partner," I said.

"Yeah," said Buckley. "I know a lot about this work."

"No," I said.

"What?" asked Buckley. "You're saying I don't know a lot?"

"I don't mean that!" I said. "Yes, you know a lot. That's not what I meant. When I said 'no,' I meant 'no, that's not why I'm glad.' I'm glad because now I am really like Dick Tracy. Because he also had a partner who was a policeman."

"Yeah!" said Sal. "Sam Catchem was his name!"

"Yes, Detective Buckley," I said. "You're Sam Catchem!"

"Still talking about those comic book detectives, huh, Trueman?" asked Buckley. "Well, as a matter of fact, my first name is Sam. And please, you all call me Sam, okay? No more of this 'Detective Buckley' stuff. We're all friends here."

I smiled widely. His first name was Sam. It was as if destiny had intended for him to be Sam Catchem. Everything was perfect. Even the sound of the rain on the windows seemed perfectly rhythmic, as if they were not random raindrops, but were ordered mathematically and were flawlessly sounding their percussion rhythm against the window panes. The sound of the rain and the laughter of my friends soothed me and calmed my mind. I wanted to stop time and preserve this perfect day.

"Three jacks!" said Buckley. "I have a feeling I'm gonna lose. I know you're going to beat me, Trueman. I'm just wondering how bad, is all. Another royal flush, I'm guessing?"

I put my cards on the table. Buckley stared at them.

"A pair of threes?" asked Buckley.

"That's right, Detective," I said. "You win."

Buckley shook his head and frowned.

"I'm not stupid, Trueman," said Buckley. "I know you're letting me win. And call me Sam, okay?"

"Can I call you Sam Catchem?" I asked.

Buckley looked at me and I couldn't interpret his emotion. But, before he could speak and make it clear to me, we were interrupted by an explosion of noise. It was so loud and horrifying that I fell to the floor and covered my head with my trench coat. I lay there, screaming, until it was over.

"What the hell is that?" shouted Buckley.

"Trueman!" shouted Nora. "Are you okay?"

I had closed my eyes tightly. When I felt Nora's comforting arms around me and the noises ceased, I dared to open my eyes. I peeked out from under my trench coat, expecting to see the entire office destroyed and smoke rising from the burning rubble. The noise had been so loud, I imagined a plane had crashed into the office building. To my surprise, the office was perfectly in order and nothing was smashed or burned.

"What happened?" I asked.

"I don't know!" said Nora. "I think the noise came from outside. Buckley and Sal went to check it out!"

"Oh, dear!" said Mrs. Levi. "What could make such a commotion? It sounds like a meteor crashed on Reade Street!"

"No!" I said. "The ratio chance of our house being hit by a meteor is 182,138,880,000,000 to 1! It's almost impossible!"

Sal walked into the room. I couldn't interpret the emotions on his face, but I had a feeling he had bad news.

"Boss, you better come out and see this," said Sal.

Nora grabbed my arm and led me out of the building. Outside, the rain was falling and the grayness of the cloudy sky made what I saw seem even more depressing.

Our neon sign had been destroyed. Pieces of glass and metal were all that remained of our agency sign. The remnants were all over the sidewalk. Only a few wires, giving off electrical sparks, remained on the side of our building. I was so shocked to see that our sign was destroyed that I couldn't react. I stood in the rain, silent and afraid.

"What was it?" asked Nora. "Lightning?"

"I don't know for sure," said Buckley. "But I've got a hunch. Give me a minute and I'll know if my hunch is correct."

Buckley climbed on top of a nearby garbage can and examined the wall near where the sign had been.

"Lightning?" I asked. "I don't understand. Maybe the electricity in the sign increases the likelihood of it being hit by lightning. But it's still very unlikely we'd be so unlucky!"

"It wasn't lightning," said Buckley.

Buckley jumped off the garbage can. He walked towards us and made a face that I interpreted as being very serious.

"Trueman," said Buckley, "everyone, I think we should get inside. Let's get off the street."

"Why?" asked Nora.

"Because," said Buckley, "someone shot that sign with some kind of gun. Seems like a machine gun of some kind. An automatic weapon. I don't want them shooting one of us!"

I heard a squealing noise. A car was speeding towards us and its tires squealed as they spun along the rain-soaked streets. Buckley pushed us back with his arm and pulled his gun from its holster. He pointed it at the approaching car.

"What is it?" I asked. "What's wrong?"

The car drove nearer to us and I noticed it was being driven by an elderly lady. I could recognize the look of shock on her face when she saw Buckley's gun. She drove away, in a hurry, and Buckley holstered his gun. His face was red.

"Oops!" said Buckley. "Well, you can't be too careful. Anyways, let's get inside, okay?"

The squealing noises, Buckley's comment about guns and my own confusion made me nervous. I covered my ears and Nora led me back into the agency building.

"No!" I said. "The surprises are supposed to be over!"

"What did you say, Trueman?" asked Nora.

"I said the surprises are supposed to be over!" I said. "I sent Rozzozzo the details of my new invention. The 'surprise revealer' invention will stop all unexpected events like this! I thought if I stayed home and didn't go anywhere I could avoid any surprises until Rozzozzo calls to say she's done the surprise revealer! But now, this horrible surprise has come!"

"Oh!" said Sal. "Mr. Bradley, that reminds me…"

"What?" I asked.

"Dr. Rozzozzo called," said Sal. "She said she's coming over to talk to you. She's said something about having 'done the invention.'"

"What?" I asked. "Why didn't you tell me?"

"Sorry, boss," said Sal. "I forgot."

I was annoyed that Sal forgot something that was so important to me, but I was overjoyed to realize the surprise revealer was ready and my days of enduring surprises were over.

"Well, that's okay, Sal," I said. "I forgive you. I don't mind this stress, as this will probably be the final surprise."

Nora led me to a chair and wrapped a blanket around me.

"Now, you relax, Trueman," said Nora. "I know this kind of thing is stressful for you. Just sit down here, in front of the window, and let the sound of the rain calm and soothe you. We'll call the police and take care of this problem. Okay?"

"Yes," I said. "I'll sit for a while."

"I'll make you some fresh tea!" said Mrs. Levi.

I listened to the calming music of the rain and watched the little raindrops as they slid down the window pane, making an endless pattern of random pathways on the glass. It was relaxing to watch the rain and ignore the world outside myself. If I could wait here, in this safe place, until Rozzozzo arrived with the surprise revealer, then I could avoid the need to experience any more unpleasant surprises.

I closed my eyes and tried to forget everything, because my memories of the smashed agency sign were causing me stress. Although I never liked surprises, the memory of that smashed sign seemed to cause me more anxiety than anything else I'd experienced for a long time. As hard as I tried to forget it, the mental picture of the broken sign was stuck in my mind.

I have a powerful visual memory, and I could see every detail of the sign clearly in my mind, as if it was physically in front of me. I could see the electrical sparks coming from the wet wires; I could see the jagged bits of broken glass on the wet sidewalk; I could see every drop of rain hitting the wall where the sign had once been. Seeing the sign caused me fear and anxiety, but I couldn't dispel the mental image.

I tried to identify what about this mental image made me so terrified. Was it the electrical sparks? Was it the holes in the wall, which I now realized were caused by bullets?

"No," I said to myself, "it's Stokowski."

"Did you say something, dear?" asked Mrs. Levi.

I was as surprised as Mrs. Levi was. It was only just now that I realized my fear was not caused by the image of the broken sign. Sometimes I saw equations as visual patterns and I could see them clearly, as if the equation were a physical thing. Subconsciously, I had applied my crime-fighting equation to the broken sign and it had indicated to me who broke it. The answer to my equation appeared in the form of Chief Stokowski, seen clearly in my mind. It was that subconscious image that had been frightening me, not the sign itself.

"Stokowski broke our sign!" I shouted.

"What?" asked Mrs. Levi.

"Call Buckley and Nora!" I said. "I need their help! Stokowski is a criminal and he's going to attack us again! We need to arrange a mission and catch him before he catches us!"

THE SURPRISE REVEALER

Twenty-four hours after our agency sign was destroyed, I was in the public washroom of an opulent casino. Earlier, I had spent the night in my room, creating the equations that would help me to nail Stokowski. Rozzozzo had arrived at my office and given me the 'surprise revealer.' I was busy all night, inputting 1,062 bits of data into it. Now, with the help of Buckley and my equations, I was in an opulent casino, on a mission to reveal the crimes of Stokowski.

The casino was decorated with marble stone and gold-plated taps. But despite the luxury, I was not comfortable. I was in a toilet enclosure, trying to balance on a toilet seat. I was peeking over the wall of the enclosure, watching a man who had just finished washing his hands. I was waiting for him to leave, so I could continue, in privacy.

"Trueman!" said Buckley.

I had forgotten that Buckley was hiding with me. He was in the adjacent toilet enclosure. His sudden comment had made me jump and lose my footing on the toilet seat. My foot slipped into the toilet. I heard a loud splash and felt cold water enveloping my foot. In my panic, I had lowered my hands onto the toilet and accidentally pushed the lever to flush the toilet.

I felt cold water swirling around my foot and I crouched down, covering my head with my hands. This was horrible. Not only was my foot very uncomfortable and my mind panicked by this unexpected occurrence, but that man who had been washing his hands may have heard me. The toilet was making a very loud flushing sound and I covered my ears until it was finished.

"Sorry," said Buckley, after the flushing stopped.

"It's okay, Buckley," I said. "It is my fault actually. I had my surprise revealer switched off. If I had my surprise revealer, or SR, switched on, it would have warned me that you would talk to me and then it wouldn't be a surprise."

"A handy tool, that SR," said Buckley. "And call me Sam!"

"Oh, yeah," I said. "I keep forgetting."

I switched on my SR. It was a small computer that strapped to my wrist, and it looked a lot like my wrist TV. I wore my wrist TV on my right wrist and my SR on my left wrist. The SR's computer screen was activated and I saw the familiar compass design. The SR was similar to the TET. The TET warned me when it was safe to do something specific, like crossing a bridge; the SR, however, warned me of any possible disturbance, at any time, doing anything. With the SR, I could be certain that my plans would never be ruined, because it warned me, ahead of time, if anything would happen that could ruin my plans.

"So, how's that SR of yours work, anyways?" asked Buckley. "And explain to me again, please, why we're hiding here. Why are we sitting on a couple of toilets here?"

"To answer your first question…" I said, "the SR's operation is very complex and you should have asked me when I had more time to explain. We can't talk about it now, we need to follow the plan exactly. To answer your second question, we are sitting on these toilets because the SR told me this is the safest place to begin our mission. Now, please, no more questions. Turn on your wrist TV. It is time to begin the mission by explaining the plan to everyone."

I switched on my wrist TV and used it to call Sal, Nora, Mrs. Levi and Buckley. The screen was split into four sections and I could see their faces.

"Trueman?" asked Nora. "What's happening? Are you okay?"

"Yes," I said. "I want to explain what exactly will be happening, so you all know what to expect. This time, because I have the SR, nothing will change the plan. So, what I tell you is exactly what will happen."

"Why can't I be there to help you?" asked Nora. "After you discovered that Stokowski destroyed our sign, you locked yourself in your room and did equations all day! And now, you and Buckley left someplace without telling us where! Now, what's going on? I'm worried about you! Let me come help!"

"I'll explain," I said. "My crime-fighting equation told me that Stokowski destroyed our sign. It also told me he would probably try to attack me personally. So I hid myself in my office with the door locked, so Stokowski couldn't get me. I was waiting for Rozzozzo to come with the SR. I knew that if I had the SR, I could create a plan to reveal Stokowski's crimes and get him arrested. The SR is designed to make plans proceed perfectly, without any surprises. So, I was in my room entering data into the SR. I explained the situation of Stokowski to the SR and it created for me a perfect plan to nail Stokowski."

"So, where did you and Buckley go?" asked Nora.

"Call me Sam!" said Buckley. "Please!"

"Sorry, Sam," said Nora.

"We are in a casino, in the district of Yonkers," I said.

"Yonkers?" asked Sal. "What are you doing there? And why didn't you ask me to drive you there?"

"Because the SR created a plan for me," I said. "I must follow the SR's plan exactly and then I can nail Stokowski without any surprises. The SR told me to take a taxicab from Reade Street to this casino in Yonkers. It didn't explain why."

"Why didn't you take me with you?" asked Nora.

"The SR told me to take Buckley!" I said. "I mean, Sam!"

"Sam, yeah. Thank you, Trueman," said Buckley.

"Okay, good," I said. "Now, the SR told me I should call you all and tell you what will be happening. So, here it is. The SR says that I need to get to the penthouse of this casino. This casino is operated by an Italian Mafia family and today is a special day. It is the birthday of one of the bosses. So the casino is full of violent gangsters with guns. They're all drunk and celebrating their boss's birthday."

"What?" asked Nora. "Trueman, are you joking? I won't let you stay in a place like that! Get out of there, now!"

"No, Nora!" I said. "It's okay! My SR is designed to avoid trouble. If I follow the SR's instructions, I will not be hurt. I am just explaining the situation to you. You see, the SR told me to come to this casino and to sneak into the building by picking the lock of an outside door. That door led into the casino's bathroom. So, we are in the casino's bathroom right now. Actually, Sam and I are sitting on the toilets."

"You're on the toilet, dear?" asked Mrs. Levi.

I could interpret the shock on Mrs. Levi's face.

"No!" I said. "I don't mean we're using them! We're hiding here because this is where the SR told us to hide. Remember, we must do everything the SR instructs us to do."

"I'm still not sure I like this, Trueman," said Nora. "Those are real gangsters out there! They might hurt you!"

"Yeah, Trueman," said Buckley, "I can't say I much like being here either. Those Mafia guys may not know who you are, but a lot of them might recognize me. When I worked for the NYPD, I probably sent a lot of their friends to jail! You sure about this, Trueman? I mean, that SR might've made a mistake."

"No!" I said. "The SR doesn't make mistakes. I used to doubt my equations and my inventions. But after that hearing and knowing how much you all trust and admire me, I have no self-doubts anymore. Please, my friends, if you trust me then please have confidence in my equations and my inventions! If we follow the SR's plan, we'll be safe. Please believe in me!"

I couldn't interpret the emotions on any of their faces, although Nora's face showed some indications of pride and love.

"Okay, Trueman," said Nora. "We trust you."

Everyone nodded their heads.

"What'll happen now?" asked Nora.

"Okay," I said. "My SR says that I should leave this bathroom in about ninety seconds. I will need to follow the SR's instructions to get through the room of dangerous criminals safely. Sam, you will continue to sit on your toilet and wait for me to call you."

"Lucky me," said Buckley. "But if I hear gunshots or something, I'm not waiting here, Trueman. I'm coming to rescue you, alright? You can't expect me to just…"

"No!" I said. "We need to follow the plan, exactly! Even if you hear gunshots, don't do anything until I tell you!"

Everyone was silent. I knew everyone was worried about me, and I appreciated how they cared about me, but I also wanted to be able to believe in myself and my equations. I didn't want anyone doubting me, or I might start doubting myself too.

"Sam," I said. "Wait on your toilet until I call you on the wrist TV. I will call you and tell you to go somewhere. I don't know where yet. The SR will tell me those details later. Be sure to follow my instructions exactly, okay?"

"Sure thing, Trueman," said Buckley. "Just as you say."

"Good," I said.

"What do we do?" asked Nora.

"I don't know," I said.

"What do you mean?" asked Nora. "Can't we help you?"

"I don't know," I said. "My SR only told me to call you. It didn't tell me anything else about you. Not yet. Just wait for me to call you, I guess."

"Trueman, dear," said Mrs. Levi. "Can we at least call the police and tell them to wait outside the casino in case you need them? Or something like that?"

"Yeah," said Sal. "My cousin Vino knows somebody who works as a bartender in that casino! He's not Mafia, but maybe he can get you out of trouble, if you need him. I'll call him!"

"No!" I said. "Please, just do what I instruct, okay?"

Everyone was silent and I could interpret the worry in their faces. But I was resolved not to let their worry affect me. I watched the clock on my wrist TV and gathered my courage.

"Ninety seconds have passed!" I said. "I must go! Bye!"

"Trueman! Wait!" said Nora.

I switched off my wrist TV before Nora could finish speaking. I hated to be rude to her, but my SR was telling me to leave the bathroom now, and if I didn't obey its instructions, the whole plan could be ruined and I might get hurt. I opened the door of the toilet enclosure and walked out.

"Trueman?" asked Buckley. "You sure you're okay?"

"Yeah!" I said. "Just wait here! I'm fine as long as I obey the SR. Wait here for me to call you."

I walked to the door that led out of the bathroom and into the casino. I could hear the sound of loud music and drunken laughter. I put on my special sunglasses and my earphones.

"Good luck, partner!" said Buckley.

"Thanks, Sam," I said.

I pushed open the door and stood for a few moments, observing the scene. It was very loud. Even with my earphones playing Mozart's music, I could still hear the sounds of the casino. This was the largest crowd I had ever seen in one building and it made me dizzy to look at it; so many unpredictable bodies moving around each other, closely, like snakes in a snake-pit, slithering over each other. I'd always hated crowds, and this was one of the worst I'd ever seen.

There were flashy gambling machines everywhere and colored lights emanated from the ceiling. At the bar, men in expensive suits were drinking alcoholic beverages and talking loudly. Their movements were drunken and aggressive and it made my stomach sick with tension to think of getting closer to them.

A singer was on a nearby stage. His music was loud, his outfit shiny and he jumped around the stage like a wild monkey. The casino stank like stale cigarette smoke and alcohol. So many different types of cigarette brands were identifiable in the air that it made me confused and dizzy. This place was so busy and fast-moving and distressing that I wanted to turn and run away.

I heard my SR beeping. That was meant to get my attention, because it was instructing me to do something. I looked at the SR and felt better. This place might have been confusing and full of dazzling sensations that made me sick, but the SR was predictable; the SR was safe. It was like my guide in a world of unpredictable phenomena. It would take this mess of unpredictable possibilities and find me a safe path through it, without any surprises or unpleasant shocks. I was so grateful to have the SR in this busy, crowded casino that I kissed it.

"I'm so glad I have you!" I said, to the SR.

The SR beeped, as if in reply. The screen lit up and I saw that it was giving me an urgent message.

"Talk to the media," I read.

"The SR wants me to talk to the media?" I asked.

I looked into the crowd and saw no media. There were no reporters or journalists, not even a newspaper delivery person.

"What media?" I asked.

The compass design appeared on the SR screen and it pointed to the bar, where the noisy gangsters were. At the bar, I could see Gwen Tone, with her cameraman. They were sitting there, watching the crowd, as if they were looking for someone. This reporter had been following me around for days, trying to get information about my love life. I wondered if she had followed me here and was looking for me. Whether or not this was the case, the SR was instructing me to go talk to her.

"I must have faith in my inventions!" I said to myself.

I lowered my gaze to the floor, so I wouldn't be dazzled by the crowds, and looked at my SR. The compass arrow would tell me where to walk. I walked through the crowds without bumping into anyone. My SR was working, helping me avoid any surprise. Finally, the compass disappeared and I looked up to see that I was at the bar. Gwen Tone was in front of me, smiling widely.

"Trueman!" said Gwen. "Imagine meeting you here! Would you like a drink? I've been wanting to talk to you for days!"

I wasn't sure what to say, because my SR screen was blank.

"Um, I don't drink alcohol," I said. "It kills brain cells. I need my brain functional to do detective work."

"What did he say?"

A man in an expensive gray suit was speaking in a loud, drunken voice. His breath smelled like bourbon and a brand of Cuban cigar named Cohiba Esplendido. From experience, I knew this was an expensive cigar. This man was rich, loud and smelly. His presence made me dizzy and sick. I looked down to my SR for help, but the screen was still blank. That usually meant that I was safe, no matter what I did. But when I looked at this drunken gangster, I could interpret the potential for violence in his eyes and I wondered if my SR was working correctly.

"Huh?" asked the gangster. "Did you hear me or what? I was telling you something! This guy here in the yellow said he's a detective? Is he joking? What's his problem, lady?"

Gwen waved her hand in front of her face.

"Your breath stinks, pal!" said Gwen. "Mind your own business, too! Me and Mr. Bradley are having a private talk!"

"Mr. Bradley?" asked the gangster. "Not Trueman Bradley? That genius detective I heard about in the papers? Hey, fellas! We got a celebrity in the room! Hey, shut up fellas!"

The gangster stood on his chair and put two of his fingers into his mouth. He whistled loudly and everyone looked at us. It seemed like every person in the whole casino stopped what they were doing and stared at us. I was so nervous, I wanted to hide under a chair. I looked at my SR, but it was still blank.

"Hey, fellas!" said the gangster. "This here's Mr. Trueman Bradley. You know, that guy what solves crimes with math! We got a detective come to wish the boss a happy birthday!"

I saw the faces of dozens of gangsters, staring at me. The big boss, who was dressed in the pinstripe suit, was also looking at me. I was too nervous to interpret very much of the gangsters' emotions. But the small amount I was able to interpret convinced me that gangsters didn't like detectives. I was starting to get scared.

"Okay, SR," I whispered. "I think this is getting close to a surprise! You have to warn me and tell me what to do!"

As if it were able to understand my words, the SR responded with a beep and instructions appeared on the screen.

"Unpleasant surprise is imminent," I read. "To avoid unpleasant surprise: Throw alcoholic drink on gangster."

My eyes widened and I was unsure if my SR was malfunctioning. I had read many clothing catalogs and memorized many details about expensive Italian suits. This gangster wore a Brioni brand suit, which was worth more than 3,000 dollars. If I were to stain his suit, I was certain he would react violently.

The SR beeped and warned me that I must obey its instructions immediately, or risk violating the plan. I knew that I was safe if I followed the SR's plans, so I gathered my courage and dismissed my fears.

I grabbed the alcoholic drink from Gwen Tone's hand and threw it at the gangster's chest. Gwen had been drinking something with chocolate liqueur mixed in it, so the gangster's expensive suit was now stained with brown streaks.

"What the hell!" shouted the gangster.

His eyes opened so wide, I could see every small red vein in his drunken eyes. I couldn't interpret his emotions, but I wasn't sure I wanted to know what he was feeling. He looked at me in a way that made me want to run away, but the SR instructed me not to move. The gangster reached into his jacket.

"You looking for trouble, punk?" he asked.

The gangster pulled a gun from his jacket and aimed it between my eyes. It was only a small Smith and Wesson double-action .45 ACP semi-automatic compact pistol; small enough to fit in his palm. But I could see from my perspective, looking down the barrel, that it had been used a lot and quite recently. Maybe it had been used to murder impolite private detectives.

"You are dead meat, punk!" he said.

"Wait!"

The big boss in the pinstripe suit had called from the other side of the bar. His voice was deep and croaking, like a frog. In fact, his bald head and wide mouth made him look like a frog in a suit. He was surrounded by big, well-dressed men.

"Don't get emotional, Emilio," said the boss. "Don't hurt him, yet. Let me talk to him. Bring him over here, will you?"

Emilio, the gangster I had offended, made a face I could easily interpret as angry and poked his gun into my back, pushing me towards the big boss and threatening me.

"You just wait, punk!" said Emilio. "No one ruins my suit and gets away with it! You're not leaving here alive, I'm telling you that for sure! You're as good as dead, punk!"

All this talk about my imminent death was starting to make me nervous. As much as I wanted to trust in the SR, this was a very dangerous situation and I started to wish I could forget about my equations and inventions and go hide somewhere safe.

"Listen!" I whispered, to my SR. "In the future, could you find a less dangerous way for me to complete my missions?"

As if in response, my SR beeped and gave me another instruction.

"Unpleasant surprise is imminent," it read. "To avoid unpleasant surprise: Give gangster boss three truthful responses."

I looked up from my SR and saw the big, frog-like face of the gangster boss. He was concentrating on me, silently studying me. He breathed heavily, as if he was asthmatic, and his eyes were so yellow they looked like they were made of amber. I felt nervous, being stared at, and tried to think of something I could say or do to make the situation less tense.

"Happy birthday!" I said.

He pulled his hand out of his pocket and pointed it at me. I jumped back, expecting another gun. But soon I realized that he wanted me to shake his hand. I took his big, moist hand and was relieved to see a smile on his face.

"Thank you," said the boss. "I'm pleased to meet you. I'm glad you could attend my birthday celebration."

The gangster boss motioned for me to sit next to him and I hastened to do so. He lit a Cohiba Esplendido.

"They call me Benvolio," said the boss. "And you? You're that genius mathematician I've been hearing so much about, is that right? You're a private detective, then, are you?"

"Yes," I answered. He had just asked me two questions. I wasn't sure if I had just answered his first or second question.

"I was only answering your second question," I said.

"Oh… right," said Benvolio. "Well, I got another question for you. Although you're welcome at my party, may I ask you exactly what is your purpose in being here?"

I knew that I needed to answer Benvolio honestly. The SR had told me to answer three of Benvolio's questions honestly. So far, I had answered one.

"I'm here to nail Chief Stokowski," I said.

Benvolio coughed. For a moment, it seemed like he was choking on his cigar. He spat the cigar out of his mouth and it flew across the room and landed at the bartender's feet.

"What?" asked Benvolio. "And you told me that? What, are you stupid? Stokowski works for me! Everyone knows that!"

I was shocked to realize that Stokowski worked for this gangster. I was starting to realize what kind of illegal activity Stokowski was involved with. Maybe this is why he wanted to cancel my license. Because he feared I would be able to expose his connection to this gangster and the local Mafia.

I was happy to finally know what sort of criminal activities Stokowski was involved with, because now I had a better idea what kind of evidence to get to send him to jail. But my happiness didn't last long. I could easily recognize the aggressive, hate-filled look in Benvolio's yellow eyes. I guessed he was not happy to know that I was trying to nail Stokowski; after all, Stokowski was his criminal partner.

"And you're supposed to be a genius?" asked Benvolio. "You walk right in here and admit that you're trying to send my partner to jail? You know you can't leave here alive now, don't you? Do you think I'm gonna let you live now? What kind of idiot do you think I am? Huh? What do I look like to you?"

I wasn't sure what he was talking about, but I knew I was in trouble. I also knew I had to follow the SR's instructions exactly, or I wouldn't get out of this dangerous situation alive. I had to answer one more of his questions honestly.

"Did you ask what you look like to me?" I asked.

"Yeah, I did," said Benvolio.

"You look like a frog," I said. "You look like a big frog in a pinstripe suit. You sound like one too."

Some of the gangsters started laughing. But they quickly stopped when they saw Benvolio's face. His anger was so intense, I could easily recognize it. He was so angry, his face had turned red. He was so red, he looked like the red poison-dart frog which I read about in my zoology book. Also called "Oophaga Pumilio," it lives in the Costa Rican jungles.

"Emilio?" asked Benvolio.

"Yeah, boss," said Emilio.

"Take him upstairs," said Benvolio.

"With pleasure, boss," said Emilio.

Emilio poked the gun into my back and pushed me across the casino, towards a big stairwell. Several large gangsters joined us. As he pushed me, Emilio continued to threaten me.

"There you go!" he said. "What did I tell you, huh? You're dead meat, punk! When the boss says to 'take someone upstairs,' you know what that means? Huh? It means you're dead, that's what! There's no escape for you now, punk!"

His threats were making me nervous and I consulted with my SR for guidance. To my horror, it was blank. Emilio continued to threaten me and poke my back with his gun. We walked across the busy casino and were soon at an elevator with a brass door.

"Alright, get in there!" shouted Emilio. "Get in the elevator! We're going upstairs!"

I don't like elevators, because it involves being very close to people. They jab me with their elbows and breathe in my face. Ever since I was a child, I hated elevators. I resisted getting on the elevator, but Emilio forced me inside.

"No!" I said. "I hate elevators!"

"Oh, do you?" asked Emilio. "Well, you're gonna hate them even more before the day's through! You know why? Huh? Do you want to know why we're going upstairs?"

The elevator was small, with little oxygen, and it smelled like cigars. I could vaguely discern that we were going up, but other than that I was too uncomfortable to notice anything about my environment or to respond to Emilio's questions.

"Well, I'll tell you anyways!" said Emilio. "Because I know you'll like this! There's an old broken elevator shaft on the other side of this casino. We use that elevator shaft to... 'get rid' of people. You know what I mean? We're taking you to the top floor. Then we'll take you to the broken elevator shaft and we're gonna push you down! Understand now? You're gonna like elevators even less when you're falling down that shaft! Now you know what the boss means when he says 'take him upstairs,' huh?"

The gangsters started laughing. The cramped elevator, mixed with the stink and the gangster's cruel laughter, made my stomach tense and I felt sweat forming on my brow. I had the vague realization that I was going to be pushed down an elevator shaft and killed and I started whining out loud.

"No!" I said. "SR! This is an unpleasant surprise! Why didn't you warn me? My inventions don't work! I'm a failure!"

The gangsters laughed some more.

"What the hell is he talking about?" asked Emilio.

As if in response to my whining, the SR beeped and it started giving me urgent instructions.

"Urgent!" it read. "Unpleasant surprise is imminent. To avoid unpleasant surprise: Call the following telephone number and let it ring only twice..."

I was able to make telephone calls on my wrist TV and I hastened to dial the telephone number specified by the SR. To my surprise, a ringing emanated from Emilio's Brioni suit. He took out a small mobile phone and stared at it. I let it ring only twice and Emilio's eyes widened in response.

"That's the signal!" said one of the gangsters.

"Yeah, I know," said Emilio.

"What do we do?" asked another gangster.

"Stop right here," said Emilio. "You heard me! Stop the elevator!"

The gangsters pressed the button to stop the elevator on the sixth floor. The doors slid open and I saw a darkened hallway. It seemed like this floor was not in use. The walls were bare and streaked with paint. The lamps on the ceiling were hanging from thin wires. Dust was everywhere. None of the lamps worked and the only light came from windows. Emilio grabbed my arm and pushed me roughly along the hallway.

"Okay, listen punk!" said Emilio. "We just got a signal that indicates maybe there's trouble…"

"No, Emilio!" said another gangster. "If your mobile phone rings twice and then stops, that's the signal that means the cops are coming and we gotta get out of here, fast! It doesn't mean 'maybe'! Come on, Emilio! Forget about him and let's go!"

"Okay!" said Emilio.

Emilio opened a door leading into an empty room and pushed me inside. He stared at me with a face I couldn't interpret.

"Me and my pals are gonna go check out what's happening," said Emilio. "I'm gonna lock you in here and I'll come back and get you later. Count yourself lucky, punk. You've got a few extra minutes to say your prayers, before you die."

Emilio slammed the door shut and I heard him lock it.

"I am lucky," I said. "Lucky to have an SR."

I kissed my SR and looked around the room. It was dark and smelled like broken plaster and dust. The walls were bare and broken in places. There was only one window and it was so dirty, it hardly let in any light. I walked to it and opened it. There was absolutely no way I could escape out the window. I was six floors up and there was no fire escape.

I sat on the floor. I was grateful to be rescued from Emilio. But how could my SR possibly get me out of a locked room on the sixth floor? Perhaps my SR had, in fact, led me into a hopeless situation. What if I remained trapped here until Emilio realized there were no police around? He'd come back and get me. He'd throw me down the elevator shaft. With horror, I imagined that Emilio may already realize the signal was false. Maybe he was already coming to get me.

The dim light and the dusty smell of the room was depressing and the hopeless situation I was in made me want to escape reality. I was tempted to comfort myself with prime numbers, something I had not done for a long time. I had become so confident in myself that I had not needed prime numbers to help me deal with reality. I didn't want to go back to the way I had been, when I was a weaker man, with less confidence. But this situation was so bleak and uncomfortable, I was tempted.

My SR beeped and the screen glowed. Urgent instructions appeared on the SR; instructions that made my stomach tense.

"Urgent!" I read. "Jump out the window!"

My heart started beating fast and I felt sick. If I jumped out the window, I would certainly die. There was no rope to grasp, like at the Marine Air Terminal. This was certain death.

And also, I had decided to never use my CCC again; I had asked Rozzozzo to destroy it. I had decided never to use it because the newspaper had reported that I jumped off a building and survived. Nora had read this story to me and she mentioned how she hoped no one would try to imitate me and jump off a building. I was worried someone with Asperger's would admire me and try to imitate my jump. If someone fell off a building and died because they were imitating me, I would be so horrified, I'd probably "become autistic" for a week! So I decided to never use the CCC again. The CCC technology was not included in my SR. So, why was the SR asking me to jump out of a window? It shouldn't be telling me to do something so dangerous. It could not have been working correctly. Maybe my invention was a failure, after all?

I had told my friends to trust in my equations and my inventions, but now I was starting to seriously doubt myself. I felt like the SR was telling me to kill myself. As if I was such a failure, my own invention wanted to me end my failed life. I was so confused and horrified, I surrendered to my temptation. I ignored the SR and thought about prime numbers.

"2, 3, 5, 7…"

The beeping of the SR interrupted my counting. I knew it was giving me an urgent warning that I was jeopardizing my mission by not obeying its commands, but I didn't want to hear it. I was sure it didn't work, because I couldn't possibly jump out of a window and live. I switched the SR off and continued counting prime numbers.

"11, 13, 17, 19…"

My wrist TV made a crackling noise and I heard Nora's voice.

"Trueman," said Nora. "I believe in you. I believe in your equations and your inventions! I admire you and your mind! So, please believe in yourself too! I know you can do it!"

At first, I was confused by this. How did Nora know to call me and give me encouragement, right when I needed it?

"How was that?" asked Nora.

Confused, I looked at my wrist TV.

"Was that a good message?" asked Nora.

I could see that Nora was on the wrist TV screen. I was also on the screen, standing beside her. Nora gave me an embrace and I smiled.

I suddenly remembered this was a recording I had made with Nora a few days ago. I had considered the possibility that I might not be able to trust in the instructions of the SR if they sounded too dangerous.

I knew, if this happened, that I might get upset and "become autistic." I would probably try to comfort myself with prime numbers. I would probably also switch off my SR, so I would not be disturbed. So, I arranged for this pre-recorded video to play on my wrist TV if I shut off my SR during a mission. I knew a message from Nora, saying how much she admired me and believed in me, would restore my confidence. And it did. I felt confident again and I switched on my SR.

It read, "Urgent: 10 seconds remain to jump out window!"

I forced myself to believe in my equations and inventions, the way Nora did and I gathered all my courage. I ran for the window and jumped out of it. I had expected to see the clear, blue sky and a scene of the street, from high above. But, instead, I hit a metal fence and bounced onto my back.

I sat up and realized I was on a platform, with cables leading up to the roof of the building. Beside me stood a tall, thin man with a cigarette in his mouth. He had a bucket of water beside him and carried a large squeegee. When he saw me fall on his platform, his mouth opened so wide, his cigarette fell out of his mouth and down towards the street below.

"You're the window washer!" I said. "This is a window washer's platform! Now I see why I could jump out the window!"

"What?" asked the window washer. "What the hell are you doing jumping out of windows? You're not allowed on here!"

I noticed we were going up, towards the roof. I started to realize what the SR had planned for me to do.

"Of course!" I said. "The window washer's platform will lift me to the roof and I can get to the penthouse!"

"Listen!" said the window washer. "I don't care what you do, but get off my stage! You want to get me in trouble? Go on! Get out of here, buddy!"

We arrived at the roof and the window washer pushed me out. He pushed a button on his platform and started lowering down the side of the building. As he lowered, he stared at me and shook his head.

"Nut!" he shouted.

I didn't understand why he was offering me a nut. This didn't seem like the type of situation to eat nuts.

"Maybe he was asking me for a nut?" I asked myself.

Before I could figure it out, my SR started beeping.

"Call Buckley," I read.

"Okay!" I said.

I activated my wrist TV and pressed the button to call Buckley. I was so happy and excited by my success that I was jumping. Buckley's face appeared on my wrist TV.

"Trueman?" asked Buckley. "Thank God! There's a lot of noise down here. Something's got the gangsters excited! Seems like someone gave a signal that cops are here! They're all leaving the building. What happened to you? Are you okay?"

"I sure am!" I said. "My SR led me safely to the roof and I can see the penthouse!"

"Okay," he said. "Well, what do we do now?"

"My SR says that you should leave the building," I said. "Go outside to a door labeled 'elevator.' Wait for the door to open and take it to the roof. Do you understand?"

"Yeah," he said, "I got it."

"Okay, I need to go! Bye!" I said.

My SR was beeping again. The compass had appeared on the SR screen and it was pointing at the penthouse. Excited and happy that my mission was almost completed, I ran across the gravelly roof, which smelled of tar. A metal back door was wide open and I entered the spacious, luxurious penthouse.

Inside, everything was decorated in expensive teak wood and adorned with marble and precious works of art. The carpet was so luxurious, I felt like I was walking on moss. The paintings were intriguing to me. I had read and memorized books about famous artists. And some of the paintings looked familiar to me. I was so absorbed in my surroundings that I hardly noticed my SR was beeping, sending me another urgent message.

"Send elevator to ground floor," I read.

The compass appeared and pointed to my left. Looking left, however, I could see no elevator. Only a wall adorned with art.

"Wait a minute," I said to myself. "Is that Jacques-Louis David's painting? 'Coronation of Napoleon'? But that's wrong!"

I examined the painting more closely and realized there was a red circle depicted there. With my keen visual memory, I could recall every detail of that painting as if it were right in front of me. On the central pillar of Napoleon's coronation hall, there was a big red circle.

"That wasn't in the original!" I said. "Besides, that painting's in the Louvre art gallery in Paris. This is a copy."

I touched the circle and it moved. I realized it was an elevator button, cleverly disguised as part of a painting.

"Wow, that's clever," I said.

I pressed the button and heard a mechanical whirring sound, like the sound of an elevator motor. Now that I knew an elevator was here, I could guess what part of the wall would open up and lead to it. It looked like a large panel of ornate teak panelling. It was very expertly disguised.

"What a fascinating place," I said.

I further examined the artworks and noticed a particular style of "cubism" art that was very familiar.

"Aha!" I said. "That is one of Marc Chagall's paintings."

"Yes, it is."

The voice made an image of Chief Stokowski form in my mind. This mental image made my body feel tense; I felt like I was frozen in ice. The voice came from behind me and I was too scared to turn around and see if Stokowski was really there.

"What the hell are you doing here?" asked Stokowski.

I looked at my SR, wondering why it hadn't warned me. To my surprise, I noticed that it had warned me. I must have been so fascinated by the artworks that I hadn't noticed it beeping.

"Unpleasant surprise is imminent," I read. "To avoid unpleasant surprise: Attack Chief Stokowski."

I was shocked to read this. I was terrible at fighting and Chief Stokowski was much stronger than me. My SR told me how to avoid unpleasant surprises, but it couldn't help me win a fight. But, trusting in myself and my inventions had taken me this far, without serious trouble, so I obeyed the SR's instructions without hesitation. I raised my fists and approached Stokowski.

"What are you gonna do?" asked Stokowski. "Hit me?"

Stokowski started laughing. I wasn't sure what to do, so I just stood there, moving my fists in a circular motion in front of me, the way I'd seen fighters do it in movies.

"You've got to be kidding me!" said Stokowski. "You seriously want to fight me? I'd kill you in a fight, kid!"

My SR beeped and I stopped to look at it.

"Urgent!" I read. "SR beeping to distract you from the fight at the ideal moment."

During the moment I was distracted by the SR's beeping, Stokowski grabbed me by the lapels of my trench coat and pushed me violently. I was thrown across the room and fell into an open plastic display case. The force of my impact against the back wall of the display case caused the door of the case to close.

"What the hell!" shouted Stokowski.

Stokowski walked towards me. I could easily recognize the anger on his face. I expected him to open the door of the plastic display case and pull me out. But when he tried to open the door, it didn't move. I noticed there was a small metal lock on the door. Stokowski had accidently thrown me into the display case and the door closed and locked behind me. I was locked in the display case and Stokowski couldn't reach me. I was safe, for a while. Maybe long enough for Buckley to use the elevator and come up to rescue me.

"You lucky little punk, you!" said Stokowski. "How the hell did you do that? I was ready to knock your head off!"

"Thank you, SR!" I said. I kissed it.

Stokowski started searching his pockets. Then he frantically searched the room, throwing things all over the floor and making a mess.

"I know I have the key to that thing somewhere!" said Stokowski. "You're not safe yet, kid! I'll get you yet!"

Stokowski didn't find the key, but he opened a fire-prevention cupboard and pulled out a large axe. He looked at me and smiled. I couldn't interpret his emotions, but I could guess what he intended to do and it made me sick from fear.

I looked at my SR, but it gave me no warnings about any "unpleasant surprises." I closed my eyes and prayed, trusting in my own equations and inventions.

"I'm safe," I said to myself. "Everything can be summed up in an equation. My equations work. My SR says I'm safe."

I expected to hear the horrible sound of the axe smashing the plastic walls of the display case. Instead I heard Stokowski yelling and swearing. I opened my eyes and saw Buckley struggling with Stokowski on the floor. Stokowski's eyes were wide open and I could recognize the fear on his face. Buckley's face had all the signs that indicated anger. Buckley had taken the axe from Stokowski's hands and was putting handcuffs on his wrists. Stokowski lay on the floor, breathing hard, and Buckley sat, looking at me with an exhausted expression.

"You okay, Trueman?" asked Buckley.

"Yes!" I said. "My SR worked perfectly! I didn't suffer any serious unpleasant surprises! Now, we have Stokowski!"

"Yeah," said Buckley. "But you managed to get yourself locked up. How'd you manage that?"

"The SR led me into here," I said. "By being locked in here I was kept safe from Stokowski until you could arrive."

"Uh-huh," said Buckley. "Let's just hope there's a key. As for you, Chief, would you care to explain what you're doing in this penthouse? According to my sources, this penthouse belongs to the Mafia boss known as Benvolio. How comes it that you're in here? Are you apartment sitting, or what?"

"Shut your mouth, Buckley!" said Stokowski. "That's none of your business! You're not a cop anymore! And you got no proof of anything! You got no right to handcuff me like this! I'll see you sent to prison for this! You and Trueman are as good as nailed! You've got no evidence I did anything here!"

Buckley sat silent for a minute. Then he stood up and walked towards the display case. Taking a long, slim lock pick from out of his pocket, he opened the lock within one minute.

"Your granddad was right, Trueman," said Buckley. "Picking locks is a useful skill for a cop. If Stokowski here had bothered to learn it, he wouldn't have needed an axe. But I'm afraid he's right, Trueman. We got no evidence. When the cops come, he'll go free and we might get in some trouble for this."

"You bet you will!" said Stokowski. "I'd like to see you find evidence! Go ahead! Show me where the evidence is!"

As if in response to Stokowski's request, the SR beeped. The SR included many of my old inventions, combined into one easy-to-use wrist device. It had my evidence-hunting invention included inside it. The compass appeared on my SR's screen, pointing me towards the evidence that would convict Stokowski.

I left the display case and ran towards the north wall of the penthouse. A large painting of a river scene adorned this wall. Buckley followed me, examining the painting closely.

"Quite an art collection this Benvolio's got here," said Buckley. "I guess a successful gangster like him has lots of money to buy expensive artwork."

"Yes," I said. "Most of this work is original. This collection must be worth millions of dollars. This painting is by a famous modern artist named George Bellows."

"Yeah?" asked Buckley. "It's beautiful. Peaceful river scenes always get to me. I grew up right beside the Hudson."

"Really?" I asked. "Well, then I'm not surprised you like this. This painting is called 'Up the Hudson.'"

"Oh, so that's the Hudson River?" he asked.

"Yes," I said, "the way it looked about a hundred years ago. Can you hand me that axe?"

Buckley was still holding the axe he had wrestled out of Stokowski's hands. He handed me the axe.

"Beautiful painting," said Buckley.

"Yes," I said. "The original is worth a lot of money."

I lifted the axe and started smashing the painting. I ripped a gouge through it, and it made a loud splintering sound as I pierced the wall behind it. Buckley's eyes widened and he stared at me. The shock on his face was easy to interpret.

"What did you do that for?" he asked. "You just said this painting's worth a lot of money!"

I gave the axe back to Buckley.

"Thanks for lending me the axe," I said. "And I didn't say this painting was worth a lot of money. I said the original painting is worth a lot of money! This is a copy!"

"How do you know that?" he asked.

I looked at Buckley in shock.

"How long have you lived in New York City?" I asked.

"My whole life," he said.

"And you've never visited the Metropolitan Museum of Art?" I asked. "The original painting of 'Up the Hudson' is hanging on a wall in that museum, so this has to be a copy! I've seen the painting there. Wow! I can't believe you've lived here all your life and never visited that museum! I've only lived here for a few months and I've already seen the museum three times!"

Buckley's face turned red.

"Well," he said, "I always meant to see the museum someday, you know. I just never got around to it. But, anyhow, I still can't figure out why you smashed this painting."

"Because my SR can detect the evidence that will convict Stokowski!" I said. "You see? Behind this painting is a secret compartment! I can see some kind of papers in there. It must be some kind of evidence that proves Stokowski's criminal partnership with that gangster, Benvolio."

Stokowski started shouting and cursing. He sat up and stared at me. I wasn't sure if he was angry or starting to cry.

"Okay!" said Stokowski. "I'm guilty, okay? You got me! I admit it! Trueman, I underestimated you. I didn't figure you were as smart as everyone said. Now, I see you're smart. How on earth you managed to get past a hundred gangsters with guns and get up here, I have no idea! But I really misjudged you and I'm sorry, okay? You're a great detective. I admit it."

Stokowski's words filled me with emotion. I felt a mixture of pride and relief, to know this man who had once mocked me and was prejudiced against me was now admitting that I was capable of being a "great detective." Everyone who had once doubted I could become a great detective now believed in me. And, what was more important, their confidence had enabled me to believe in myself. Believing in myself, my equations and my SR had solved this case, and now even Stokowski, my worst enemy, admitted that my Asperger's didn't stop me from being a great detective. I became so emotional, I smiled at Stokowski.

Stokowski's face suddenly changed. He stopped shaking and no longer seemed like he would start crying. He smiled at me.

"Yes, Trueman," said Stokowski. "Yes, you're a great detective. I admit it! And, what's more, I'm sure you're a good man. I'm sure you'll let me explain what happened, right? I mean, everyone's got a right to explain their actions, right?"

"I guess so," I said.

"Yeah!" said Stokowski. "Well then, just hear me out. I may've been partners with Benvolio, but it wasn't my fault! You've got to believe me, Trueman. Just let me tell my story and I think you'll see that I'm a victim here, not a criminal."

"Okay," I said. "Tell your story."

"Thank you!" said Stokowski.

He licked his lips for a minute and seemed to be thinking of what to say. When he did speak, he spoke in a pleading way. It reminded me of a child I had once seen, in a mall, explaining to his mother why he needed a video game.

"I'm not a criminal, Trueman!" said Stokowski. "I was being blackmailed. You see, I've got a pretty serious gambling problem. I've had this problem for years. Since before I was Chief, even. Well, I'd go out and gamble most nights. I'd win a little, lose a little. Some nights I'd make a couple thousand. But some nights I'd lose almost everything I had."

Stokowski started blinking his eyes. Sweat was dripping down his face and he was unable to wipe it off, because he was still wearing handcuffs. Buckley took a handkerchief out of his pocket and wiped Stokowski's face.

"Thanks, Sam," said Stokowski. "You're a good man. I'm sorry for the way I treated you too, Sam. I hope, when I finish telling my story, you'll realize that I had no choice."

"Go on," said Buckley. "Finish your story."

"Well," said Stokowski, "one night I was in this very casino, and I was having miserable luck. I tell you, I lost so much money, I was left with nothing. I almost had to give them the shirt off my back, I lost so much. Well, I'd had a few drinks too, so my mind was a little, um, fuzzy. I wasn't thinking too good. I did something stupid. This guy, Benvolio, he comes up to me and starts talking to me. Like I said, I had no money. I lost everything I had. I told this Benvolio guy that I had no money and couldn't even afford a taxi to get home. Well, he offered to give me a loan. He gave me 10,000 bucks! Just like that! Well, I shouldn't have done it, but I took the loan."

"And just what were you thinking, doing that?" asked Buckley. "You know who Benvolio is! Every cop in this city knows Benvolio's a gangster! And you took a loan from him? And you expect me to believe all this wasn't your fault? No, it is your fault. You did a stupid thing, Chief!"

"I was drunk!" said Stokowski. "When I sobered up, the morning after I took the loan, I paid Benvolio back. I paid back every penny! But then he started blackmailing me! He said he recorded our loan transaction on the video surveillance cameras of this casino and he said he'd show the video to the media if I didn't do what he says. It's shameful for a cop to get a loan from a gangster, right? What could I do? I'd lose my job! I didn't mean to do anything illegal! I was drunk!"

"That's no excuse," said Buckley. "What kind of things did Benvolio ask you to do, anyways? What are those papers there, in the wall? Something about your and Benvolio's partnership?"

"We weren't really partners," said Stokowski. "Benvolio just asked me to make sure the police didn't discover any of the criminal activities he was doing. As for what he asked me to do, well… you recognize that bottle over there, Trueman?"

Stokowski pointed his finger at a whiskey bottle on a nearby table. I recognized the label immediately.

"Yes," I said. "That's a bottle of Orkafend's Blend Whiskey. The same kind of whiskey bottle you showed me that day I was in jail. You dropped it on the floor."

"Yeah," said Stokowski. "Well, did you ever wonder why I showed you that bottle and offered you a drink?"

"Well," I said, "I guess because you're an alcoholic."

"No!" said Stokowski. "Well, yes. I mean, I am an alcoholic, but that's not why I showed you the bottle. You see, Benvolio was illegally making that whiskey here in Manhattan. He produces tons of that stuff every year and sells it on the black market. Benvolio was blackmailing me, like I said. So, I had to do what he said. He told me to make sure the cops never found out about his illegal alcohol production. I showed you the bottle because I wanted to see if you knew anything about it. I was watching you closely as I showed it to you. I've been a detective a long time and so I can read a man's face. If you knew anything about the illegal alcohol, I would have seen it on your face. Of course, I could see right away you didn't know anything about it. But, still you made me nervous. All this talk in the media about your miracle crime-fighting equations and all that. Well, it made me think you might discover everything about me and Benvolio. That's why I charged you with the State Department and tried to get your license revoked. Then, when you won the case, I guess I panicked. I'm the one who shot at your building and destroyed your sign. I thought, if I frightened you, you might close your agency or leave the city or something. I was scared of you, Trueman. I was scared you were really as good a detective as the newspapers said. Now, of course, I can see that you are."

"That explains why you were always trying to interfere with my detective work," I said. "So, you didn't really want to do anything illegal or to discriminate against me? You were forced to do it by Benvolio? He blackmailed you and forced you to hide his illegal alcohol production from the police?"

"Yeah!" said Stokowski. "Exactly."

"I still don't see what Malcolm Vrie and Eddie Sipple have to do with all this," said Buckley. "Why were you trying to stop us from investigating their deaths?"

"Well, you see," said Stokowski, "any time Benvolio did a crime, I couldn't send police to investigate, because I had to keep his crimes secret. So who did I send? I sent this private investigator, Malcolm Vrie! He was actually a friend of Benvolio's, so he wouldn't expose Benvolio's crimes!"

"Malcolm Vrie was a criminal?" I asked. "A gangster?"

"Yes," said Stokowski.

"That still doesn't explain why you wouldn't let us investigate their deaths," said Buckley. "Who killed them?"

"They killed each other," said Stokowski.

"What?" I asked.

"Yeah," said Stokowski. "You see, Malcolm Vrie and Eddie Sipple were criminal partners. But Eddie was a bit crazy. I hear he was an alcoholic, too. Eddie had an argument with that Eric Lendalainen guy and killed him. When Malcolm heard about it, he came to me and told me Lendalainen was killed by Eddie. I knew Eddie was one of Benvolio's men, so I couldn't let the police investigate. So, I let Malcolm investigate the case."

"So that's why you didn't give the case to Nora," I said.

"Oh, yeah!" said Stokowski. "Of course not! No, I couldn't let her investigate. She might've found out everything. Then Benvolio would've been real mad at me."

"You still didn't explain how they killed each other," said Buckley. "What happened? How did Malcolm and Eddie die?"

"Well, you see," said Stokowski, "Malcolm was sick and tired of Eddie's wild and drunken behaviour. He thought, if Eddie kept acting so wild, he'd end up doing something stupid and risk exposing their crimes to the police. So, what does Malcolm do? He decides to get rid of Eddie. He meets Eddie at the Hickson warehouse one day, where they both worked together, counterfeiting money, and he tried to kill him, by giving him a bottle of whiskey laced with this kind of poison, called thallium or something like that."

"Thallium sulphate," said Buckley. "A tasteless, odorless poison that kills very slowly."

"Yeah, that's the one," said Stokowski. "Well, Malcolm figured Eddie would be dead soon, so he decided to take the credit for solving the Eric Lendalainen murder. He told the press that he solved the case, and that Eddie was the murderer."

"Why would he do that to his own partner?" asked Buckley.

"I guess he figured Eddie would already be dead by the time they came to arrest him," said Stokowski. "And I guess he got greedy. He wanted credit for solving a murder case. He thought Eddie would be dead and wouldn't be able to tell anyone they were criminal partners. But Malcolm thought wrong. Eddie was a pretty strong guy. He didn't die too fast. He was sick, but still alive. And when he heard that Malcolm betrayed him, he went looking for him. Well, he found him at the Hickson warehouse and that's where Malcolm's life ended. Soon after, the cops found Eddie and arrested him. But, you know, since Malcolm couldn't be found to present any evidence against Eddie, the cops had to let him go. I guess Eddie was at the airport trying to get out of the city when the poison finally killed him."

"Wow, so that's the answer to the mystery," I said. "Eddie Sipple and Malcolm Vrie killed each other. And they were criminals. And you were only doing these illegal things because you were forced. You didn't really want to hurt anybody?"

Stokowski looked at me like the little boy who wanted a video game. He seemed to be pleading for my help and sympathy.

"Of course not!" said Stokowski. "Look, I'm no criminal, Trueman! The only things I'm guilty of is having a gambling problem and a little bit of an alcohol problem! Since when is that against the law, huh? I tell you, Trueman, I'm a victim here. I didn't do anything wrong! I only did what anyone else would do. I mean, what could I do? I couldn't let him show that video to the world or I'd be fired. I might even go to jail! You understand me? I shouldn't have to go to jail for one stupid decision I only made because I was drunk! I mean, that's just not fair! I got a problem with gambling and alcohol. I shouldn't be punished for it! Someone should be trying to help me, not punish me! I'm a victim. Can't you see that? You've got to help me, Trueman! You just got to!"

I could recognize the fear on Stokowski's face and I was sympathetic to him. I had assumed that he was just an evil man, a criminal, and I hadn't considered the possibility that Benvolio was forcing him to be his criminal partner. I hadn't considered that Stokowski had any serious problems and needed help and compassion. After being so discriminated against by this man, it felt nice to have his acceptance. Not only was he accepting of me, he was pleading for me to help him. I decided the only compassionate thing to do was to try to help him.

"Of course I'll help you," I said, smiling.

Stokowski let out a deep sigh and smiled widely.

"Oh, good," said Stokowski. "You're a good man, Trueman."

Buckley walked between Stokowski and me, waving his finger.

"Trueman, Trueman, Trueman," said Buckley, "you're a total genius with equations and you're a damn good detective, I admit. But some things, you just can't see. Stokowski's trying to butter you up, understand? He thinks you're a sucker."

"Butter?" I asked. "Sucker? Butter sucker? Do you mean a butterscotch lollipop? I had one of those candies before. I didn't like them much. So, if Stokowski's trying to give me one, I don't want one."

Buckley put his head in his hands.

"No, Trueman," he said. "Sorry, I got to remember not to use expressions around you. A 'sucker' is someone who's easy to fool, understand? Stokowski's trying to fool you! He doesn't respect you, he doesn't think you're a good man. He thinks, if he acts friendly to you, you'll think he's your friend and you'll let him escape."

"Oh…" I said.

Stokowski's face changed as he listened to Buckley. His friendly smile changed to a frown. I could recognize the anger and hatred in his frown. I jumped back, away from Stokowski. His face had changed so rapidly, from friendly to hate-filled, that I realized Buckley was right. He had only been pretending to be friendly. He was trying to fool me, because he thought I was a sucker. He didn't really think I was smart.

"You liar!" I said. "I'm no sucker! Thanks for telling me, Sam. I had no idea he was trying to give me butter."

"No," said Buckley, "the expression is 'butter you up.' It means he's trying to trick you by being friendly to you."

"Oh," I said. "I'm lucky I have you here to tell me these things. I was ready to free him. I felt sympathy for him."

"Yeah," said Buckley. "Well, I'm mighty lucky to have you here with me too, Trueman. If it wasn't for you, we wouldn't have caught him at all! So, we both help each other out."

I smiled in response. We were a good team. Exactly like Dick Tracy and Sam Catchem.

"We're a good team, Sam Catchem," I said.

Buckley smiled and put his hand on my shoulder.

"We sure are, Dick," said Buckley.

Stokowski stared at us. He had an excited look in his eyes. He seemed ready to cry again and spoke in a whiny voice.

"Look, guys!" said Stokowski, "I'm not asking for sympathy. I'm not asking for you to believe anything I've said, okay? Just give me a little compassion! I made one mistake, and for that, I'm looking at life in prison! When the cops see that evidence, they'll put me away for life! You can't condemn me to life in prison, just because I got drunk one night and did one dumb thing! I'm begging with you, just let me go. Take these handcuffs off me and let me run. I'll leave the country! You'll never see me again! Just, please, have some compassion for me. Let me walk away from here and try to start my life over again, in some other country. What do you say, fellas?"

Stokowski looked like a pathetic, whining child and I was moved to sympathy again. Previously, he had been so commanding and powerful, and now he was a pitiful man, begging for mercy. I wanted to let him run away, but I remembered how Buckley had warned me about Stokowski's tricks. I looked at Buckley, trying to guess his reactions. I couldn't interpret his emotions.

"How about it, Trueman?" he asked. "Should we let him go?"

I thought about it for a minute.

"No," I said.

"But why not?" asked Stokowski.

"Because I am like Dick Tracy," I said. "And Dick Tracy exists to get the gangsters and stop the criminals. As Chester Gould, the creator of the Dick Tracy comics, said, 'I decided that if the police couldn't catch the gangsters, I'd create a fellow who could.' So that is why I'm here, to get the gangsters. And you, Chief, are one of the police who couldn't catch the gangsters. You did even worse. You helped them commit their crimes, so that makes you a gangster too. So, it's my duty to catch you, too. It's what Dick Tracy would do and so it's what I'll do. I sympathize with you. But you chose to help the gangsters. It was your decision and so it was your fault. I know you don't like comic books, but maybe if you read Dick Tracy, like I did, then you would have learned that it's not good to help gangsters and you wouldn't have this trouble."

Stokowski lowered his head onto his chest and sighed.

"There you go, Chief," said Buckley. "Looks like you might've been wrong. Seems like maybe a police detective could learn a few things from reading comic books, after all."

My SR started beeping and gave me another message.

"Unpleasant surprise is imminent," I read. "To avoid unpleasant surprise: Put earphones in your ears and play relaxing music."

I hastened to put my earphones into my ears and played Mozart's Symphony #41 in C major. I also put on my special sunglasses, just to be sure I'd avoid the unpleasant surprise.

Only moments after I put on my sunglasses I could see police lights on the street below. I could vaguely hear the sound of sirens. Buckley walked towards the windows and looked down at the street. Following him, I looked down and saw a dozen police cars, ambulances and fire engines. There were also at least a dozen news vans on the street below. Reporters and journalists were everywhere. If I hadn't been wearing my earphones, it would probably be very loud. I thanked my SR for saving me from some ear pain and gave it an appreciative kiss.

The sirens stopped and the lights stopped flashing, so I took off my sunglasses and stopped the music.

"Aha, I can see Gwen Tone down there," said Buckley. "Looks like our friend, Gwen, brought the police with her, as well as a couple dozen of her media friends."

Buckley walked to Stokowski and pulled him up by his arm. He stared at me as if expecting me to do something.

"Well, Trueman?" asked Buckley. "Go ahead and take his other arm. We'll take Stokowski downstairs and introduce him to the media. Just grab that evidence out of the wall, will ya?"

I took the papers and put them in my trench coat. I then took Stokowski's other arm and we took him into the elevator.

As the elevator went down to the ground floor, Buckley put on a pair of sunglasses. He looked at me and smiled.

"You might want to put your sunglasses back on," said Buckley. "If you thought you were famous before, just wait and see how famous you're gonna be after this story gets out!"

I put my sunglasses back on.

As the elevator door opened onto the street, I saw what seemed like a hundred faces staring at us. Reporters swarmed like bees and the cameras flashed like a lightning storm.

I closed my eyes and increased the volume of my portable music player, so I wouldn't be disturbed by the noise and lights of the media. I could feel someone pulling my arm. I struggled against the pulling hand, but I couldn't free myself from it. I recognized the scent of Nora's lilac shampoo. I opened my eyes and saw that I was surrounded by three people.

"The triangle of friendship!" I said.

"Yes, Trueman," said Nora, "we've come to take you home."

Nora, Mrs. Levi and Sal were surrounding me, protecting me from the media and leading me towards the Lincoln car.

"What have you been doing?" asked Nora. "There must be a hundred reporters here! We've been waiting outside, in case you needed help. Journalists have been gathering here for an hour!"

"We arrested Stokowski," I said.

"What?" asked Sal. "You arrested the chief of police?!"

I was about to answer him, but instead I was led into the Lincoln car and Mrs. Levi and Nora used their coats to block the windows and keep the flash of the media's cameras from disturbing me. We drove through the crowds and onto a highway.

"Okay, Trueman," said Nora. "What happened in there?"

"I think you'll know soon, Mrs. Nora," said Sal. "I think a lot of people will know! This will be all over the news!"

TWO ENDS OF A PERFECT CIRCLE

The Trueman Bradley Detective Agency was closed for the evening and it was very quiet. We had returned home, soon before sunset, and had spent all evening and most of the next day watching the news on TV. My friends heard the entire story of what happened to me at the casino. Now, it was evening and we were enjoying some relaxation after the excitement of the last few days.

Only a few dim light bulbs lit my office, making everything seem peaceful and calm. Sal had arranged for walls to be constructed around my desk, so I could have privacy when I was working and would never be unpleasantly surprised again. This was my new, private office. Nora and I were taking my boxes of possessions from my old room and moving them into my new office. I'd been so busy since my arrival in New York City that I hadn't even unpacked most of my boxes. I was unpacking, placing my possessions on the desk and remembering the past.

Outside was dark and only the blinking lights of New York City and a full moon were visible. I could smell a blend of car fumes, garbage and mildewed drainage pipes; this was the smell of New York City. I had gradually begun to love this smell, because this city had been the site of my successes and the place where I'd found so many friends. I loved everything about this city, even that astringent smell.

I walked to the window and breathed deeply, savoring the scent of the city. I looked out at the large, pale moon and admired the sights and sounds of this big, fascinating city.

Nora came into the room, carrying my large mirror. She seemed to be struggling to carry it, so I ran to help her.

"Let me help you, Nora," I said.

"Thanks, Trueman," said Nora. "This is one really big mirror! And I like its ornate frame. Is it an antique?"

"I think so," I said. "It belonged to my granddad."

We carried the mirror to a place on the wall where Sal had hammered a nail. We hung the mirror on the nail and stepped back to look at it. I could see Nora's reflection in the glass.

"Beautiful," said Nora.

"Yes, you are," I said.

Nora's face turned red.

"No!" said Nora. "I meant, the mirror's beautiful."

"Oh," I said. "Sorry, I was thinking of something else."

Nora looked at me and smiled.

"Yes, I can see that," said Nora. "But let's concentrate on the mirror's beauty for now, okay?"

"Okay," I said.

I looked at the mirror and admired its beauty. I could see my reflection. I was lit by the moonlight that came through my office window. With my yellow trench coat and hat, my suit, my wrist TV, I really looked like a detective. But there was another reason I looked like a real detective.

I thought back to the day I had first arrived at Reade Street. I remembered how I had doubted myself. I had looked into this same mirror and I had asked myself if I could do it; I had asked myself if I could really succeed as a detective. I remembered how I could see the doubt in my eyes; I remembered how I looked like a frightened child, unsure of his own worth.

Looking into the mirror now, I saw something else in my eyes. I saw confidence; I saw bravery; I saw a man who had the support of his friends; I saw a man who could be a great detective, despite all of the challenges he faced. I looked like a different man. The Trueman I saw in the mirror answered the question I had asked him, a long time ago. He answered it with the confidence I saw on his face and the pride in his eyes.

"Yes, I can do it," I said. "I did do it."

"What did you say?" asked Nora.

"Oh..." I said, "I was just thinking about the past. When I first arrived here, in New York City, I wasn't sure if I could be a detective. I thought my Asperger's and my inexperience would mean that I could only fail as a detective. I looked into this mirror and asked my reflection if I could do it. Now that I see myself in the mirror, I see the answer."

"How can you see the answer?" asked Nora, stepping closer and looking at my reflection.

"Because the Trueman I see in the mirror has changed," I said. "Now he has confidence. My granddad always said, confidence makes anything possible. So I know I can do it now."

Nora put her arm around my shoulders and embraced me.

"Now, he also has friends," said Nora. "Friends who will defend and help him. With good friends, anything is possible."

"I'm glad I have a friend like you," I said.

Nora's eyes became moist and I could recognize that my words had touched her. She moved closer and embraced me again.

"I'm glad too, Trueman," said Nora.

I could smell the lilac shampoo she used and her hair was soft on my face. Her embrace was warm and filled me with joy.

"Does this mean you're my girlfriend now?" I asked.

Nora's arms became rigid and she moved away from me quickly. She laughed in a way I couldn't interpret. She seemed embarrassed, by her red cheeks, but she was also smiling widely.

"Trueman!" said Nora. "Really. You say the most unexpected things sometimes!"

"Oh, sorry," I said. "I know you said you weren't in love. But I just wanted to check if maybe you had changed your mind."

"It's okay," said Nora. "I'm just glad that reporter, Gwen Tone, wasn't here to hear you say that. Or it just might've been on the front page of tomorrow's newspapers."

"Yes," I said. "Maybe it would."

Nora stood nearby, doing nothing. She stared at the moon through the window and I couldn't guess what she was feeling. My confusion about the situation made me feel awkward, so I started opening boxes again. But before I could begin Nora interrupted me and started pulling me from the room.

"Let's do that later, Trueman," said Nora. "Okay? Sal and Mrs. Levi invited us to play poker with them. Let's go play."

Nora pulled me out of the room and I looked back at the boxes, not sure if I wanted to leave or finish my task.

"What?" I asked. "Poker? Well, okay. I guess we can unpack later. But wait, Nora! Wait!"

Nora let me go and I ran to my desk. I picked up my checklist of today's activities.

"Just let me write that down," I said. "Because I hadn't planned to play poker tonight. I'll just add it to the plan."

I wrote "play poker" in my notebook and put it into my trench coat pocket.

"Okay," I said. "Let's go."

Nora took my hand and we walked into the big front office, where Sal and Mrs. Levi were sitting.

Sal sat smoking his pipe near an open window and reading the evening newspaper by moonlight. Mrs. Levi sat at the table, arranging tea cups and cutting a freshly baked raspberry lemon cake. The sights and sounds of my good friends made me feel warm and cozy. I could smell the raspberry lemon cake, which always reminded me of Mrs. Levi. Even the smell of Sal's pipe had become a pleasant aroma, because I associated it with him. Entering this familiar room, for another night-time poker game with my good friends, along with all these familiar sensations, made me feel safe and content. I felt a sudden desire to embrace my friends and tell them how much I loved them all.

"Hello, friends!" I said, with affection in my voice.

Mrs. Levi and Sal looked up at me and smiled.

"Hello, dear!" said Mrs. Levi. "I just finished baking a raspberry lemon cake for you. I know it's your favourite! Please, have a seat, dears. Would you like a cup of tea?"

Nora and I sat down and took our tea cups.

"I'd love a cup of tea, Mrs. Levi," I said.

Sal extinguished his pipe and moved to sit beside me. He embraced me and patted my shoulder with his hand.

"Trueman!" said Sal. "My famous friend! How are you?"

"I feel great, Sal," I said.

"Did you see tonight's newspaper?" asked Sal. "A lot of big news! All of it about you! Have a look at this!"

Sal passed me the newspaper and everyone gathered around me, reading over my shoulder. The front page had a picture of me, Buckley and Stokowski. Stokowski was in handcuffs.

"Chief Stokowski arrested," I read. "The celebrated private detective, Trueman Bradley, along with ex-NYPD detective Samuel Buckley, recently teamed up to bust NYPD Chief of Police, Paul Stokowski, on charges of conspiring with gangsters to conceal criminal activities. Evidence was presented to the police, implicating Stokowski in conspiring to conceal the activities of an illegal alcohol production enterprise. The evidence also implicated Stokowski in attempting to conceal the criminal acts of more than fifty local gangsters. If the evidence is proven valid by a court of law, Stokowski is likely to serve life in prison for his crimes."

Everyone was silent.

"Wow!" I said. "So Stokowski is going to jail."

"Yeah," said Nora. "If they can prove the evidence you found is valid."

"Oh, I think they will," said Sal.

"Really?" asked Nora. "Why do you think that?"

"You remember that hearing officer, Tritch?" asked Sal. "The one that really hated Chief Stokowski?"

"Yes," I said.

"Well, then keep reading!" said Sal.

"Sidney Saul Tritch," I read, "an officer of the State Department, has launched an independent government investigation into Stokowski's activities. After thoroughly examining the evidence against Stokowski, Tritch was reported to say: 'There is no doubt, based on this evidence, that Chief Stokowski will spend his retirement years in a New York State prison.'"

"So, he thinks the evidence is valid?" asked Nora.

"I would say so," said Sal. "Definitely."

Sal took a deck of playing cards out of his pocket and we started playing poker. He dealt me my cards and I sat staring at them. I tried to think of my poker strategy, but I was distracted by thoughts of Chief Stokowski.

I had always seen life's villains as inherently evil, like the ugly caricatures in comic books. I had always seen people as good or evil. Life was full of good guys and bad guys, and people were from one group or the other. But for a few short minutes, I had pitied Chief Stokowski. This thought nagged at me, because it brought to my mind a realization I had never previously considered: that evil may not always be entirely evil and that even villains were human beings who could be pitied.

"Poor Stokowski," I said.

"What?" asked Nora.

"Well, I know he's a criminal," I said. "But, he did have a problem with alcohol. That is what caused him to become a criminal. If someone had helped him to defeat his addictions, maybe he wouldn't have gotten drunk and made that mistake of associating with Benvolio. Then his life would be better now."

"Yes, dear," said Mrs. Levi. "Alcoholism is a sad thing. It can really ruin lives. Stokowski's an example of that."

"Sure, it's sad," said Sal. "Of course. But don't forgot, he was a police chief! That's an important responsibility! If he can't quit alcohol maybe he should've resigned, if it affected his job. Police are there to protect the citizens, and if he couldn't do that, he was putting people at risk! Who's going to protect us from the gangsters?"

"We will," I said. "Dick Tracy will."

"Ha!" said Sal. "Sure! But what I'm saying is, don't waste your pity on Stokowski! We should be happy he's gone! Because now we have a police chief that can protect the people."

"Oh, really?" asked Nora. "Who?"

Sal's eyes opened wide and I could interpret his shock.

"Are you kidding?" asked Sal. "Didn't you hear?"

"Hear what?" asked Nora.

"Look at this story!" Sal gave the newspaper to Nora.

Nora looked at the story that Sal indicated and her eyes widened.

"Buckley's the new chief of police!" she shouted. "Trueman! Buckley's the chief! Did you know that?"

"Yes," I said. "He told me."

"He did?" asked Nora. "You saw him?"

"Yes," I said. "I had lunch with him today at the Metropolitan Museum of Art. I showed him some of my favourite paintings by George Bellows."

"Oh my God!" said Nora. "I can't believe it! It says here, 'the citizens of New York City were so impressed by Buckley's integrity and his ability to expose the corruption of Stokowski that they successfully lobbied the police commissioner to promote him to chief of police.' That's amazing! Buckley will be taking Stokowski's old job!"

"And he'll do a better job too!" said Sal. "Now New York City will have a real police chief! Not a criminal and a liar."

"Yes," I said.

Nora's excited face soon became calmer and she frowned. I could see signs to indicate that she was suddenly worried.

"What's wrong, Nora?" I asked.

"Oh, nothing," said Nora. "I was just thinking… this means Buckley's not working for us anymore, right? We probably won't see him here much anymore. He's back with the NYPD."

"Yes," I said.

"Well," said Nora, "are you okay with that, Trueman? I know you two have become pretty close friends. I know I'll miss him, so I can just imagine how sad you'd be about it."

"I'm not sad," I said. "In the Dick Tracy comics, Sam Catchem also exposed criminal acts of the chief of police. And Sam Catchem also became chief of police! So, do you understand? It's perfect! Buckley is exactly like Sam Catchem. This is how it should be. This helps me to feel even more like Dick Tracy."

"Oh," said Nora.

We played poker for a minute, in silence.

"A pair of twos?" asked Sal. "Trueman has a pair of twos? That's the worst hand in poker! You're not fooling anyone, Mr. Bradley! You're letting us win, aren't you?"

"Oh, sorry," I said. "I wasn't thinking of what I was doing. Last time I played with Buckley I was letting him win."

"Well, don't do that with us!" said Sal. "I'm determined to beat you some day. Even just to win one game of poker against Trueman, the mathematical genius! If I could do that, then I could brag about it for the rest of my life!"

Nora and Mrs. Levi laughed.

"Ah, okay," I said. "I'll try to win again."

"Trueman?" asked Mrs. Levi.

"Yes?" I asked.

"You explained this whole mystery to me," said Mrs. Levi. "But there's one thing I still don't understand. If Eddie and Malcolm killed each other, then why did your crime-fighting equation identify that black-haired guy at the Marine Air Terminal as the murderer? Was your equation wrong?"

"No, it wasn't wrong," I said. "That's one of the reasons why I met Buckley today. We met to use my equation and find that black-haired man we were chasing at Marine Air Terminal."

"And did you find him?" asked Nora.

"Yes," I said.

"Wow!" said Nora. "Well, what happened?!"

"Oh, well…" I said, "he's an employee at a chemical factory. He's the one who manufactured the thallium sulfate Malcolm used to kill Eddie."

"What?" asked Nora. "But he didn't kill Eddie!"

"Yes, I was also confused about that," I said. "But now I realize my equation can't identify a murderer if the murderer is already dead. When I used the equation, Malcolm was already dead. Malcolm was the one who was most responsible for Eddie's death, but he was no longer available because he died. So my equation led me to someone who was less responsible, but still responsible. It led me to the person who made the poison."

"But the factory employee didn't kill Eddie!" said Nora. "Why would your equation call him the murderer? He was just doing his job, making chemicals. He didn't commit any crimes!"

"I know that," I said, "but my equation doesn't know that. My equation is logical. And, logically, the person who made the poison is responsible for Eddie's death. If he didn't make it, Eddie would be alive. Do you understand what I'm saying?"

Nora sighed.

"Not really," said Nora, "but never mind. Why did the factory employee run away from us if he wasn't guilty?"

"Oh," I said. "He said he ran from us because I startled him. He was robbed in that airport last summer. He panicked, and when he saw your gun, he assumed we were trying to rob him."

"So he climbed down from the roof of a two-storey building to escape us?" asked Nora. "That seems a bit extreme to me!"

"I don't think so," I said. "He told me he had over three thousand dollars in his coat. For three thousand dollars I'd climb down from the roof of a two-storey building too."

"Me too!" said Sal.

"Why did he have so much money with him?" asked Mrs. Levi.

"I asked him," I said. "But then Buckley said it was not our business to ask him questions like that. He was an innocent man, not the murderer, so we should respect his privacy. That's what Buckley said and I decided he was correct. I apologized to the factory employee for bothering him and we left him alone."

Nora sighed.

"I'm glad for Buckley, of course," said Nora. "He deserves to be chief. But I'm gonna miss having him around here."

"Miss him?" I asked. "I don't understand why you think you won't see him anymore. I just saw him today."

"And what did he say?" asked Mrs. Levi. "Is he still going to come visit us as often as before? Did he actually say that?"

"Well, he didn't say that," I said.

Mrs. Levi frowned and I could recognize her disappointment.

"But," I said, "I imagine he'll need to come here often, considering we're working on a case together."

"What?" asked Nora.

"Yes," I said. "That was the other reason why I met Buckley today. We met to discuss our new case. He said he'd give all his cases to our agency from now on. He thinks we're a good team, so we'll be doing all the available police cases. We'll be really busy and Buckley will spend a lot of time here."

"Wow!" said Nora. "That's such good news, I don't even know what to say! I never thought we'd succeed like this when we first started this agency! I'm just speechless!"

"I think you're wrong," I said.

"What?" asked Nora.

"You said you're speechless," I said. "But you just said something, so you have the power of speech. You were wrong when you thought you were speechless."

"No Trueman!" said Nora. "Sorry, that's just an expression! It means I'm so excited I don't know how to react!"

"Oh," I said. "I'm excited too."

"I'm so proud of you, dear!" said Mrs. Levi.

"Thank you," I said.

Sal put his arm around me and patted my shoulder.

"Trueman!" said Sal. "The best detective I know! Let's drink to our good friend Trueman, and his many successes!"

Everyone raised their tea cups and knocked them against each other lightly, making a musical sound. I learned, from experience, this was called "making a toast" and was a way of celebrating a success. I lifted my tea cup and smiled.

"Thank you, my friends," I said.

Everyone was smiling, and we played cards in silence.

"Trueman?" asked Nora.

"Yes?" I said.

"What case are you and Buckley working on?" she asked.

"Oh, nothing too complicated," I said. "A group of men robbed a house in the area of Riverdale."

"Robbed a house?" she asked.

"Yes," I said. "Well, also, it was the house of a military commander and they stole documents that could cost the United States hundreds of soldiers' lives. Buckley thinks it was gangsters who stole them. I was going to do some math and figure out who stole the documents. But then Nora wanted me to play cards. So, I guess I'll do it after we're done."

My friends were silent and they became perfectly still. I couldn't recognize what they were feeling. They vaguely resembled mannequins I had seen displayed in a shop window on Broadway, but that didn't help me to interpret their emotions.

Nora jumped out of her chair.

"I don't want to play anymore!" said Nora. "I'm so excited about this case, I want to work on it right now!"

"Oh, me too, dear!" said Mrs. Levi. "I can drive to the station and get the military records of the commander! I know just how to do that, dear! Sal, can you drive me there? My car's got engine troubles!"

Sal jumped from his chair and slapped his thigh. He was smiling widely and I could recognize that he was very excited.

"With pleasure, Mrs. Levi!" said Sal. "Now, this is what I've been hoping for! Another case! We're back in action, my friends! We'll nail those gangsters and get those documents!"

"Yes!" said Nora. "I can't wait! I'm going to go home and get my toothbrush and pack my things! I'm spending the night here with you guys! We'll spend all night solving this case!"

Everyone was so excited, that I could feel it. I couldn't normally interpret emotion very well. But their enthusiasm was so intense that I could actually feel it in the room, as if it were an electrical force, moving through us all. I realized that I was excited too. I loved detective work and so did my friends. My dreams to be a detective were also their dreams and our dreams had come true. I became as excited as they were.

"Yes!" I said. "We'll work all night to solve this case!"

Nora gave me a kiss and ran out of the room. Mrs. Levi and Sal followed and I heard the door slam closed as they left the building. I got up from my chair and was so excited, I didn't know which way to run. I stopped and closed my eyes to think.

"Charts!" I said. "Yes, I will use my charts to make a visual list of everything I must do to solve this case!"

I ran into my new office to make a chart. I opened my boxes, looking for my paper and geometrical instruments. I looked into a small box, covered in packing tape, and found a photo of my granddad. The sight of his familiar, smiling face made me stop what I was doing. I examined his features: the wide smile, the small, unshaven chin, the kindly eyes, the gray fedora. Every feature of his face brought back memories of my childhood; they brought back memories of every kind word he'd given me and everything he'd done to support me and help me through life. He always told me I could do anything, and finally, I believed him.

"Thank you for believing in me, Granddad," I said.

I felt moisture forming in my eyes and I wiped away my tears with the sleeve of my trench coat. I put the photo in a nearby picture frame and positioned it on my desk.

"Now you can continue to inspire me, Granddad," I said.

I found some paper and geometric instruments at the bottom of the box and sat down at my desk to trace some perfect circles on the paper. As I considered the predictable perfection of the circle, I found myself delighting in its beauty. Some things were indescribably beautiful. Like this circle; like this moment in time where everything was as I had hoped it would be and life was perfect. This moment was perfect, like a circle.

The circle was beautiful for obvious mathematical reasons. Because it was a perfect circle, with perfect degrees and balanced symmetry. But if there were mathematical reasons why this moment of my life was perfect, I couldn't identify them.

"Everything can be summed up into an equation," I said.

I wondered if there were any mathematical reasons that could explain why this moment was perfect, or why George Bellow's paintings looked perfect, or why Nora's hair felt perfect against my hand. But I couldn't identify any pattern or formula that could even begin to explain the beauty of these things.

"Maybe I'll discover that equation someday," I said. "Then I can make an invention that can fill my life with perfect moments. But, I'll stop thinking about it. I don't want to do anything right now, except to enjoy this perfect moment."

I savored the scent of New York City and the calming light of the moon. I looked at the photo of my granddad and smiled. I continued making my chart and observed, with keen delight, the perfect arc of my compass as it spun around the diameter to bring together the two ends of a perfect circle.